Levinas and the
Philosophy of Religion

INDIANA SERIES IN THE PHILOSOPHY OF RELIGION
Merold Westphal, *general editor*

Levinas and the Philosophy of Religion

Jeffrey L. Kosky

INDIANA UNIVERSITY PRESS
Bloomington and Indianapolis

This book is a publication of

Indiana University Press
601 North Morton Street
Bloomington, IN 47404-3797 USA

http://iupress.indiana.edu

Telephone orders   800-842-6796
Fax orders   812-855-7931
Orders by e-mail   iuporder@indiana.edu

Portions of chapters 7, 8, and 9 were previously published as
"After the Death of God: Emmanuel Levinas and the Ethical Possibility
of God," *Journal of Religious Ethics* 24, no. 2. Portions of chapter 4 were previously
published as "The Disqualification of Intentionality: The Gift in Derrida, Levinas,
and Michel Henry," *Philosophy Today* (1997, supplement).

© 2001 by Jeffrey L. Kosky

The paper used in this publication meets the minimum requirements of American
National Standard for Information Sciences—Permanence of Paper for
Printed Library Materials, ANSI Z39.48-1984.

Manufactured in the United States of America

Library of Congress Cataloging-in-Publication Data

Kosky, Jeffrey L.
Levinas and the philosophy of religion / by Jeffrey L. Kosky.
p.   cm. — (Indiana series in the philosophy of religion)
Includes bibliographical references and index.
ISBN 0-253-33925-1 (alk. paper)
1. Lévinas, Emmanuel—Religion. 2. Religion—Philosophy. 3. Lévinas,
Emmanuel—Ethics. 4. Ethics, Modern.   I. Title.   II. Series.

B2430.L484 K67 2001
210'.92—dc21   00-050637

1 2 3 4 5   06 05 04 03 02 01

To Benjamin or Emma,
whoever you will have been . . .

CONTENTS

ACKNOWLEDGMENTS

How difficult, probably impossible, to write or describe here what I seem on the verge of describing. Perhaps it is impossible to hold a discourse which holds itself at this moment saying, explaining, taking note of E. L.'s work.

—Jacques Derrida, "En ce moment même dans cet ouvrage me voici"

If it is so difficult for a reader as keen as Jacques Derrida to describe, explain, or take note of Levinas's work, how much more so for one like myself, who can hardly claim the years of experience and a comparable reputation! My task has been made much easier, however, by the fact that friends and family, teachers and peers have sustained me along the way.

I was first put on that way by my professors as an undergraduate at Williams College, Mark C. Taylor and H. Ganse Little. I remain amazed by Taylor's incomparable teaching and his dedication to students both during their time in class and well after they leave. In Little, I found someone who inspired me with a passion for questions, paradoxes, associations, and everything else that makes life much richer and more worth living. Having learned immensely from them as teachers, I am now fortunate to count them as friends and to have benefited from their advice and wisdom as I negotiated the many twists and turns that led me to this book and beyond it.

Were it not for John D. Caputo and Merold Westphal, this book undoubtedly would not have seen the light of day. I offer my heartfelt thanks to them for that, though readers might offer them something else. Between the time this began as a dissertation project and the time it came to a close as a book, I had the happy occasion to meet and become friends with Jean-Luc Marion. In his writings, his teaching, and his conversation, he brought philosophy alive in a way that opened immeasurable possibilities for me. I thank him for that expansive gift and more.

The task itself, like all work of writing, was completed alone during long hours at the library or, more often, at my desk in a small circle of light illuminating myself and the words I read and wrote. The perhaps more important task of transforming this day-to-day accomplishment into cause for daily celebration was not, however, something that I did or could have done on my own. For that, I owe my gratitude to others: to my parents, Michael and Marsha Kosky, and my sister, Rachelle Kosky, who never let their incomprehension stand in the way of their love; to Tom Carlson for his good humor and, dare it be said, an optimism that I see each and every time I am with him; to Peter Struck and Natalie Dohrmann for the time we shared; to my friends at Redmoon Theater in Chicago—especially, Jim Lasko, Kristi Randall, Tria Smith, as well as Sheri Doyel and Blair Thomas—who knew more than enough to celebrate in me what they did not understand about what I was doing; and finally, to Stephanie Hodde, who came along when all seemed nearly said and done and showed me that the best was yet to come.

May 2000
Williamstown, Massachusetts

ABBREVIATIONS

The following works are cited in abbreviated form in this book. I have sometimes modified the translations cited.

Jacques Derrida

GD *The Gift of Death,* trans. David Wills (Chicago: University of Chicago Press, 1995). *Donner la mort, l'éthique du don* (Paris: Métaillié Transition, 1992).

VM "Violence and Metaphysics." In *Writing and Difference,* trans. Alan Bass (Chicago: University of Chicago Press, 1978). *L'écriture et la différence* (Paris: Editions du Seuil, 1967).

Martin Heidegger

BT *Being and Time,* trans. John Macquarrie and Edward Robinson (New York: Harper and Row, 1962). *Sein und Zeit,* 16th ed. (Tübingen: Max Niemeyer, 1986).

HCT *History of the Concept of Time: Prolegomena,* trans. Theodore Kisiel (Bloomington: Indiana University Press, 1992). *Prolegomena zur Geschichte des Zeitbegriffs,* Gesamtausgabe, vol. 20 (Frankfurt am Main: Vittorio Klostermann, 1979).

Edmund Husserl

CM *Cartesian Meditations: An Introduction to Phenomenology,* trans. Dorion Cairns (The Hague: Martinus Nijhoff, 1960). *Cartesianische Meditationen und Pariser Vorträge, Husserliana,* vol. 1 (The Hague: Martinus Nijhoff, 1963).

Id *Ideas Pertaining to a Pure Phenomenology and to a Phenomenological Philosophy,* First Book, *General Introduction to a Pure Phenomenology,* trans. F. Kersten (The Hague: Martinus Nijhoff, 1982). *Ideen zu einer reinen Phänomenologie und phänomenologischen Philosophie, Husserliana,* vol. 3 (The Hague: Martinus Nijhoff, 1950).

IP *The Idea of Phenomenology,* trans. William P. Alston and George Nakhnikian (The Hague: Martinus Nijhoff, 1964). *Die Idee der Phänomenologie, Husserliana,* vol. 2 (The Hague: Martinus Nijhoff, 1958).

PIT *The Phenomenology of Internal Time Consciousness,* trans. James S. Churchill (Bloomington: Indiana University Press, 1964). *Vorlesungen zur Phänomenologie des inneren Zeitbewusstseins,* ed. Martin Heidegger (Halle an der Saale: Max Niemeyer, 1928).

Emmanuel Levinas

AQS *Autrement que savoir, Emmanuel Levinas* (Paris: Editions Osiris, 1988).

BTV *Beyond the Verse: Talmudic Readings and Lectures,* trans. Gary D. Mole (Bloomington: Indiana University Press, 1994). *L'au delà du verset* (Paris: Les Editions de Minuit, 1982).

DEHH *En découvrant l'existence avec Husserl et Heidegger* (Paris: Librairie Philosophique J. Vrin, 1967).

EE *De l'existence à l'existant,* 3rd ed. (Paris: Librairie Philosophique J. Vrin, 1990).

EN *Entre Nous: Thinking of the Other,* trans. Michael B. Smith and Barbara Harshav (New York: Columbia University Press, 1998). *Entre nous: Penser à l'autre* (Paris: Grasset, 1991).

GCM *Of God Who Comes to Mind,* trans. Bettina Bergo (Stanford: Stanford University Press, 1998). *De dieu qui vient à l'idée* (Paris: Librairie Philosophique J. Vrin, 1990).

ITN *In the Time of the Nations,* trans. Michael B. Smith (Bloomington: Indiana University Press, 1994). *A l'heure des nations* (Paris: Les Editions de Minuit, 1988).

NTR *Nine Talmudic Readings,* trans. Annette Aronowicz (Bloomington: Indiana University Press, 1990). Includes: *Quatre lectures talmudiques* (Paris: Les Editions de Minuit, 1968); and *Du sacré au saint: Cinq nouvelles lectures talmudiques* (Paris: Les Editions de Minuit, 1977).

OBBE *Otherwise than Being, or, Beyond Essence,* trans. Alphonso Lingis (Dordrecht: Kluwer Academic Publishers, 1991). *Autrement qu'être ou au-delà de l'essence* (The Hague: Martinus Nijhoff, 1974).

TI *Totality and Infinity,* trans. Alphonso Lingis (Pittsburgh: Duquesne University Press, 1969). *Totalité et infini: Essai sur l'extériorité* (The Hague: Martinus Nijhoff, 1961).

INTRODUCTION

A comedy played out in the ambiguity of the temple and the theater,
but where the laughter sticks in your throat at the approach
of the neighbor . . .
—Emmanuel Levinas, "Dieu et la philosophie"

When Nietzsche and then Heidegger, standing at the brink of the twentieth century, announced the end of metaphysics, what they most put in question was something everyone knows: God and morality, or morality and God. Whatever the appropriate order might be, it has appeared ever since Nietzsche, if not before, that the destinies of morality and religion are linked. This connection is at times one of proportionality (as seems to have been the case during most of the subsequent history of the twentieth century), at times one of inverse proportionality (as Nietzsche himself noted in the triumphant moralism of the godless culture he denounced), and at times both, according to who is speaking. An entire genealogy of religion, at the very least of modern religion, could be written in the wake of Nietzsche, reflecting backwards and beyond, in which the significance of religious notions was reduced to the meaning they have for corresponding various forms of the moral consciousness.

As the twentieth century comes to a close, this paired destiny seems to be confirmed by important strands of cultural and academic discourse—but with an important difference. A century that began by dismissing or ignoring religious and ethical categories is now ending with a renewed interest, taking every opportunity to show the relevance of religious and ethical questions to readings of literature, psychoanalysis, philosophy, and culture in general. To be sure, the religion and the ethics of such renewed interest bear little resemblance to the religion and the ethics dismissed after Nietzsche and Heidegger; but the fact remains that there seems to be a twofold and paired opening to religious and ethical questions in disciplines previously closed to them.

The present work takes as its point of departure this observed connection between the destiny of ethics and that of religion. It asks if there might be another form of morality besides the morality of *ressentiment* denounced by Nietzsche and the morality of metaphysics criticized by Heidegger. Nietzsche himself admits this possibility by speaking not just of a slave morality but of a morality of the masters. Would another interpretation of the ethical subject open a new significance of religious categories? On the other hand, this book also asks if there might be another notion of God or religion besides the metaphysical ones attacked by Nietzsche and Heidegger. Nietzsche admits this possibility, too, when the madman, even before announcing "God is dead," cries out, "I seek God! I seek God!"[1] Would another religion or another God open the possibility of a new discourse on ethical life?

In this book, I raise these questions in and through a reading of the work of Emmanuel Levinas. I have chosen Levinas for at least two reasons. First, he represents one of the twentieth century's most powerful examples of this inseparable destiny, even suggesting how and why the two might be connected. Second, a canonic figure in the list of post-Nietzschean, post-Heideggerian, or, chronologically speaking, postmodern thinkers, Levinas nevertheless causes us to question the common perception of postmodern thought as irreligious and immoral, unconcerned about God and about the neighbor. Levinas's insistence on the importance of ethical considerations goes back to a date well before such concerns were fashionable; and he was delivering Talmudic lectures to Jewish audiences at a time when it was an academic heresy to speak about religion. The time thus seems right to turn to Levinas's work, and a growing body of literature from across the disciplines has done so. Many articles and a steadily increasing number of books have treated Levinas's ethics, and many are now turning to the religious significance of his thought. The questions that have been raised or that serve as points of contention are these: just how are ethics and religion related in Levinas's thought, and what is the relation of the religious themes found in his work to that of particular, historical religious traditions? These questions are the subject of this book.

To the many postmoderns who suspect that thanks to Nietzsche, they are through with religion and morality, the reading of Levinas proposed here suggests otherwise. For within the postmodern context of the end of metaphysics and the death of God, Levinas nevertheless proposes an ethical understanding of who we are, and he articulates this "proposal" in terms that are undeniably and unmistakably religious. Inversely, to those who remain secure in their commitments to religious traditions and moral systems and have deplored the century of thought after Nietzsche, after metaphysics, as decadent and exhausted, wholly incompatible with religion and morality, this reading of Levinas might suggest a way to understand how the age after modernity might still signify ethically and religiously.

It can hardly be doubted that the study of religion was crucial to the birth of many, if not all, of the disciplines which dominate modern thinking. No one less than Marx stated this clearly and precisely: "Criticism of religion is the presupposition of all criticism."[2] Marx's statement could represent the slogan not only for his own sociology but for those other great thinkers and the disciplines they founded at the culmination of modernity, namely, Freud and Nietzsche. The most important and dominant forms of thought in the twentieth century—Freudian psychoanalysis, Marxist sociology, and Nietzschean philosophy and existentialism—have evidently borne the stamp of this critical turn to the religious beliefs and institutions that structure personal, social, and cultural life.

With these names figuring the cultural paternity of the twentieth century, it is no wonder that the early years after the dawn of modernity were characterized by a marked antipathy or dismissal of religious issues and questions from the dominant cultural discourses. During this period, for instance, the mainstream view of psychoanalysis could be summed up by this remark from Philip Rieff: "It is on the subject of religion that the judicious clinician grows vehement and disputatious. Against no other strongpoint of repressive culture are the reductive weapons of psychoanalysis deployed in such open hostility."[3] In art criticism, Clement Greenberg represented the dominant voice. Claiming that modern and contemporary art was determined solely by a tendency toward purity and autonomy, Greenberg ignored the role of religious or spiritual concerns in shaping the history of art—despite the views frequently expressed by artists themselves. Discussing the origin of art in the then recently discovered caves of Lascaux, Greenberg evidenced his dismissal of religion from the field of art history when he wrote: "The art of Upper Paleolithic man was part of his *economy*."[4] By situating Paleolithic art in an economic site or function rather than in what now might seem to be the appropriate choice of a ritualistic or magical context, Greenberg clearly evidenced the ignorance (willed or not) of religion prevailing among dominant cultural discourses in the wake of modernity.

By the end of the century, however, the landscape was cast in a quite different light. Just as it cannot be doubted that the century began with a critical turn to religion, so too one can hardly avoid seeing that it ended with another turn to religion, though one with a far different outcome than the first.[5] Addressing past oversights, such theologians as Mark C. Taylor and David Tracy have suggested the important role that religion and religious issues have played in shaping cultural forms and discourses.[6] While Taylor and Tracy represent theologians arguing for the significance of religious studies to disciplines other than their own, the shift has also taken place from within individual disciplines. In literary theory, for example, Harold Bloom has suggested that the mystical Jewish kabbalah is a powerful theory of hermeneutics that should be of significance to anyone concerned with the interpretation of texts. Bloom has even promoted the notion that kabbalah foreshadows and anticipates key aspects of deconstruction, the theory which dominated literary circles at the time he was writing.[7] In psychoanalysis, Julia Kristeva has turned to a consideration of religious writers and texts in order to illuminate her psychoanalytic concerns with love and transference, abjection and repression, speech and desire. For Kristeva, psychoanalytic theory proves not to be hostile to religion but to greatly benefit from listening to it. In general, then, it could be said that what was once taboo, namely religion and religious texts, has gained acceptance in circles where it had been forbidden.[8]

Across all the humanistic disciplines, throughout the print and televisual media, and in major representatives of artistic and literary culture, a renewed interest in thinking, discussing, and seeking religious themes can be detected. The strength of the movement is nowhere more evident than in its rewriting of its own paternity—as when it is claimed that "there is another Freud: not the secular scientist, but the genuinely religious thinker."[9] Recent readings of Jacques Derrida are emblematic of this move to rewrite the history of postmodernism in terms that bring to light a religious concern. These readings are especially significant in that the name Derrida is, for most, synonymous with postmodernism. As anyone will agree, the earliest reception of Derrida in the English-speaking world was in departments of English or comparative literature. Kevin Hart, a trained literary critic and accomplished poet, has pointed out that the reception Derrida found there was framed by contexts that were avowedly atheistic or secular. In particular, Gayatri Spivak's "Translator's Preface" to Derrida's *Of Grammatology* situates Derrida's deconstruction in the context of Freud, Nietzsche, and Heidegger—more importantly, of atheistic readings of these authors. Thus, not only was the reception of deconstruction framed by a decision to place it in a nonreligious setting (Bloom's counter-example of kabbalah as a precursor showing that such a decision was arbitrary), but this context was built by particularly atheistic readings of the texts making it up. As Hart notes, the reception of Derrida was thus guided by Spivak's "stern warning to the reader: 'Let me add yet once again that this terrifying and exhilarating vertigo is not 'mystical' or 'theological.'"[10]

Against this framing, Hart proposes that we "put in question the often unspoken assumption that there is a natural or inevitable link between deconstruction and atheism."[11] He then goes on to offer a very compelling account of how deconstruction could be read in an explicitly religious or theological context: he suggests that certain forms of apophatic or negative theology might operate deconstructively and that deconstruction might serve to liberate theology from metaphysical forces. Along the same lines, John Caputo's *The Prayers and Tears of Jacques Derrida* argues that we will have understood Derrida less well if we have not understood his religion, what Caputo—citing Derrida—calls his "religion without religion." In opposition to the context that has dominated previous interpretations of Derrida, Caputo puts forth the bold hypothesis that "Jacques Derrida has religion, a certain religion, his religion" and that "deconstruction is set in motion by an overarching aspiration, which on a certain analysis can be called a religious or prophetic aspiration."[12]

In a sense, the present work proposes that a similar task be undertaken with regard to Levinas's work. It argues that an understanding of religion and the religious life is essential to understanding his work. To the all too many postmoderns who believe that the dawning of modernity thankfully put an end to religion and religious questions, my study of Levinas suggests that religious traditions and theological forms of thought are not as foreign to contemporary discourse as they would like to believe. And to those who, in the wake of modernity, still seek a religious dimension of life but cannot identify with religious traditions, I suggest that Levinas offers a way to think and speak about religion within the contemporary horizon of thought.

A parallel story about the concern for ethics and ethical language could perhaps be written. In recent years, critics both within the academy and in culture at large have expressed a growing interest in questions of alterity, or otherness; decision and responsibility; care for the self versus commitment to the other. They speak from varying perspectives, including not only those of feminism, postcolonialism, and gender studies but also in the traditional disciplines of literary and psychoanalytic studies, philosophy and theology.

The morality of modernity was critiqued by such writers and critics as Dostoevsky and Nietzsche. In their wake, postmodern culture reveled in newly found freedom from the repressive voices of old, exhausted authorities. What Dostoevsky analyzed in the declaration "God is dead! Everything is permitted!" was not received frightfully, as a terrifying burden carrying the weight of dislocated selfhood and infinite possibility, but enthusiastically, as an invitation to become oneself and satisfy one's desires. For one strand of postmodernity, this became the revolutionary proclamation of a dawning age of emancipated individuality or collective salvation. The most obvious example of unlimited emancipation being Gilles Deleuze's and Félix Guattari's dream of a collective not structured by the Oedipus myth, and so one not determined by the logic of repression or exclusion.[13]

Against this liberated, postmodern consciousness, something of a backlash arose. It was more and more frequently lamented that the postmodern twentieth century had lost everything that makes ethics and morality possible. Like Nietzsche on the cusp of his own century, these arguments look into the next century and fear an encroaching nihilism. Unlike Nietzsche, however, they ward off their despair with conviction, conviction of the value of the highest (metaphysical) values. Without such conviction, they conclude, the twenty-first century is threatened with the dissolution of all that holds together individual, social, and cultural life; having lost God, the twenty-first century threatens the collapse of all that made Western culture great. Without a God, what sanctions moral action? How can one do what is right and good without believing in God? And without moral certainty, how can we survive? When metaphysics is discredited, on what basis can we argue for the rightness or legitimacy of one code of morality over another? And doesn't our tired, decadent, wayward age need most of all some sense of what is right and what is wrong? To resist the encroachment of nihilism, these arguments often go, we must fight to retain or reinstate the

God and the systems of metaphysics that render it possible to make normative judgments and to hold certain convictions about our acts and those of others.

I do not believe that either of the above alternatives will bring salvation with the new millennium. Instead, I find myself joining camp with a growing number of authors who are rethinking crucial ethical categories—decision, responsibility, good and evil, agency, altruism or generosity—precisely within a horizon defined by the end of metaphysics and the death of God. Authors such as John Caputo and Edith Wyschogrod and, dare it be said, Mark C. Taylor and Jacques Derrida, have turned to considerations of the ethical dimensions of existence.[14] For these authors, the long list of questions above are real questions, not to be put to rest with premature answers from obsolete and discredited systems of thought. Before any advance in morality is to be made, if it is to be made, these questions must be inhabited—which is what these authors try to bring us to do. In keeping with the collapse of metaphysical transcendence and the Nietzschean critique of morality, the ethics they explore does not provide an alternative moral theory or normative standards, nor does it offer much consolation for the responsible self. Lacking the certainty and rewards offered in metaphysical systems of morality, it does nothing—and even resists all attempts to justify ethical action or make one feel good about one's involvement in good deeds. Nevertheless, these thinkers' work aims to articulate the terms within which we can think and question ethical experience in the wake of Nietzsche and Dostoevsky.

The reading of Levinas proposed here shares this aim. Without avoiding the unavoidable postmetaphysical, posttheoretical, post-Heideggerian horizon, subjective existence will be described in terms compatible with ethical concern. Indeed it was precisely reading Levinas that inspired many of these authors, not only with the passion to pursue this course but also with much of the vocabulary to articulate their position. As with its position regarding religion, this book turns to Levinas precisely because Levinas challenges us to think what was most put in question at the dawn of modernity (morality) without denying the postmodern horizon of thought (the end of metaphysics and the death of God).

Levinas is perhaps most well known for his claim that "ethics is first philosophy." It has been used to title two volumes of critical commentaries on his work in two different languages—one in French, one in English.[15] It has been repeated by those critics anxious to correct what they see as a crucial lack in postmetaphysical or postmodern thinkers, namely, its perceived indifference to ethical questions and concerns. This book, however, is premised on my belief that the claim "ethics is first philosophy" implies something other than an attempt to correct the ethical failings of the postmetaphysical era. In claiming ethics is first philosophy, Levinas not only elaborates a meaning of ethics but also, in this very discovery, uncovers a new figure of philosophy and philosophical intelligibility. To say that ethics is first philosophy not only means that ethics is a very important, the first or most important, concern of our age. It is a claim about philosophy. It says something about philosophical thought. I intend to give this claim a full hearing, allowing it to speak about philosophy and not just about ethical life.

When understood in this way, the claim "ethics is first philosophy" is the point of entry for illuminating the relation between the ethical and the religious in Levinas's thought. My thesis is this: *the analysis of responsibility opens onto a philosophical articulation of religious notions and thus makes possible something like a philosophy of religion.* As first philosophy, ethics opens philosophy to a new figure of its subject, namely, responsibility. A broader range of phenomena appear with this subject than its previous figure (consciousness). These phenomena include religious meanings that have traditionally been consigned to the unintelligibility of faith or else reduced to the intentions (conscious and unconscious) of the self. I argue that Levinas's ethical philosophy can be applied to a philosophy of religion which relieves theological thought of sacrificing the significance of religious notions at the threshold of intelligibility and understanding. This philosophy of religion gives significance to religious meanings by reducing them to the responsible subject where they appear. Achieved through a reduction to subjectivity, the significance of religion is accessible to those not committed to a particular religious tradition.

My reading of Levinas necessitates that he be wrested somewhat from contexts in which he has most often been read. Since he is, apparently, an ethicist or philosopher of ethics, it is not evident at first sight why Levinas is relevant to the current interest in religion and religious questions. Readings that ignore the religious significance of Levinas's work often presuppose it to be divided in two parts. The first part, represented by the major works *Totality and Infinity* and *Otherwise than Being, or, Beyond Essence,* would be philosophical. The second, comprising his several volumes of Talmudic commentaries and a volume of essays entitled *Difficult Freedom: Essays on Judaism,* would be deemed religious. In the logic of this frame, the first part of Levinas's work is not matter for a discussion of religion and religious issues since it is philosophy. This framing of Levinas's work serves as the unstated premise justifying the fact that many, not all, early and popular commentaries on Levinas did not consider the religious dimensions operative in his work. With few exceptions, it was not until the most recent collections of critical commentaries on Levinas that sections devoted to religion are to be found. What is more, this framework has meant that when religious issues and questions are considered in Levinas's work, they are most often assigned to, quarantined in, a section or chapter of their own, safe from traffic with philosophy and saving philosophy from having to traffic with them.

My reading of Levinas shows that such categories oversimplify the complex relation and often blurred boundaries between the philosophical and religious aims of Levinas's thought. This all too tidy categorization of the work leads interpreters to ignore or remain dumb before crucial theses put forth in Levinas's admittedly philosophical work: namely, the attempt announced in the preface to *Otherwise than Being, or, Beyond Essence*, "to hear a God not contaminated by Being" (OBBE, xlii) and the claim that "what is at stake for the self in its being is not to be. Beyond egoism and altruism, it is the religiosity of the self" (OBBE, 117). The prominence of these claims in philosophical work suggests that understanding religion, religious language, and religious concerns is crucial to understanding even the philosophical work.

The work of reading Levinas in the context of religious questions and concerns has already been undertaken by authors who seek to emphasize the particularly Jewish aspects of the responsible self. These authors suppose the influence of Judaism to be the chief reason for reading Levinas and position him as a "Jewish philosopher."[16] Though I admit the importance of Judaism to Levinas, I must argue against reading him as a Jewish philosopher, first because he says he is not one,[17] and second because such a reading fails to appreciate the sense in which the discovery of the subject's religiosity happens through a phenomenology of the subject as such, a subject that we all are (even if each says I alone am responsible). In suggesting that the responsibility and hence the religiosity of the subject is identifiable with the religion of an historical people and religious tradition, these readings restrict the possible signification of Levinas's thought in the posttraditional context of much of late twentieth-century and early twenty-first-century culture. When they do argue for a broader significance of Levinas's ethics, they do so, it seems to me, by risking a repetition of the crime with which nineteenth-century Christian theology has been charged: the crime of making one particular religion the archetypal or consummate religion.

The operation of Jewish tradition and a commitment to Judaism in Levinas's phenomenology has also been noted by Dominique Janicaud; but for him, this is precisely why Levinas is not of interest to philosophy, why his work is best left to those who can identify with particular religious traditions and why it should not be influential in university or public discourse. Janicaud argues that the presence of religious language in Levinas's phenomenology represents something like a "theological hijacking" of phenomenology.[18] Levinas's phenomenology is not imposed by philosophical rigor but dogmatically, that is, by a "Jewish philosopher" philosophizing in accord with commitments to religious dogma and on the basis of a revelation kept in the tradition. This would amount to a betrayal of the phenomenological reduction and the claim to a first philosophy. Thus, that for which the first camp praises Levinas, that which they claim makes him of utmost importance to philosophy—namely, his commitment to Judaism and his position within the Jewish tradition—is precisely what renders his phenomenology unphenomenological according to the second.

Seeking to cut across this debate, I suggest instead that Levinas's analysis of responsibility can be seen as a discourse on religion that, at least in its intentions, holds forth without recourse to the authority of any faith or religious tradition. I argue, against readings that identify Levinas as a Jewish philosopher, that the religiosity met in Levinas's phenomenology of responsibility is not an actual religion but the possibility or nonnoematic meaning of religion. In his great philosophical works, *Otherwise than Being, or, Beyond Essence* and *Of God Who Comes to Mind,* everything happens as if the phenomenological analysis of responsibility alone sufficed for, and even necessitated, discovering the significance of religious notions. Levinas's ethical phenomenology therefore becomes a way for those who cannot or will not subscribe to religious traditions—philosophers and others—to nonetheless approach the significance of religious issues and religious language.

At this point, the religiosity of the responsible subject might seem like a sort of secular transformation of religion into ethics. It might seem as if the religiosity I am proposing to discover in Levinas is just another example of what the sociologists, psychologists, and historians of religion have taught us to see everywhere today: namely, the dissemination of religiosity throughout cultural life. I argue, however, that the religiosity of the responsible self is distinguished from a secular transformation of religion by Levinas's attempt to give significance to the meaning of divine *transcendence*.[19] Not only is the significance of transcendence unanimously excluded from these secular disseminations of religion, it is also the one phenomenon which has almost never appeared in the philosophy of religion of the twentieth century. This absence can be traced back to the founding moment of the modern philosophy of religion and so into those postmoderns who still think to think about religion. In those figures who mark its birth (namely Kant, Hegel, and Nietzsche), the emergence of the philosophy of religion is closely connected to the death of God—either consummating, conditioning, or coming as the result of it. I will argue that a philosophy of religion issuing from Levinas's phenomenology might surpass the beginnings of this tradition in what Hegel described as "the feeling that 'God Himself is dead,' upon which the religion of [modernity] rests."[20]

In pursuit of these points, this book is divided into three parts. The first is devoted to a reading of Levinas's project as it is expressed in *Totality and Infinity.* Sounding a note long unheard in the reigning avant-garde, post-Nietzschean philosophy and culture of 1961 Paris, Levinas's work opens with the declaration "everyone will readily agree that it is of the highest importance to know whether we are not duped by morality" (TI, 21). It then goes on to offer a not so readily agreed upon account of metaphysics itself in precisely ethical terms. Taking the author at his word when he claims "it would be false to qualify [his ethical thought] as theological" (TI, 42), my reading of *Totality and Infinity* begins with a strictly philosophical reading of Levinas. Through reference to Jacques Derrida's "Violence and Metaphysics," I then argue for a theological reading of *Totality and Infinity*, thus proposing that even an avowedly philosophical thought can be complicit with a certain theology. In this way, I claim that what Levinas claims is the hidden foundation of all thought and language, even and most expressly of theological language, is already guided by a theologic, already ordered by a theological conceptuality.

Having detected an underlying theological conceptuality operative in Levinas's *Totality and Infinity*, the stage is set for parts 2 and 3 of the book. There, I turn to Levinas's later ethical thought as it is expressed most forcefully in the two works *Otherwise than Being, or, Beyond Essence* and *Of God Who Comes to Mind*. In thus dividing the book, I do not intend for it to trace the development of Levinas's work or to argue that Derrida's monograph was responsible for any such development; many authors have undertaken these most interesting and sometimes illuminating tasks. I do hope, however, to address thereby the well-recognized fact that there are significant differences between the language and even the intentions of *Totality and Infinity* and that of the later work.

Part 2 attempts to position Levinas within a philosophical tradition. It is meant to lay the groundwork for my discussion of his contribution to the philosophy of religion. *Otherwise than Being, or, Beyond Essence* and *Of God Who Comes to Mind* are situated within the phenomenological tradition insofar as their thought is achieved through the practice of the reduction and is carried out as an analysis of subjectivity. Part 2 means to give a full hearing to the claim that "ethics is first philosophy" by investigating first the meaning of philosophy as it was promoted phenomenologically by Husserl and then the question why ethics—and not, for example, ontology or the phenomenology of consciousness—leads phenomenology to its ideal. My investigation is presented as something like a comparison of the three major claimants to the office of subjectivity (however displaced or decentered this subject might be): Husserl's consciousness, Levinas's responsibility, and Heidegger's *Dasein* or existence. Through this comparison, I hope to show what phenomenology is capable of when it takes first consciousness then responsibility as its subject. As responsibility, subjectivity is first or originary in a new way. No longer are phenomena accounted for by tracing them back to the conscious I that makes them appear or that constitutes the conditions of their appearance. Rather, in responsibility, phenomena appear without this appearance being limited by conditions set in and by the priority of the I of consciousness.

I also use such a comparison to pose a question that I believe is not asked frequently enough when reading Levinas. To the degree that it reaches an ultimate figure of the subject where phenomena appear, Levinas's phenomenology constitutes a first philosophy. However, it is not entirely clear why this subject has to be thought in terms of ethics. When Levinas claims "no language other than ethics could be equal to the paradox that phenomenology enters" (OBBE, 193) when it practices a reduction to the ultimate figure of subjectivity, one should immediately wonder: why no language but ethics? What is so special about ethical language that it can relieve phenomenology in this way? Might there be another horizon in which the subject is structured in ways similar to that of responsibility such that it too could play the role of nonoriginary origin? I want to raise these questions through a reading of Heidegger's Dasein analytic. By showing the striking similarities between the subject in Levinas (responsibility) and in Heidegger (Dasein), I suggest that there is no reason why the new phenomenological ultimate needs to be described in ethical terms. The same figure of the subject could be presented in existential terms, and might even be generalizable to a thought of subjectivity freed from any horizon whatsoever.[21] In noting these similarities, I want to challenge the privilege that Levinas accords ethics in the phenomenological account of the subject.

It is in part 3, then, that I treat the relation between Levinas's ethical phenomenology and religion. Levinas's position within phenomenological philosophy having been established and tested in part 2, part 3 poses a question which Husserl himself asked after his own practice of the reduction arrived at the subject as consciousness: "What can I do with [it] philosophically?" (CM, 27). Having shown in part 2 that a broader range of phenomena appear when the subject is construed as responsibility than will appear for consciousness, I argue in part 3 that this extended range includes religious phenomena. Husserl's question can be addressed, therefore, and the responsible subject used philosophically to articulate a philosophy of religion. I contend that this philosophy of religion evades the alternative of either consigning religious phenomena to a faith that knows not of what it speaks or constituting them as phenomena known by consciousness.[22] Religious notions such as creation, election, martyrdom, and sacrifice are all given significance by a reduction that leads them back to the responsible subject where they signify.

I conclude by suggesting that Levinas's phenomenology of responsibility surpasses the origin, and outcome, of the philosophy of religion in the death of God. By saving the significance of the transcendence of God, a philosophy of religion that issues from Levinas's phenomenology distinguishes itself from most secularizations of religion as well as from the majority of modern philosophies of religion. This is perhaps the most remarkable possibility opened by the phenomenology of responsibility. But, it is a possibility that remains haunted by an ineradicable shadow of doubt, undecidability, and confusion. For, in accepting the postmetaphysical, posttraditional horizon of philosophical thought, phenomenology can only name this transcendence anonymously. Having distinguished the subject as responsibility from the subject as consciousness, and having located responsibility in a quasi-transcendental realm outside historical traditions, the attempt to save the name "God" for what signifies in responsibility is troubled in several ways. The responsible self cannot tell, and certainly cannot tell anyone else, whether its responsibility witnesses God or something else since both it and God are outside the order (metaphysics and consciousness) where identification would be possible. What is more, the anonymity of this God and the trauma suffered by the self are disturbingly close to a more menacing form of the anonymous as that anonymity was described in Levinas's earliest work under the "name" *il y a*.

The book ends with this undecidability, not at all a reassuring point at which to arrive but one rich with possibility: is it God or the anonymous menace of some other other that is witnessed in responsibility? The religiosity that signifies in this postmodern responsibility, is it religion or an absurd comedy? I believe that arriving at this point of indecision, the point where the question is asked, is the most important lesson we have to learn from reading Levinas. As responsibility, subjectivity is played out "in the ambiguity of the temple and the theater."

PART 1
Beyond *Totality and Infinity*

1

Ethics as the
End of Metaphysics

It is not often well-enough remarked that Emmanuel Levinas's *Totality and Infinity* seeks *not* to overcome or destroy metaphysics but to retain a positive sense of it. The author even goes so far as to proclaim that "[metaphysics] is the ultimate relation in Being" and that "ontology presupposes metaphysics" (TI, 48). In this way, *Totality and Infinity* marks an end of metaphysics where the end is not so much a disappearance or vanishing as it is a sort of completion, a place where metaphysics comes to itself after a long history of being distorted by its traditional appropriation.

This is why *Totality and Infinity* begins not with a denunciation of metaphysics and a call to overcome it but with a description or definition of the desire of metaphysics.

> [Metaphysics] is turned toward the "elsewhere" and the "otherwise" the "other." For in the most general form it has assumed in the history of thought it appears as a movement going forth from a world that is familiar to us . . . toward an alien outside of oneself, toward a yonder. . . . The metaphysical desire tends toward *something else entirely,* toward the *absolutely other.* (TI, 33)

Thus, for Levinas the end of metaphysics can be defined as the absolutely other; metaphysics is the movement unto exteriority or the absolutely other. This is the essence, distillation, or "most general form it has assumed in the history of thought." Elsewhere in the work, this description of the desire of metaphysics is joined to a somewhat more widely accepted formulation of metaphysics. In it, metaphysics is defined as a movement unto a transcendent being:

> The absolute exteriority of the metaphysical term, the irreducibility of the movement to an inward play . . . [is] claimed by the word transcendent. The metaphysical movement is transcendent. . . . The transcendence with

which the metaphysician designates it enters into the way of existing of the exterior being. (TI, 35)

The end of metaphysics is "this relation with a being [*un étant*]. . . . It is the ultimate relation in Being. Ontology presupposes metaphysics" (TI, 48).

What these texts show is that, for the author of *Totality and Infinity*, the metaphysical desire thinks together a being, exteriority, transcendence, and the absolutely other. That is, aiming at a being as such or a being itself, metaphysics aims at the absolutely other in its exteriority or transcendence. As a corollary, these texts suggest that Levinas's true target in *Totality and Infinity* is not so much metaphysics as it is a tradition of thinking metaphysics which has obscured or failed to enact its essential desire. The tradition has obscured this desire, according to Levinas, in two ways: by thinking the absolutely other in terms of negativity (Hegel) and by thinking the being as such within the prior comprehension of Being (Heidegger).

The question, then, for Levinas is the following: at what does metaphysics aim such that it moves toward the absolutely other, the being as such? Anyone familiar with even the least bit of Levinas's work knows the answer: metaphysical desire is desire for *Autrui*, the personal other. Ethics accomplishes the metaphysical desire (an accomplishment which does not mean arriving at an end) because it is in ethics that a being that is absolutely other or exterior presents itself as such. This presence is the face of *Autrui*: "Our relation with the Metaphysical is an ethical behavior" (TI, 78). This implies that in failing to accomplish the end of metaphysics, the history of metaphysics is guilty of denying or forgetting the alterity (the face) of *Autrui*;[1] it is at once *violence* against *Autrui* and a *falsification* of the metaphysical quest. In other words, violence against *Autrui* is as much an ethical crime as it is a disaster for metaphysical thought of *l'étant*. In failing to admit *Autrui*, the tradition has been unable to reach the reorientation of metaphysics which alone, according to Levinas, will allow it to accomplish itself.

In *Totality and Infinity*, then, it is not a question of abandoning metaphysics but of leading it toward the end it has always sought—the being as such, being itself, which means the absolutely other or exteriority: the face of *Autrui*. By thinking the ethical encounter with *Autrui*, Levinas redirects metaphysics to *l'étant* that presents itself as such or *l'étant* itself by purging metaphysics of what the tradition has interposed between it and its end. According to Levinas, this purgation entails a confrontation with the Hegelian thought of negativity as much as with the Heideggerian comprehension of Being.

Without Negativity

The "Same" is the single term with which Levinas characterizes the violence integral to the traditional appropriation of metaphysics: all metaphysics insofar as it has thought of the Same has been constituted by violence against the otherness of *l'étant*. Hence it is important to begin by understanding what Levinas means by the Same. One will miss the radicality of

Levinas's thought of the absolutely other if one mistakes the Same for an undifferentiated unity or unchanging substance. Echoing Hegel's determination of the Absolute, the Same is not substance but subject, the I, namely, "the being whose existing consists in identifying itself, in recovering its identity throughout all that happens to it . . . the primordial work of identification. The I is identical in its very alterations" (TI, 36). Again following Hegel, the subjective work of identification or recovering self in difference, the work which distinguishes the subject which is "for-itself" from the substance which is "in-itself," is the "labor of the negative." Negativity is the work by which the subject identifies itself in otherness and confirms what Levinas calls thought of the Same.

Established in and through identification, the Same comprehends otherness, grasping it in knowledge and possession. The same "carries out an act of violence and of negation. A partial negation, which is violence. And this partialness can be described in the fact that, without disappearing, beings [*l'étant*] are in my power. The partial negation which is violence denies the independence of beings [*l'étant*]: they are mine" (EN, 9).[2] The other partially negated is preserved, but it is preserved in its negation, that is as the same. Its absolute alterity is reduced to an other that is integral to the Same or I. On Levinas's reading, this reduction of alterity is the violence against the other: the same is integrally violent insofar as it necessitates that otherness appear only on the condition that its alterity be reduced to a comprehensible alterity. In *Totality and Infinity*, then, violence is the necessity that the other dissimulate itself in its appearance for the same.

In describing the same as constituted by a negativity that negates and preserves the other, Levinas describes it in terms strikingly similar to those used by Kojève to describe the Hegelian I. In his seminal *Introduction to the Reading of Hegel*, Kojève writes that, for Hegel,

> negating action is not purely destructive, for if it destroys an objective reality, for the sake of satisfying the Desire from which it was born [a Desire such as this would be what Levinas calls need], it creates in its place, in and by that very destruction, a subjective reality. . . . The I of Desire [need] is an emptiness that receives a real positive content only by negating action that satisfies Desire in destroying, transforming, and "assimilating" the desired non-I.[3]

On Kojève's reading of Hegel, negation is not total destruction or annihilation of otherness but the "transformation" and "assimilation" of the other, an activity which is constitutive of the I. While Levinas, too, holds that the I is constituted not by the pure annihilation of alterity but by the partial negation and mastery of otherness, he claims that, for this very reason, the I is integrally violent. Contrary to the opinion common in recent political and social thought, where it is held that exclusion constitutes the violence against marginalized groups, subjectivity for Levinas is inherently violent not because it is constituted by excluding otherness but because in its very constitution it includes the other within it while mastering its otherness.

Within the same, there would be only the otherness designated by Hegelian phenomenology. This is an otherness that I distinguish from myself
and that is consequently an otherness identified at once as the same as
myself. Levinas cites a passage from Hegel's *Phenomenology of Spirit* to illustrate this:

> I distinguish myself from myself; and therein I am immediately aware that
> this factor distinguished from me is not distinguished. I, the selfsame be-
> ing, thrust myself away from myself; but this which is distinguished,
> which is set up as unlike me, is immediately on its being distinguished no
> distinction from me. (TI, 36)[4]

Within the same, I alter myself within myself by at once negating myself
and identifying myself in this difference from myself. Negation would be
the movement whereby I make these distinctions and at once recover myself in these distinctions. In this way, negativity is the negation of the negation, which by negating what is posited as other constitutes the same or the
identity of the I.

At this point, the attempt to think the other seems integral to the constitution of the same and therefore bound to violence against alterity. As
Jacques Derrida has pointed out, if we do not notice the theses concerning
the constitution of the same in and through an intrinsic other, we will miss
what is essential in Levinas's attempt to think the otherness of the being as
such (VM, 94). For, to *both* the same and the other comprehended by it,
Levinas juxtaposes the absolutely other, which he will call the Infinite and
the transcendent. The absolutely other would be beyond the same, that is,
it would be neither the I nor the (false) other (falsely) distinguished from
the I.[5]

Within *Totality and Infinity*, the Same is equivalent to the I. This strange
conceptuality means that any protest against totality on behalf of subjective
existence, the I, is just as much a promotion of the same as is Hegelianism.
Hence, Levinas writes that "it is not I who resist the system, as Kierkegaard
thought; it is the other" (TI, 40).[6] For Levinas, it is not the thought of subjective existence that escapes the totality but the approach of the infinite or
the other. This pits his thought against two thinkers who, as some argue—
most notably Mark C. Taylor—mark the extreme limits of Western thought:
Kierkegaardian thought, in its obsession with the I that neither comprehends nor is comprehended by the system, would be guilty of the same
violence against the other as would be the Hegelian philosophy that comprehends the system in its totality.[7]

According to Levinas, the absolutely other, the transcendent, is a being
that is other by itself, without its otherness depending on its being distinguished from the I, though nevertheless it is not identical with this I. As not
depending on any distinction from the same, the difference between the I
and the absolutely other is not a difference that follows after an antecedent
sameness or commonality. The absolutely other is "a being that stands beyond every attribute, which would precisely have as its effect to qualify

him, that is, to reduce him to what is common to him and other beings" (TI, 74).[8] In other words, alterity is not attributed to a being that is fundamentally the same as me. For Levinas, then, the thought of the absolutely other is, as Derrida says, a "thought of original difference," a difference that precedes and is not reducible to the integration of the I and its intrinsic other in the same (VM, 90). What Derrida here calls "original difference" is called, in the lexicon of *Totality and Infinity*, "separation." In asserting separation to be original, Levinas stands opposed to a thought for which difference, the distinction between the same and the other, signals and results from a fall from primordial unity.

This separation is not the distinction of two finite terms that limit one another and therefore define the finitude of each other. Such would be the case in the Hegelian dialectic of the master and the slave, each of which limits the other and is at the same time integral to defining the identity of the other: the master is master only when recognized as such by the slave that the master is not, and vice versa. For Levinas, if separation is to respect the absolutely other, this other must not arise on the border or limit that distinguishes while defining finite beings. Such respectful separation is, according to Levinas, the distance in and through which the absolutely other appears.[9] Not defined by its opposite, the absolutely other is distant without this distance depending on its relation to another term. "The transcendence with which the metaphysician designates it is remarkable in that the distance it expresses, unlike all distances, enters into the way of existing of the exterior being. Its formal characteristic—to be other—makes up its content" (TI, 35). Unlike other distances, the distance of the transcendent is not relative to a finite term which it would limit but is constitutive of the transcendent itself. It is in keeping with the strictures of distance that Levinas wants us to understand the "and" of *Totality and Infinity:* this "and" is, according to Levinas, a nonconjunctive conjunction; it presents the Same with what remains at a distance from it. In admitting a conjunction with what it cannot join (since it is given in distance), the Same renounces its claim to totality, or at least acknowledges that its claim to totality cannot include all.[10]

Levinas describes the relation that exceeds the movement of negativity, the relation with the absolutely other who remains forever in distance, as the idea of infinity. Unlike a concept that conceives or grasps the finite, the idea of infinity is "exceptional in that its ideatum surpasses its idea" (TI, 49). For this reason, Levinas sees the idea of infinity as a way of approaching the other that does not grasp the other but lets it remain in distance. When the metaphysician thinks the idea of infinity,

> the distance that separates ideatum and idea here constitutes the content of the ideatum itself. Infinity is characteristic of a transcendent being as transcendent; the infinite is the absolutely other. The transcendent is the sole ideatum of which there can be only an idea in us; it is infinitely removed from its idea, that is exterior, because it is infinite. (TI, 49)

Unlike concepts which grasp or contain that which they conceive, the idea of infinity does not grasp that of which it is an idea precisely because it is an idea of the distance that separates this *ideatum* from thought.

Since the absolutely other remains forever in distance without limiting the Same, Levinas will write that "this separation is not simply a negation . . . [it] opens upon the idea of infinity" (TI, 105). With this notion of the Infinite, Levinas opposes the Hegelian notion of the Infinite which becomes truly infinite by negating the finitude which opposes it. Leaving out no other, Hegel's true Infinite is that from which nothing is separate because it grasps or comprehends within it its own negation and every other. In contrast to the true Infinite of Hegel, Levinas sees the idea of infinity as the idea of that which exceeds comprehension and is excluded from a supposedly limitless totality. As Infinity, the absolutely other escapes comprehension not because it is simply lacking from the same but because it overflows it: "infinity overflows the thought that thinks it. Its very infinition is produced in this overflowing" (TI, 25). Levinas describes this overflowing or exceeding the same as the ab-solution of the absolute. The exceptional idea of infinity is thus a relation with the absolute that does not render it relative but respects its very absolution from every relation it enters.

Since negativity is the movement that constitutes the Same, the absolutely other can never be conceived by reference to the category negativity. In one of the more intriguing sections of *Totality and Infinity*, "Transcendence Is Not Negativity," Levinas argues that the absolutely other would be expressed in the idea of perfection or the idea of infinity. But,

> precisely perfection exceeds conception, overflows the concept; it designates distance. . . . This passage to the limit does not remain on the common plane of the *yes* and the *no* at which negativity operates. . . . The idea of the perfect and of infinity is not reducible to the negation of the imperfect; negativity is incapable of transcendence. (TI, 41)

According to Levinas, affirmation and negation, yes and no, remain negative determinations of each other. As such, concepts of neither one sort nor the other are capable of containing the absolutely other. In distinguishing the absolutely other from the negation of its opposite, Levinas attempts to introduce a form of negativity—if it can still be called that—which does not constitute the Same. On this reading of negativity, the negation of the negation would not return to the same (as in the passage cited from Hegel) but would transcend the same.

We thus encounter what Derrida has described as the "nature of Levinas's writing[:] . . . to progress by negations, and by negation against negation. Its proper route is not that of an 'either this . . . or that,' but of a 'neither this . . . nor that'" (VM, 90). That is to say, neither affirmative nor negative propositions can contain or conceive the absolutely other. Though Levinas's conceptuality demands that the other be inconceivable by negativity, there is nevertheless an excessive abundance of negations in his thought. But, these negations progress otherwise than in the Hegelian dialectic of opposites. By using the formula 'neither this . . . nor that' to describe Levinas's writing, Derrida remarks that Levinas's thought of the absolutely other can proceed only by way of a non-Hegelian negation, that is a negation that does not determine opposites and that consequently moves beyond the same. In progressing by negation against negation, the Levinasian neither/nor does not contain or aim to secure an affirmation in its negation, as does the negativity that returns to or affirms the same. As such, it would be an infinite negation or a negation ad infinitum. If it contains no affirmation, the Levinasian negation would not finally determine the other, would never be definitive, would never pretend to define or to grasp the absolutely other.

But where might we find a relation that meets the perhaps impossible requirements of a metaphysics of this absolute other? Up until now, Levinas's analyses have failed to offer any description of this situation; they have remained almost formal and logical. On Levinas's reading, the relation without negativity, the one that evades violence and the constitution of the same, is discourse. "It is prior to the negative or affirmative proposition; it first institutes language, where neither the no nor the yes is the first word. The description of this relation is the central issue of the present research" (TI, 42). But, before turning to this description, I must examine another way in which the Same violates the alterity of the other and so fails to achieve the dream of metaphysics.

The Same Revisited: Ontology

For Levinas, the tradition has constituted metaphysics as the promotion of the Same before the other, the reduction of the other to the Same. This understanding of metaphysics and the traditional (mis)constitution of it allows Levinas to include Heidegger in the tradition that has failed to realize what metaphysics has always sought. This is a very strange move because it was Heidegger who had claimed to undertake a destruction of the tradition that was responsible for blocked access to the original question of metaphysics. To include Heidegger in the tradition, then, is a remarkable move, one possible to the degree that the metaphysical task has been reimagined.[11]

Heidegger's destruction of the tradition and his attempt to think what remains unthought by it differ markedly from Levinas's. For Heidegger, the metaphysical tradition has failed to think the meaning of Being because it remains ontically preoccupied with beings, never passing beyond what is to ask after the meaning of the Being of what is. The task of thinking is to think the unthought meaning of Being presupposed by any ontic thought, that is, any thought of what is, be it anthropological, biological, theological, or metaphysical thought. Each such region of ontic thought presupposes an understanding of Being, an ontology that determines the being of what is ontically studied by it. However, even ontological inquiry into the Being of what is studied ontically "remains itself naive and opaque if in its researches into the Being of entities it fails to discuss the meaning of Being in general"

(BT, 31). For this reason, Heidegger proposes a fundamental ontology that will lay bare the meaning of Being in general, a meaning that is presupposed in every ontic science of what is and in every ontological understanding of the Being of what is.

At the point when he takes as his task to explicate the meaning of Being, Heidegger recognizes the necessity of securing the correct point of departure for his fundamental ontology: fundamental ontology can begin only if one first considers a being for whom Being is at issue before it is determined by scientific inquiry, namely, *Dasein*. This being is the one that we ourselves are before our Being is determined as subjective or as scientific inquirers. Heidegger justifies his choice of *Dasein* as the point of departure on the grounds that *Dasein* is the entity whose mode of being is to ask the very question of the meaning of Being. In fact, when *Dasein* is first named in *Being and Time*, it is determined precisely as the possibility of asking this question:

> the very asking of this question [the question of Being] is an entity's mode of *Being;* and as such it gets its essential character from what is inquired about—namely, Being. This entity which each of us is himself and which includes inquiring as one of the possibilities of its Being, we shall denote by the term "*Dasein.*" (BT, 25)

Dasein is selected as the point of departure for fundamental ontology for a second reason; namely, it is the being for whom "Being in a world is something that belongs essentially. Thus Dasein's understanding of Being pertains with equal primordiality both to an understanding of something like a 'world,' and to the understanding of the Being of those entities which become accessible within the world. . . . Dasein accordingly takes priority [because it possesses] an understanding of the Being of all entities of a character other than its own" (BT, 34). *Dasein* thus receives a second equally fundamental determination (Being-in-the-world) from which its privilege in the work of *Being and Time* derives. In contrast to Levinas, who sees the path to the transcendent other as the way out of the traditional appropriation of metaphysics, Heidegger attempts this egress by approaching the unthought meaning of Being in and through *Dasein*, determined minimally as being-able-to-question and being-in-the-world.[12]

On Levinas's reading, however, Heideggerian thought remains complicit with the violence constitutive of that tradition insofar as, according to Levinas, it promotes the Same before the other.[13] On Levinas's reading, the very framing of the question of Being and understanding of Being in the world, as articulated in *Being and Time*, violate alterity because they subject its appearance to the conditions imposed by a horizon previously disclosed in the understanding.

To understand how Heidegger remains a thinker of the Same and consequently an accomplice to the tradition of thought that denies, reduces, or violates the alterity of the other, I want to discuss what Levinas means by the comprehension of Being or Heideggerian ontology. On Levinas's reading, the comprehension of Being means at least two things. First, it names the entire Heideggerian interrogation of Being, the fundamental ontology of *Being and Time* just as much as the later thought of Being. Second, comprehension of Being is existence itself (the *Dasein* of *Being and Time*). As he writes in the article "L'ontologie, est-elle fondamentale," "the so called authentic ontology coincides with the facticity of temporal existence. . . . The comprehension of Being does not suppose only a theoretical attitude but the entire comportment of man. All of man is ontology. . . . [And], to comprehend Being is to exist" (EN, 14–15). In other words, when Levinas speaks of the comprehension of Being, he means both Heideggerian thought as a philosophical questioning and *Dasein* or existence, Being-in-the-world.

It is not hard to find in *Being and Time* passages that explicitly acknowledge the near synonymy of *Dasein*'s existence and authentic questioning:

> If to interpret the meaning of Being becomes our task, Dasein is not only the primary entity to be interrogated; it is also that entity which already comports itself, in its Being, towards what we are asking about when we ask this question. But in that case the question of Being is nothing other than the radicalization of an essential tendency-of-Being which belongs to Dasein itself—the preontological understanding of Being. (BT, 35)

What Levinas calls comprehension of Being includes both the "preontological understanding of Being," which definitively characterizes *Dasein*, and the explicit formulation of this "preontological understanding" in the developed ontology of *Being and Time*. In terms of comprehending Being, the difference between existence and the question of Being would be only one of degree; the latter is a modification of the former: it renders explicit what was only implicit in the former. In what follows, when I plot the structure of the question of Being and of existence in the world, I am, implicitly at least, describing the comprehension of Being. By doing so, I hope to show ultimately how, for Levinas, such comprehension reduces the other to the same.

The question of Being is formulated in paragraph two of *Being and Time*. Since it is a "kind of seeking," according to Heidegger, the question of Being is "guided beforehand by what is sought. So the meaning of Being must already be available to us in some way. . . . We always conduct our activities in an understanding of Being" (BT, 25). In other words, the question of Being is posed as one which already understands what it seeks (the meaning of Being) but understands it in a vague or unclarified way. In thus framing the question, Heidegger announces what he will later call (§32) the forestructure of the understanding. The understanding is not the result of willed acts of knowing on the part of *Dasein* but belongs, always and in advance, to the unavoidable existential constitution of *Dasein*. According to Heidegger, *Dasein*'s position in the world is to be the very place where there is an understanding of Being, the very opening from which Being shines forth. While commenting on *Being and Time* nearly twenty years after its

publication, Heidegger emphasized this point: "the only way the 'understanding of Being' in the context of the 'existential analysis' of 'being-in-
the-world' can be thought . . . [is as] the ecstatic relation to the light of
Being."[14] Because it always and in advance understands Being, *Dasein* is
where the question of Being takes place and thus where it is possible to
explicate the meaning of Being.

The question of Being comprises two moments: the understanding of
Being, which has always already happened in advance, and interpretation,
which probes the forestructure of the understanding of Being in order to
seek out the meaning of Being. The "development of the understanding we
call 'interpretation' [*Auslegung*]. In it the understanding appropriates understandingly that which is understood by it. In interpretation, understanding does not become something different. It becomes itself" (BT, 188). Being has already been disclosed for the understanding in such a way that, to
proceed with the question, we need to "interpret this average understanding of Being" (BT, 25). The movement of interpretation is not one that
passes to what is absolutely other or surprisingly different, but one in which
existence "becomes itself," becomes what it already understands itself to
be. In seeing interpretation as the becoming itself of the understanding of
Being, Heidegger describes the question of Being, and hence existence, as a
movement within what is already understood.

It is necessary that the question comprise these two moments, understanding and interpretation, not only because it is formulated as the becoming itself of what is already understood but also because Heidegger for-
mulates it in terms of three elements: that which is asked about, that which
is to be found out by the asking, and that which is interrogated. In the
question of Being, "what is asked about is Being—that which determines
entities as entities . . . what is to be found out by the asking [is] the meaning
of Being. . . . Insofar as Being constitutes what is asked about, and 'Being'
means the Being of entities, then entities themselves turn out to be what is
interrogated" (BT, 25–26). The first element, Being, is that which is already
disclosed in any understanding, though in an unclarified and implicit way,
while the second element, the meaning of Being, is the explicit thematization of this understanding. Here, it is important to note the irreducibility
of what is asked about, Being, and that which is sought by the asking, the
meaning of Being. It is this irreducibility that gives rise to the second moment of the question, the interpretation that moves from the understanding of Being to the meaning of Being.

As comprising three elements, the question of Being comprises two moments: the first moving from what is interrogated to what is asked about,
the second moving from what is asked about to what is sought. In the first,
beings are "questioned as regards their Being" (BT, 26). That is, beings as
such are not asked what they are but as what or of what they are: beings
are asked about that to which they refer and that by reference to which
they are: namely, Being. Approached by the question of Being, beings are
seen not as what they are of themselves but in terms of a relation or an

involvement which they have with Being. This moment of the question plots the implicit understanding of the Being of beings. In it, Being is understood. But, for this understanding to be authentically, a second moment must be added to it, the interpretation that moves from what is asked about to what is sought by the asking. In this movement, the question is conducted without beings. This movement departs from the understanding of the Being of beings, by involvement with which beings are, and proceeds, by interpretation of this previous understanding, to the meaning of Being.

The question of Being is thus formulated in such a way that it encounters beings only as they arise for it as it makes its way toward the meaning of Being. The question of Being does not aim at a being alone or exclusively since, for it, the being is itself a view through which the question aims at Being. In Heidegger's own words,

> In the disclosure and explication of Being, entities are in every case our preliminary and accompanying theme; but our real theme is Being. . . . As entities so encountered, they become the preliminary theme for the purview of a 'knowing' which, as phenomenological, looks primarily towards Being and which, in thus taking Being as its theme, takes these entities as its accompanying theme. (BT, 95)

Far from aiming first and foremost at beings exclusively, the question of Being casts its sights in a broader scope or purview, aiming "primarily towards Being." It aims at beings only insofar as beings fall within the purview of, and therefore accompany, this broader, more far-reaching, gaze. As aiming "primarily towards Being," the question of Being encounters beings, since in *Being and Time* Being is the Being of beings. However, it encounters them only in the context of its aim at Being, which is beyond them.

If this is how Being and beings come up in the question of Being, how are they encountered within existence? According to Heidegger, *Dasein* encounters being proximally and for the most part as equipment dealt with in its concernful dealings in the world.

> To the Being of an equipment there always belongs a totality of equipment in which it can be this equipment that it is. . . . [Equipment] always is in terms of [*aus*] its belonging to other equipment. . . . These 'Things' never show themselves proximally as they are for themselves, so as to add up to a sum of realia. . . . Before [an equipment shows itself] a totality of equipment has already been discovered. (BT, 97–98)

In other words, beings encountered by existence are only in terms of the totality to which they belong. Beings are not first encountered by an aim that sets its sights simply on what is but by broader, circumspective aims that see *of* what beings are, aims that refer them to the context or totality beyond merely what it is.

Heidegger claims that the Being of these beings is an assignment or reference relationship. In *Being and Time*, an entity, considered in terms of its Being, "is discovered when it has been assigned or referred to something, and referred as that which it is. With any such entity there is an involvement which it has in something" (BT, 115). For existence to encounter a being in its Being, therefore, does not mean to contemplate it in abstraction from the world, a posture that aims at what is but arrives only at what is in its objectivity; rather, it means to let it be involved in the world to which it refers, by using it in the task with which it is involved. Letting a being be (usefully) involved in the world is thus the condition on the basis of which existence in the world encounters beings in their Being. This implies that before any being is encountered the world is already disclosed. It is important to note here that the assignment or reference relationship which a being is is not a reference to another being or to the sum total of beings but to the world, the lighting of Being. The world is thus neither a being nor the sum of beings but a context of reference relationships or a totality of possible involvements.

> An involvement is itself discovered only on the basis of the prior discovery of a totality of involvements. So in any involvement that has been discovered [that is, in any entity which we encounter] what we have called the worldly character of the ready-to-hand has been discovered beforehand. In this totality of involvements which has been discovered beforehand, there lurks an ontological relationship to the world. (BT, 118)

For existence to encounter a being by letting it be involved, the totality of possible involvements, that is to say, the world, must have been disclosed in advance.

Once again, Heidegger has recourse to the forestructure of the understanding of Being to explain how existence in the world encounters a being. As I have said, this understanding is constitutive of *Dasein*'s place in the world: *Dasein* is the there where Being comes to light or is understood. In the understanding, "the relations indicated above [those that are comprised in the referential totality] must have been previously disclosed; the act of understanding holds them in this disclosedness. It holds itself in them with familiarity" (BT, 120). According to Heidegger, because it includes the disclosure of such a context of involvements, the understanding of Being is the condition for the discovery of beings. Beings are encountered only out of the familiarity which existence has with the world, a familiarity that it has unavoidably by virtue of its position, there, where Being is understood.

Heidegger claims, finally, that the relational totality or context of references out of which beings are encountered is called "significance." From the very fact of its existence, *Dasein*, insofar as it is familiar with or understands the world of references, is the source of significations. Within the world, beings are significant only and precisely insofar as they are encountered by *Dasein*, whose understanding is or contains the network of signification in which beings appear. "The significance thus disclosed is an existential state of Dasein—of its Being-in-the-world" (BT, 121). From this, Heidegger will claim that

> Meaning is the upon which of a projection in terms of which something becomes intelligible as something. . . . Meaning is an *existentiale* of Dasein, not a property attaching to entities, lying "behind" them, or floating somewhere as an "intermediate domain." . . . This Interpretation of meaning is ontologico-existential in principle; if we adhere to it, then all entities whose kind of Being is other than Dasein's must be conceived as unmeaning. (BT, 193)

Beings have a meaning, but they themselves are not the source of this meaning; rather, it is a product of their position within the network of significance whose disclosedness constitutes *Dasein* and makes up its understanding of the world.

On Levinas's reading, the Heideggerian project remains complicit with the violence of the Same: "the relation with Being that is enacted as ontology consists in neutralizing the existent [*l'étant*] in order to comprehend or grasp it. It is hence not a relation with the other as such but the reduction of the other to the same" (TI, 45–46). Approached in and through Being which is not a being, the other as such, the otherness of *l'étant*, *l'étant* as such (however it may be called), is encountered only within a horizon that embraces or comprehends it, a horizon which, as horizon, measures, only and precisely, the same and hence reduces or forgets the absolutely other.

There are two interdependent ways in which, according to Levinas, the absolute otherness of *l'étant* is neutralized or betrayed when it is encountered within the luminous horizon of Being. First of all, *l'étant* is encountered only after and in the light of the prior disclosedness of Being. Levinas claims that the comprehension of Being affirms the "priority of Being over existents . . . it is to subordinate the relation with someone who is an existent [*un étant*] (the ethical relation), to a relation with the Being of existents, which, impersonal, permits the apprehension, the domination of existents (a relation of knowing)" (TI, 45).[15] The comprehension of Being remains complicit with the thought of the same because it first understands neutral, anonymous Being and only on the basis of and within the scope of this understanding does it encounter the otherness of *l'étant*. The alterity of *l'étant* thus does not appear absolutely but relatively, relative to limits measured by the comprehension of Being. As Heidegger himself writes, "a being can be encountered by us as a being only in the light of the understanding of Being."[16] On Levinas's reading, such a staging of the encounter is in fact the betrayal of otherness; in betraying themselves within the light of Being, beings are betrayed.

Second, within the horizon measured by the comprehension of Being, we never encounter the absolute otherness of *l'étant* because, here, *l'étant* itself is only by reference to the totality of Being. According to Levinas, "to say that *l'étant* is disclosed only in the openness of Being is to say that we are never directly with *l'étant* as such" (TI, 52). Though not stated explicitly, this would be Levinas's reading of the Heideggerian notion that beings are a reference relationship to the totality of significant references. Approached through the prior openness (disclosure) of Being, *l'étant* is never exclusively *l'étant* as such but *l'étant* included in the context of the world or within the horizon of Being.[17] For the comprehension of Being, beings do not present themselves solely from themselves but only by appearing together with the worldly context or horizon of Being. On Levinas's reading of Heidegger,

> the relation of the subject to the object is subordinated to the relation of the object to light—which is not an object. This understanding of beings [*l'étant*] consists in going beyond that being [*l'étant*]—precisely in openness—and perceiving it upon the horizon of Being. Which is to say that, in Heidegger, understanding rejoins the great tradition of Western philosophy: to understand particular beings is already to place oneself beyond the particular. (EN, 5)[18]

The understanding of Being is never exclusively with *l'étant* as such insofar as it approaches *l'étant* only by having already gone beyond it toward the horizon whereupon it comprehends it.

On Levinas's reading, the otherness of *l'étant* is betrayed when it is broached in and through the prior comprehension of the impersonal or anonymous Being of beings. The "mode of depriving the known [or possessed] being of its alterity can be accomplished only if it is aimed at through a third term, a neutral term, which itself is not a being; in it the shock of the encounter of the same with the other is deadened" (TI, 42). According to Levinas, by aiming through the anonymity or neutrality of Being, *Dasein* and the question of Being are never shocked or surprised by what they encounter. On Levinas's reading, they never encounter an other who remains infinitely strange or foreign. This is so because the neutrality of Being suspends the difference separating the same and the other by including both terms within a common light. Appearing only in its betrayal, otherness, the absolutely other or *l'étant* as such, by definition falling outside the light or horizon of Being, would remain forgotten.

Autrui: The Name of the Absolutely Other or *L'étant* as Such

If even the Heideggerian fundamental ontology, according to Levinas, remains a violent reduction of the otherness of beings, how is metaphysics to proceed toward the absolutely other? If Levinas were to leave this question unanswered, his thought would be a purely reactive denunciation of the entire history of thought. But, he does propose a way out: according to Levinas, "the terms must be reversed" (TI, 47). Whether or not a reversal actually opens a way out is a question to defer until the next chapter, but it seems clear that for Levinas an other being is approached outside of and before seeking the meaning of Being. But, this is not simple. For in the Heideggerian formulation of the question, it is meaningless to encounter a being as such, the absolutely other, without presupposing the disclosure of Being. It is meaningless to encounter a being as such, the absolutely other, without seeing it in the light of a context of references, the world, to which it belongs and through which it is. Levinas thus takes as his task the description of (1) "events whose ultimate signification (contrary to the Heideggerian conception) does not lie in disclosing. . . . No prior disclosure illuminates these essentially nocturnal events" (TI, 27–28), which implies that he describe (2) "the possibility of a signification without context" (TI, 23). Such a nocturnal event without context is the upsurge of language in the ethical encounter with the face.

In "Is Ontology Fundamental?" an essay whose importance to these questions is attested by its being cited in the section of *Totality and Infinity* that most explicitly presents Levinas's critique of Heideggerian ontology (TI, 45), Levinas claims that the relation with a being can be independent of the prior comprehension of Being only when that being is *Autrui*, the personal other (EN, 5). This is repeated in *Totality and Infinity* when Levinas claims that "the absolutely other is the Other [*Autrui*]" (TI, 39). *Autrui* is a being who is as such without reference to Being. He is, therefore, encountered without the horizon of Being disclosed in advance conditioning his appearance. Because of this, the relation with an other being, provided that being is *Autrui*, precedes and overflows the comprehension of Being, thereby rendering it impossible for the question of Being to totally comprehend *Autrui*.

As preceding and overflowing the Same, *Autrui* occurs as infinity or is the occurrence of the idea of infinity. The encounter with *Autrui* thus opens the possibility of approaching the absolutely other without either of the conditions which constitute the Same, Heideggerian comprehension of Being and Hegelian negativity. "The relationship with a being infinitely distant, that is, overflowing its idea, is such that its authority as an existent [*un étant*] is already *invoked* in every question we could raise concerning the meaning of Being" (TI, 47). Here, Levinas describes the relation with *Autrui* in terms that bring together the infinitely other, the infinite without negativity, and *l'étant* without the comprehension of Being. The question of Being has recourse to, or "invokes," a being with whom I speak; but this recourse, while necessary to provoke the question of Being, also necessitates that the question fall short of comprehending the meaning of Being. For

> I cannot disentangle myself from society with *Autrui*, even when I consider the Being of the existent [*étant*] he is. Already the comprehension of Being is said to the existent [*étant*], who again arises behind the theme in which he is presented. This "saying to *Autrui*"—this relation with *Autrui* as interlocutor, this relation with an existent [*étant*]—precedes all ontology. (TI, 47–48)

The relation with *Autrui* undoes the comprehension of Being precisely insofar as *Autrui* is the being to whom I speak in interrogating or understanding Being.

This can be understood by relating speech with *Autrui* to the threefold structure of the question of Being in Heidegger. Speaking with *Autrui* undoes the question of Being because, when the being questioned is one with whom I speak first, I can never pass beyond the first moment of the question. Since the question (*Dasein* itself) "cannot disentangle" itself from the being with whom it speaks, the question remains at only the first moment of the interrogation. It never progresses to the second moment of the question, the interpretation of the already understood Being of beings. Always and already invoked in every question relating to the Being of this being *Autrui,* "the claim to know and reach the other is realized in the relationship with *Autrui* that is cast in the relation of language, where the essential is the interpellation, the vocative" (TI, 69). As the addressee of the word that purports to comprehend it, *Autrui* exceeds what is comprehended in and through this word and thus denies that comprehension be total. According to Levinas, language is not essentially a means of communicating or of representing thoughts for myself and my community nor is it essentially a means of ordering experience and the world. Rather, language is essentially an interpellation or an invocation. "The invoked is not what I comprehend: he is not under a category. He is the one to whom I speak" (TI, 69). Language maintains the other as other because, far from being an instrument to represent, generalize, or otherwise comprehend the other, language addresses all comprehension to it. It thus denies that comprehension achieve the other, for it maintains this other as the addressee (outside) of all comprehension.

According to Levinas, the intentionality, if it can still be called an intention, which aims at a face is the question, if it can still be called a question, "who?" In contrast to how it is traditionally understood, Who? does not aim at an identity and thus does not aim at what might be identified as fundamentally the same as the I. The response to the question Who?—if it can still be called Who?—is not a my-self or your-self, an identity, but the face of the infinitely other. "To the question who? answers the non-qualifiable presence of an existent [*un étant*] who presents himself without reference to anything, and yet distinguishes himself from every other existent [*étant*]. The question who? envisages a face" (TI, 177). In the question Who? a being manifests itself such as it is without reference to a context in terms of which it is; the approach of the face, thus, is not conditioned by a horizon wherein it appears. Though presenting itself without reference to anything else, the face is distinguished from all beings. This means that, strangely, the face manifests itself as other without its presentation as other being conditioned by its distinction from anything else. The face thus manifests the being which, as infinitely other, is not a simple negation of the same, an other who is neither this . . . nor that. . . .

For the comprehension of Being, both the question of Being and existence in the world, *l'étant* is manifest as such only as a reference relationship that positions it within the context of the world or the horizon of Being. The question that contemplates the quiddity of *l'étant*, asking "what is it?" is thus superseded by the existential question, which asks "as what" the being gives itself out to be or "for what" the being is to be used. According to Levinas, for ontology,

> to ask *what* is to ask *as what:* it is not to take the manifestation for itself. . . . [But,] if the question who? does not question in the same sense as the question what?, it is here that what one asks and he whom one questions coincide. To aim at a face is to pose the question who? to the very face that is the answer to this question; the answerer and the answered coincide. (TI, 177–78)

Unapproachable by the question that asks 'as what,' the face is not the appearance of something other than that which it is not nor does it appear as something which it is not. This is why Levinas claims it is encountered by the question Who?: this question does not aim beyond what is interrogated since for it the answerer and the answered coincide. In the question Who?—unlike the question of Being—the being interrogated is precisely and exclusively what is asked about. The face is itself, not a reference to something else sought by the questioning, 'something' like Being that would be dissimulated in its appearance as. . . .

Since it precedes all questions posed to it, even the question of Being, the presence of the face, according to Levinas, arises from itself; it presents itself absolutely, not as an other relative to us as is the otherness of beings that appear on the basis of a previous disclosure of the worldly context: "to recognize truth to be disclosure is to refer it to the horizon of him who discloses. . . . The disclosed being is relative to us and not καθ' αὐτό" (TI, 64). Whereas disclosure manifests a false or relative otherness, according to Levinas, absolute otherness is manifest καθ' αὐτό (as itself) in expression: "manifestation καθ' αὐτό consists in a being telling itself to us independently of every position we would have taken in its regard, in *expressing itself*" (TI, 65). In expression, a being "expresses himself without our having to disclose him from a point of view in a borrowed light" (TI, 67).

In expressing itself, the absolutely other, *Autrui*, reveals itself: "the absolute experience is not disclosure but revelation: the coinciding of the expressed with him who expresses, which is the privileged manifestation of *Autrui*, the manifestation of a face over and beyond form" (TI, 66). The revelation of the face resists the play of veiling/unveiling or revealing/concealing that characterizes the appearance of Being in and through—as—beings which it is not. As expression of *Autrui*, the face is not a figure; it does not signal *Autrui* but reveals *Autrui* in person.

With the notion of expression, Levinas describes the way in which *l'étant* as such, the absolutely other, irreducible to the Same, presents itself as other by signifying in the face. I have already shown how the face of *Autrui*, the interlocutor, arises or upsurges continually behind the theme by which the Same pretends to grasp the other. "This way of undoing the form adequate to the same so as to present oneself as other is to signify or to have a meaning. To present oneself by signifying is to speak" (TI, 66). Since, according to Levinas, to signify is to present oneself as other, signification entails the disruption of the Same: there would be no signification where the Same has not been interrupted or breached by the presence of the other. For this reason, Levinas maintains that the worldly significations, so admirably analyzed by Heidegger, terminate finally insofar as the totality of involvements refers ultimately to a being, *Dasein*, who refers from self to self in care (see TI, 94–95). In contrast to the world in which signification terminates in *Dasein*, Levinas describes society with the face, in which the presence of the face undoes the same by signifying ad infinitum. At this point, it is important to explain just how the expression of the face, its presence, signifies.

As expressing itself before we have disclosed it, the expression of the face bears its own meaning, is the very production of meaning, and means prior to the meaning produced by projecting possibilities-of-being upon the always already disclosed totality of worldly significance. In a certain sense, the face does not signify; for, in its presentation καθ' αὐτό, in its appearance outside and prior to the context of worldly signification, it does not signal anything other than itself. At the very least, it does not signify in the way that, traditionally understood, a sign signifies something other than itself or coordinates different items. Expression does not signify as do signs but presents the face, the other as other.

According to Levinas, the face presents itself as other, that is signifies, by expressing itself in speech. In the expression of the face, *Autrui*, far from being signified by a spoken sign, is itself present as the face which bears or gives the sign. As that which bears the sign, Levinas will call the face the signifier [*signifiant*], a naming that disturbs the traditional distinction between the speaker and the signs he utters.

> Expression does not manifest the presence of being by referring from the sign to the signified; it presents the signifier [*signifiant*]. The signifier [*signifiant*], he who gives a sign, is not a signified. It is necessary to have already been in the society of signifiers for the sign to be able to appear as a sign. Hence the signifier [*signifiant*] must present himself before every sign, by himself—present a face. (TI, 182)

In a similar passage, Levinas writes that "he who signals himself by a sign qua signifying [*signifiant*] that sign is not the signified of the sign—but delivers the sign and gives it" (TI, 92). According to Levinas's extraordinary conceptuality, the expression of the face emits or signifies the sign and thus presents the signifier: "the signifier, he who emits the sign, faces . . . *Autrui*, the signifier, manifests himself in speech" (TI, 96). In the expression of the face, therefore, *Autrui* never separates himself from the sign that is given precisely because the face in which he presents himself is the signifier that delivers this sign. *Autrui* is, in this way, present to its own manifestation in speech. Insofar as in the face the expressed coincides with the expresser, *Autrui* attends or comes to the assistance of its own presence.[19] "Speech consists in *Autrui* coming to the assistance of the sign given forth, attending his own manifestation in signs" (TI, 91).

The face is the signifier in which *Autrui* presents himself. But Levinas does not understand the signifier as that which indicates or refers to a signified. Rather, he makes an interesting play on the French word *signifiant*. As a participle, the word can be used either in a quasi-verbal sense, what might be thought of as "the act of signifying," or in a substantive sense, "the signifier." Levinas will use the word *signifiant* in both senses and will locate this double meaning in the expression of the face: the face is both the (verbal) signifying of significance and the (substantive) signifier of significance. As *signifiant*, then, the face is irreducible to the sign function—namely, the connection of ordinary signifiers with their signifieds—a function which ultimately terminates when signified meaning has been reached. Insofar as the face is the very signifying [*signifiant*], in the quasi-verbal sense of bearing or emitting, of the signifier [*signifiant*], signification is operative to the degree that the signifier is not surpassed or discarded. If above I said that the face does not signify, now I must say that the face always and only signifies and for that very reason does not signify as does a sign.[20] Since in expression the revealer and the revealed coincide, Levinas writes that in speech "the signifier never separates himself from the sign he delivers, but takes it up again always while he exposes" (TI, 97). As I just noted, the face is a signifier that can never be discarded or abandoned when the sign refers it to the signified. As only and incessantly signifying, the face undoes the finality of the sign function by renewing the signification of all signs. "And this renewal is precisely presence, or [its] attendance to itself" (TI, 182). The presence of *Autrui* is its attendance to and incessant renewal of its own speech.

Levinas distinguishes the presence of the face in speech from the absence of the other symbolized in his works. While the absent other can be deduced from his works and, according to Levinas, thereby comprehended in his absence, speech manifests "the incomprehensible nature of the presence of *Autrui*" (TI, 195). Levinas here claims that, strangely, the presence of *Autrui* in speech is his incomprehensibility or irreducible otherness. How so? Insofar as, in speech, the face is signifying [*signifiant*] incessantly, it undoes the reduction of the sign to a finite, and therefore comprehensible, signification. The face by which the other is present thereby undoes the bounds in and through which it would be contained. The exceptional presence of the other in the signifying face implies the absence of the other from every image, concept, or horizon within which the Same might contain or grasp it. Its exceptional presence in expression is absolute presence, in the special sense that Levinas gives absolute: ab-solute, loosened, freed, separated, or unbound—absolved from the presence it enters.

Generosity and the Origin of the Universal

Having seen how discourse presents the exceptional or incomprehensible presence of *l'étant* as such, the absolutely other, in the face, the necessity of ethics in Levinas's conception of philosophy can now be understood. "The relation with *Autrui*, or conversation [*discours*], is a non-allergic relation, an ethical relation" (TI, 51). Ethics, the nonviolent approach of the other, is presupposed in, and encountered only in, speech with *Autrui*. According to Levinas, "the formal structure of language thereby announces the ethical inviolability of *Autrui* and, without any odor of the 'numinous,' his 'holiness'" (TI, 195).[21] In language, the other is inviolable because, as the interlocutor, he "upsurges inevitably behind the said," which pretends to grasp it within the same (TI, 195).

But, it might be objected, if the presence of the Other has remained uncomprehended by the traditional constitution of metaphysics, hasn't that tradition evidenced the highest degree of respect for the absolutely other? Isn't the absolutely other precisely that which resists comprehension, and doesn't the history of metaphysics, by Levinas's own admission, exclude the absolutely other? Therefore, wouldn't the history of metaphysics evidence the greatest ethics? Though the possibility that such an objection can be raised merits consideration,[22] such a line of reasoning omits the positive description of the ethical encounter in *Totality and Infinity*. For Levinas, the incomprehensible presence of the excluded other is acknowledged not in forgetting but in generosity. In addition to announcing the incomprehensibility of *Autrui*, language is essentially an ethical acknowledgment of the incomprehensible presence of the other. Levinas claims that this acknowledgment is generosity, the "offering which language is" (TI, 174).

The ethical inviolability of the other, of *Autrui* with whom I speak, is announced in the face. The otherness of the face, according to Levinas, is distinguished from the (false) otherness negated and preserved within the same in that the face is not grasped but killed: "The alterity that is expressed in the face provides the unique 'matter' possible for total negation. . . . *Autrui* is the sole being I can wish to kill" (TI, 198). In a strange paradox, the face alone resists inclusion in the same precisely because it is the sole being that can be annihilated. Its murder differs from the negativity that constitutes the same in that negativity is always only partial, preserving the other at the same time as neutralizing its otherness, whereas "murder alone lays claim to a total negation" (TI, 198), such that the other is not reduced to the same but annihilated sovereignly.[23] The fact that the face is either killed or spoken to means that the same finds itself paralyzed before the face. The face always remains absolutely other than the same; for no possible approach to it, not even violence, can include it in the same.[24]

The face resists the same in and through its primordial expression: the command "thou shall not commit murder" (TI, 199).[25] With this, we again see how Levinas binds ethics to language and language to ethics such that each arises with the other, with *Autrui:* the expression of the face speaks an imperative which commands its respect. Since "thou shalt not commit murder" is the expression of the face, murder, while no doubt really committed against a being in the world, is an impossibility when directed against the face. Murder always aims at the face but thereby always overlooks the expression definitive of that face. On this reading, murder is violent insofar as it overlooks or forgets the face; in fact, all violence, the violence inherent to the history of metaphysical thought, would be founded on such forgetfulness.

Faced with *Autrui*, the same is unavoidably and incessantly in society with the other. The same cannot rid itself of the other's face, neither by comprehending it nor by partially negating it and assimilating it nor by totally negating it and murdering it. How then does the same respect the alterity of the other? "To recognize *Autrui* is to give" (TI, 75). According to Levinas, the same respects the other in generosity by giving to the other in and through language. The essence of language is thus ethical not only because language announces the inviolability of *Autrui* but also because language is generosity—it designates things for the other.

According to Levinas, though *Autrui* is not a part of the world, the relationship with him "is not produced outside the world, but puts in question the world possessed. The relationship with Autrui, transcendence, consists in speaking the world to Autrui. . . . To see the face is to speak of the world" (TI, 173–74). In other words, when *Autrui* presents himself to me, the world is no longer mine, no longer what I possess, but what I give to him by speaking to him. On this reading, language is primordially an act of generosity that responds to the advent of the face by offering my world to him. When before I noted that, for Levinas, the essence of language is the vocative by which one is interpellated, I now must say that the essence of language is the dative, by which the world is given *to Autrui*. In offering what is mine to *Autrui*, language is not preceded by community or commonality but is the foundation upon which the world is put in common. "To recognize the Other is therefore to come to him across the world of possessed things, but at the same time to establish, by gift, community and universality. . . . To speak is to make the world common, to create commonplaces. Language does not refer to the generality of concepts but lays the foundation for a possession in common" (TI, 76). Far from relying on the already constituted universality of concepts, language, in creating commonplaces, establishes such universality where before there was none.

For Hegel, too, language marks the passage from the immediate here and now of the thing possessed into the universal. It is the "divine nature" of language to utter the universal in which the particular thing that is meant and possessed (*meinen/mein*) by immediate sense certainty, the first shape of consciousness, is negated and preserved in a new shape of consciousness. By uttering the universal, language is the "labor of the negative" by which consciousness embarks on a journey that will ultimately arrive at absolute knowledge.[26] Levinas agrees with Hegel, for once at least, in claiming that "the universality a thing receives from the word extracts it from the *hic et nunc*" (TI, 173). Like Hegel, Levinas believes that language cannot utter the particular or sensuous thing, what is mine and what I mean, and in fact marks the entry of the thing into the sphere of the universal or the general.[27]

However, for Levinas, language dispossesses me of what is mine not simply by the act of designating the thing, of uttering it, as Hegel argues, but because "in designating a thing, I designate it to *Autrui*. The act of designating modifies my relation of enjoyment and possession with things, places things in the perspective *Autrui*. . . . The word that designates things attests their apportionment between me and the others" (TI, 209). On Levinas's reading of designation, a thing is designated only insofar as it is given to *Autrui*. The act of utterance, designation, is not the act of subjectivity ascending to the universal in and through the dialectical negation of particularity and otherness; rather, it presupposes the presentation of *Autrui*, the upsurge of language in the face, to which every act of designation responds. In other words, language, generosity, is essentially a response to the presence of the face in speech.

Not only does designation presuppose *Autrui*, it also institutes a world in common between myself and *Autrui*. In designating the thing that I possess, language gives it to *Autrui*; in doing so, it institutes the order of the universal or general where things can be shared, held in common. Language confers universality to the sensuous thing only insofar as language is essentially the gift of what is mine to *Autrui*.

> The *hic et nunc* itself issues from possession, in which the thing is grasped, and language, which designates it to *Autrui*, is a primordial dispossession, a first donation. The generality of the word institutes a common world. The ethical event at the basis of generalization is the underlying intention of language. The relation with *Autrui* does not only stimulate, provoke generalization . . . but is this generalization itself. (TI, 173)[28]

On Levinas's reading, generalization, the becoming universal of the thing in the word, is not what is entered when language negates what is mine (*meinen*), the sensuous thing. Things become general in language because language offers what is mine to *Autrui*, dispossesses me, thereby "putting in common a world hitherto mine" (TI, 174). In this way, Levinas provides an ethical explanation of how language generalizes. Language generalizes, universalizes, insofar as it puts the world in common; but such putting in common is an essentially ethical event, if by ethics is understood the donation of what is mine to *Autrui*.

2

Theology and the Unthought Constitution of Ethical Metaphysics

Because in *Totality and Infinity* the discourse on the absolutely other is ethical, my reading in the previous chapter was decidedly not theological. In this, I acknowledged the express intentions of the author of *Totality and Infinity* when he writes "it would be false to qualify [the relation to the absolutely other] as theological" (TI, 42). However, on another reading, an other's reading, what Levinas claims to be the foundation of all thought, even and most programmatically of theological thought, is seen to be already determined by a theologic, a theological conceptuality. If this reading is accurate, ethical metaphysics is neither first philosophy—for it would be determined by an uninterrogated horizon anterior to it—nor is it as free from violence as it claims. That is, if it is true that ethical metaphysics remains theologically determined, then one would expect it to maintain the consistency of the very tradition it intends to overcome. In this case, one should be able to find that *Totality and Infinity* is composed necessarily by means of references to the tradition it pretends to have evaded.

In part, this chapter will argue for the necessity of reading *Totality and Infinity* as a disguised or displaced theology, and, heeding this necessity, as assuming the texture of the tradition it intends to overcome. Such an argument goes against the declared intentions of the author and so is necessarily suspicious. Since just such a suspicious reading of ethical metaphysics is developed by Jacques Derrida in his essay "Violence and Metaphysics," this chapter will present itself as a reading of that essay. On Derrida's reading, the theological determination of *Totality and Infinity* betrays the strange necessity that the step beyond the totality appear only in and through the language of the totalizing tradition—leading one to wonder if at the end of metaphysics, thought can do anything but uphold that end.

The Ethical Conditions the Appearance of God

In *Totality and Infinity*, Levinas rejects any description that characterizes the originary relation with the absolutely other as in any way theological. As Derrida has noted, "the messianic eschatology from which Levinas draws inspiration . . . is developed in its discourse neither as a theology nor as a Jewish mysticism (it can even be understood as the trial of both theology and mysticism)" (VM, 83). Levinas himself asserts that "our relation with the Metaphysical [that is, the transcendent] is an ethical behavior and not theology, not a thematization, be it a knowledge by analogy of the attributes of God" (TI, 78). Whatever misunderstandings or excessive generalizations about theology such a statement contains, it is clear that the author of *Totality and Infinity* reads theology as a theoretical or thematizing discourse.[1] As theoretical, or thematizing, theology would know only a false other, an other that is constituted by the conscious I. Since Levinas's ethical metaphysics desires the absolutely other beyond the I, it will distance itself from theology: "no theology, no mysticism is concealed behind the analysis I have just given of the meeting with *Autrui*" (EN, 8).

In *Totality and Infinity*, Levinas prefers the term "religion" when describing the relation with the absolutely other: "we propose to call 'religion' the bond that is established between the same and the other without constituting a totality"; "for the relation between the being here below and the transcendent being . . . we reserve the term religion" (TI, 40, 80). Unlike theology, religion would escape the totalization or promotion of the same which defines thought as violence. Whereas theology thematizes God and therefore approaches a God that it has itself conceived, religion does not conceive any God but, through the idea of infinity, has an idea of the separation in which the absolutely other appears: "Religion where relationship subsists between the same and the other despite the impossibility of the Whole—the idea of Infinity—is the ultimate structure" (TI, 80).

Insofar as theology approaches a false other conceived by the I, it is the atheist metaphysician, the atheist I, who relates to the transcendent or absolutely other.

> Only an atheist being can relate himself to the transcendent and already absolve himself from this relation. Transcendence is to be distinguished from a union with the transcendent by participation. The metaphysical relation, the idea of infinity, connects with the noumenon which is not a numen. This noumenon is to be distinguished from the concept of God possessed by the believers of positive religions ill disengaged from the bonds of participation, who accept being immersed in a myth unbeknownst to themselves. (TI, 77)[2]

On this reading, theistic concepts are complicit with the bonds of (mythic and mystical) participation insofar as both deny the absolution of the absolute. That is to say, by conceiving the transcendent and by grasping it, theological concepts approach a God that participates in the same totality as does the theistic I, the totality that in fact this I constitutes.

By a gesture that is not thought explicitly in *Totality and Infinity*, Levinas denies the difference between theological theoretism and mystical (or mythical) communion. Within the logic of this work, both theological transcendence and mystical immanence ignore the separation between the absolutely other and the I. In theology as much as in mysticism, for Levinas, the I is closed to the outside or beyond: in theology because conceiving God reduces the absolutely other to a participant in the same; in mysticism because mystical participation in the divine annihilates the separation in which the absolutely other appears.[3] As Derrida has noted, "the complicity of theoretical objectivity [of which theology is a form] and mystical communion will be Levinas's true target. The premetaphysical unity of one and the same violence" (VM, 87).

Neither a theologian nor a mystic, the atheist I, lacking an adequate concept of God, a concept that pretends to be adequate to God, is absolutely separate from God and therefore enters a religious relation with this uncomprehended God. On such a reading, atheism is not the simple opposite of theism; it does not merely hold to the negative of what the theist holds. Unlike the theist who affirms his concept of God while denying other misconceived concepts of God, the atheist I is the I who relates to the absolutely other outside of the categorical alternative between yes and no, affirmation and negation. "By atheism we thus understand a position prior to both the negation and the affirmation of the divine, the breaking with participation" (TI, 58).[4]

It might be objected at this point that the references to the idea of Infinity, to the Good beyond Being, and to creation indicate a theological project of *Totality and Infinity*. In claiming that the transcendent is best approached through the ideas of Infinity and of the Good, Levinas seems to invoke theological notions in describing the approach to the absolutely other. These ideas certainly have theological status in the case of Jean-Luc Marion's *God without Being* for whom the Good is preeminently a theological name taught not by philosophers but by Christian theologians—most importantly by Dionysius and Bonaventure—and the Infinite a name which Descartes inherited from his theological predecessor Lessius, the Jesuit student of Suarez.[5] Levinas, however, claims that these ideas are not theological inheritances but the legacy of philosophers: namely, Descartes and Plato.

> Greek metaphysics conceived the Good as separate from the totality of essences. . . . The place of the Good above every essence is the most profound teaching, the definitive teaching, not of theology, but of philosophy. The paradox of an Infinity admitting a being outside of itself which it does not encompass, and accomplishing its very infinitude by virtue of this proximity of a separated being—in a word, the paradox of creation—thenceforth loses something of its audacity. (TI, 102–103)

On this reading, thought would be conducted to the originary event of separation not by theology but by philosophy, specifically Greek philosophy. Even the notion of creation, a notion that for Levinas conveys the paradox of separation, belongs more to a properly conceived philosophy than to theology.

> Theology imprudently treats the idea of the relation between God and the creature in terms of ontology. It presupposes the logical privilege of totality, as a concept adequate to being. . . . If the notions of totality and being are notions that cover one another, the notion of the transcendent places us beyond categories of being, we thus encounter, in our own way, the Platonic idea of the Good Beyond Being. . . . What embarrasses the traditional theology, which treats of creation in terms of ontology—God leaving his eternity in order to create—is incumbent as a first truth in a philosophy that begins with transcendence. (TI, 293)

In such a passage, Levinas makes it clear that his critique of ontological thought implies a critique of theology insofar as theology is penetrated by ontology, a penetration that nowhere seems not to exist for the author of *Totality and Infinity*.[6] Whereas theology presupposes the privilege of totality and therefore is scandalized by the idea of a created being separate from God, philosophy, in its openness to the Good beyond Being, can start with separation and hence make sense of creation.

Far from being a theological work, *Totality and Infinity* characterizes itself as a description of the ethical events that precede and open the very possibility of theological thought of God. Levinas writes,

> The dimension of the divine opens forth from the human face. *Autrui* is the very locus of metaphysical truth, and is indispensable for my relation with God. He does not play the role of mediator. *Autrui* is not the incarnation of God, but precisely by his face, in which he is disincarnate, is the manifestation of the height in which God is revealed. It is our relations with men . . . that give to theological concepts the sole signification they admit of. (TI, 78–79)

Levinas here submits the appearance of God to certain conditions, ethical ones, under which God can appear for thinking in general and for theology in particular. These ethical conditions are proper neither to God nor to theology. Only by admitting the prior advent of the face in ethics can theology begin to approach true height, and only through true height can theology accede to God.[7] Though *Totality and Infinity* describes the approach of the absolutely other, Levinas aims thereby not to establish the proper theological thought of God but to describe the irreducible structure of ethics upon which the very significance of any theology is founded.

Levinas himself claims that the appearance of God is conditioned by ethical relations among men, relations which are not determined by theology but which in fact determine the possibility of any theology. But, an author's intention does not always have the last word in matters of interpretation, and Levinas's portrayal of the relations between ethics and theology need not be taken at face value. One such suspicious reading has been put forward by Jacques Derrida in his seminal essay "Violence and Metaphysics." On Derrida's reading, ethics is not the condition of theology but is already guided by a certain theologic. Far from describing the foundation or pre-theological source of all signification and every concept, ethical metaphysics is part of what Jean-Luc Nancy has called an "interminable post-theology," a phrase which could just as well describe Derrida's position regarding Levinas in "Violence and Metaphysics."[8] It says that despite the pretension to have passed beyond theology by advancing to what precedes it, Levinas's thought can only come after theology, after a theological tradition has passed on, for better or worse, its conceptuality and its determination of Being. In the wake of this passing theology, Nancy asks, "is there any statement about the divine that henceforth can be distinguished, strictly speaking, from another about . . . [here Nancy lists many, including those relevant to this discussion], 'others' (*autrui*), 'the Other'. . . ."[9] Though Nancy responds to this confusion of the divine (God and the gods) with others and the Other in different ways than does the author of "Violence and Metaphysics," such a confusion seems essential to Derrida's argument in that essay. Just as Nancy implies that the blurring of distinctions between the divine and the Other is symptomatic of our "interminable post-theology," Derrida shows the theological consistency of *Totality and Infinity* by suggesting that what was once said of God is now said of *Autrui*. Speaking broadly, this has at least two significant consequences: (1) the absolutely other is a determined form of otherness, otherness determined as *Autrui* by the Judeo-Christian theological tradition; and (2) ethical metaphysics assumes the position of first philosophy only by inheriting and maintaining the consistency of this theological conceptuality. Supposing such a theological determination of the ethical, Derrida asks "independent of its 'theological context' (an expression that Levinas would most likely reject)[,] does not this entire discourse collapse?" (VM, 103). In answer to this (rhetorical) question, Derrida's reading suggests that *Totality and Infinity* be read theologically.

Autrui Resembles God

Though the theological determination of ethical metaphysics may not be evident explicitly,[10] if Levinas wants to liberate ethics from the worst violence possible, the absolutely other met in ethics can only be God or his resemblance.

> Asymmetry, non-light, and commandment [the ethical in *Totality and Infinity*] then would be violence and injustice themselves—and, indeed, so they are commonly understood—if they established relations between fi-

> nite beings, or if the other was but a negative determination of the (finite
> or infinite) same. . . . This is why God alone keeps Levinas's world from
> being a world of the pure [*sic*] and worst violence, a world of immorality
> itself. (VM, 107)

Though Levinas nowhere says that the infinitely other is God, instead claiming it is *Autrui*, Derrida suggests that it must be God if only because no thought of finite or worldly being would think asymmetry and nonviolence together. Only if the infinitely other is God or is determined by his resemblance to God could one understand how an asymmetrical relation might be pure of violence. "The face-to-face, then, is not originally determined by Levinas as the vis-à-vis of two equal and upright men. The latter supposes the face-to-face of the man with bent neck and eyes raised toward the God on high. Language is indeed the possibility of the face-to-face and of being-upright, but it does not exclude inferiority, the humility of the glance at the father" (VM, 107). Though the author of *Totality and Infinity* describes the face-to-face as an interpersonal relation, a relation among men, on Derrida's reading, it appears only in a "space" that is theologically (and paternally) determined. Its asymmetry is meaningful, or means the peace which Levinas wants it to mean, only if one presupposes that the other is not another man like me but an other determined as God or resembling God. As Levinas himself admits, "this 'curvature of space' is, perhaps, the very presence of God" (TI, 291).

Derrida's reading also suggests that the ethical notion of expression, in which the absolutely other reveals itself in the face of *Autrui,* is profoundly theological, for it is essentially a notion of divine speech. Derrida asks,

> is the frankness of expression essentially an aspect of living speech for him
> who is not God? This question is meaningless for Levinas who conceives
> the face in terms of the 'resemblance' between man and God. . . . It is only
> in God that speech, as presence, as the origin and horizon of writing, is
> realized without defect. (VM, 102)

For Levinas, it is meaningless to ask whether or not expression is possible in human speech since for him the face is the resemblance of God. Without developing Derrida's views on the relation between speech and writing, it suffices here to notice that, according to Derrida, the notion that speech perfectly presents the speaker is profoundly theological. As I showed in chapter 1, such a notion is at work in how *Totality and Infinity* conceives expression. Both the face and the Christian Word of God, the Logos, are the perfect expression of that which they reveal and present καθ' αὐτό: in the first case Infinity or the absolutely other, in the second the Christian God. The coincidence of the expresser and expressed in the face bears a striking resemblance to the presence of God in his Word or Logos.

In defense of the author of *Totality and Infinity,* it should be noted that the notion of expression cannot be convicted unqualifiedly of logocentrism simply because it privileges speech and debases writing. When Derrida attacks the privilege of speech (logocentrism) in Western metaphysics, a privilege which for Derrida rests profoundly on a theology,[11] he attacks a notion of presence in which the speaker's presence to his speech guarantees, stabilizes, and fixes the meaning of language. Such a notion of presence is *not* operative in expression as it is described in *Totality and Infinity*. Far from fixing or stabilizing meaning, the presence of the face undoes by exceeding every attempt to reduce meaning to a finite signification comprehensible finally and once and for all. Insofar as it undoes the fixity or finitude of meaning and recognizes the impossibility of surpassing signification and arriving at a transcendental signified, expression functions for Levinas in ways that are very similar to those that Derrida attributes to writing.[12]

Though these precisions suggest that Levinas might avoid the unqualified charge of logocentrism and all that it implies about determinations of speech and writing, presence and absence, Derrida nonetheless still holds that Levinas's use of speech and expression betrays a profoundly theological conceptuality. According to Derrida, it would be possible to invert all of Levinas's statements about the relation of speech and writing such that what Levinas says of speech is true of writing, and, in fact, for finite or worldly being, is more true of writing:

> [one could show] that writing can assist itself . . . [,] that, by neutralizing the demands of empirical 'economy,' writing's essence is more metaphysical (in Levinas's sense) than speech. That the writer absents himself better, that is expresses himself better as other. . . . And that . . . the writer more effectively renounces violence. (VM, 102)

For a thought of finitude, a worldly thought, a thought before or without theology, writing—not speech—can serve as expression. Levinas, however, holds that the frankness of expression is an aspect only of speech, and not of writing, precisely because his is not a worldly thought, not a thought without theology.[13] Since the face is not only human but the resemblance of God, it is possible for Levinas to debase writing and the written work and privilege speech and the face-to-face. If the face were only human, one might be led to ask, as Derrida here does, if writing, not speech, better expresses the other as other, that is, as absenting or absolving himself from the sign put forth.

To pursue the suggestion of a theological determination of ethical metaphysics, "one would have to show that only [the] reference to the speech of God distinguishes Levinas's intentions from those of Socrates in the *Phaedrus*; and that for a thought of original finitude this distinction is no longer possible" (VM, 103). As Derrida notes, in *Totality and Infinity*, the notion of expression and the relation between speech and writing are quite close to positions taken by Socrates in the Phaedrus. Levinas, however, is quite clear that his use of these concepts should be distinguished from Socratic maieutics, the dialogue that endeavors to give birth to knowledge already contained in the interlocutors. For Levinas, speech is teaching or command, the putting in me of an idea that I cannot find in the contents of my own mind. It is not a dialogical relation between interlocutors meeting on even terrain in order to aid one another in recollecting what they already know. Instead, the speech that transpires between master and disciple happens in a "space" that is theologically determined: "the essence of discourse is prayer" and "the interlocutors are not equal; when it has reached truth discourse is discourse with a god" (EN, 7; TI, 72 [modified]). It is the relation of a master or god coming from on high to teach his disciple, to put in him an idea of what he did not know before and can never contain. From this, Derrida concludes that Levinas's description distinguishes speech from Socratic dialogue by situating it in a theological context.

As Derrida notes, this determination of the ethical implies, at least, "the resemblance between man and God, man's visage and the Face of God" (VM, 108), a resemblance that Derrida finds to be stated in an obscure passage near the end of *Totality and Infinity*, "*Autrui* . . . resembles God."[14] On Derrida's reading, the phrase "*Autrui* resembles God" describes the condition which makes it possible for man to present the face, a condition upon which the primacy of ethics in *Totality and Infinity* depends. If ethical metaphysics and not another thought is primary, this is because ethics describes a relation with *l'étant* as such or *l'étant* itself before its appearance is determined, violently, by conditions other than its own. This being (*l'étant* as such) is presented in the face of *Autrui*, the interpersonal other met in ethics. But, it is possible to ask the simple question: why is *l'étant* as such presented by the face of *Autrui* and not by any other *étant* among *l'étant*? Why is *Autrui* the only being of all the beings who presents being as such?

On Derrida's reading, ethical metaphysics (the face of *Autrui*) acquires its primacy only because Levinas's thought situates itself within a theological conceptuality in which the other met in ethics, *Autrui*, resembles God.

> "The encounter with the face is not only an anthropological fact. It is absolutely speaking a relation with what is. Perhaps man alone is substance, and this is why he is face." Certainly. But it is the analogy between the face and God's visage that, in the most classical fashion, distinguishes man from animal, and determines man's substantiality: "[*Autrui*] resembles God." Man's substantiality, which permits him to be face, is thus founded in his resemblance to God. (VM, 142)

Only insofar as *Autrui* is determined by its resemblance to God does the face appear in interpersonal relations and not in relations with other beings, say, with animals or the "things" of the world. If in *Totality and Infinity* the primacy of the same is undone not by the relation with any being but with human-being, on Derrida's reading, this is because human-being alone resembles God. In other words, Levinas's theological conceptuality, a conceptuality in which man alone among beings resembles God, permits him to identify the absolutely other as this other, human-being, and not that other, for instance animal-being. When otherness has been determined in accord with a theologic, it becomes possible to say that this other (*Autrui* or the face, human-being) presents the absolutely other while that other (a stone, an animal, for instance, or any other other) does not. The true other is other than the other other and is recognized as such by means of the resemblance to God.

The effects of this theological conceptuality can also be seen if the word *Autrui* is read in ways suggested by Derrida. Citing Littré, he writes, "*Autrui,* from *alter-huic,* this other" (VM, 105). Read this way, *Autrui* would obviously be a determinate form of otherness, this (*huic*) and not that other (*alter*). The specifically theological determination of otherness is then visible in the opposition between *Autrui* and *heteron,* the Greek genre or category of otherness relative to a point or term. Recognizing both *Autrui* and *heteron* to presuppose an other otherness, an otherness which they subsequently determine, Derrida asks a question unheard of in Levinas: "What does *autre* mean before its Greek determination as *heteron* and its Judeo-Christian determination as *Autrui*?" (VM, 105).

The suggestion of a theological conceptuality thus helps bring to light what remains unthought in *Totality and Infinity*—namely (1) the prior difference between the true and false other, the perspective that, without his remarking it, has already been operative so as to permit Levinas to distinguish true from false otherness; and (2) otherness prior to its being determined as this and not that other, human- and not any other-being. Such otherness might be approached, according to Derrida, if we consider "this *Huic* of *Autrui,*" the this of this other (*alter-huic*) (VM, 105). Such an analysis, according to Derrida, is presented in the opening chapter of Hegel's *Phenomenology of Spirit.* According to Hegel's analysis of the this, it is already part of the parade of consciousness, already interior to consciousness from the moment it is designated "this." *Autrui,* as *alter-huic,* would no longer be infinitely other or determined entirely by itself since *huic,* this, is a determination of consciousness. What escapes consciousness, then, would not be *Autrui, alter-huic,* but *alter,* otherness before being designated as this other. But, this reading continues, there is *alter* to escape consciousness only insofar as consciousness designates it as this or that other. For without this designation *alter* is nothing at all. *Autrui,* when the *huic* is considered, would be the name by which language retrospectively constitutes the ineffable *alter* and keeps it as what it is not.

Some Brief Historical Remarks

The theological determination of ethical metaphysics can be seen just as strikingly when Levinas's thought is shown to bear a resemblance to historical figures considered to be theological thinkers. Thus, Derrida often names negative theology when discussing the auto-erasure of Levinas's discourse; and throughout "Violence and Metaphysics," he suggests comparisons between Levinas and thinkers belonging to this tradition of theological thought—thinkers such as Nicholas of Cusa and Meister Eckhart.[15] For these theological thinkers, the process of neither . . . nor . . . denies that God is this or that, that God can be named exhaustively by either affirmative or negative terms. To name the God who is beyond both positive and negative names, beyond this and that, this tradition makes frequent use of terms with the prefix "hyper" (beyond or above), claiming that such names designate what is beyond the totality of what is.

However, according to Derrida, the redoubled negation of these negative theologies does not transcend the realm of ontical determination insofar as it reserves a God outside or beyond negativity, a hyper-essential God who is and is eminently. On Derrida's reading, the hyper-essential terms do not name a God without Being but a God who is still a being, though a being beyond the totality of beings.

> When Meister Eckhart seeks to go beyond these determinations, the movement which he sketches remains enclosed in ontic transcendence. "When I said that God was not a Being and was above Being, I did not thereby contest his Being, but on the contrary attributed to him a *more elevated Being*" (*Quasi stella matutina . . .*). This negative theology is still a theology and, *in its literality at least,* is concerned with liberating and acknowledging the ineffable transcendence of an infinite *étant,* "Being above Being and superessential negation." (VM, 146)

Crucial to Derrida's reading of this passage from Eckhart is his interpretation of the phrase "a more elevated Being." As Derrida reads it, a more elevated Being is not beyond or otherwise than Being, but the Being of an infinite being.[16] Thus, for Derrida, the redoubled negation of negative theology is part and parcel of a progress that aims not beyond Being but to an infinite being.

By situating Levinas's thought in relation to figures of negative theology, Derrida suggests that such a theologic is also at work in *Totality and Infinity.* I have already shown in chapter 1, how Levinas's discourse, like that of a Meister Eckhart when he denies that God is this or that, employs the neither . . . nor . . . in its approach of the infinitely other. This comparison can be developed further by showing that *Totality and Infinity* often uses terms similar to those used by the negative theologians when they name the God beyond this and that, the God that cannot be designated by positive or negative terms. In ways that resemble the "more elevated Being" of Meister Eckhart, Levinas writes: "eschatology institutes a relation with being beyond the totality (*l'être par-delà la totalité*). . . . It is a relationship with a surplus always exterior to the totality. . . . [The eschatological relationship announced in ethics] institutes a relation with the infinity of being which exceeds that totality (*l'infini de l'être, qui dépasse la totalité*)"; and "we have broached the exteriority of being (*l'extériorité de l'être*)" (TI, 22–23, 296). Just as Eckhart employs the term a "more elevated Being" to designate the God who cannot be designated as this or that, so Levinas calls the absolutely other beyond affirmative or negative propositions "being beyond the totality," "the infinity of being," or "the exteriority of being."

These phrases oscillate in the same ambiguity as those of a theological figure like Meister Eckhart. Just as the "more elevated Being" of the God-head is for Eckhart ambiguously beyond beings and the being of a supreme being, so too in the discourse of ethical metaphysics the infinity of being, the exteriority of being, and the being beyond the totality can always be read as beyond the totality of beings and as the being of a supreme being. In short, it is always possible to reattach this beyond to a being. Levinas himself admits that "the production of an infinite entity is inseparable from the idea of infinity" (TI, 26). In other words, while the idea of infinity is an idea of neither this nor that, an idea of the surplus always exterior to the totality of beings, it refers inevitably to an entity who exists infinitely or exteriorly. Without this reference to a being beyond the totality, or if the being beyond or infinity of being were not also a being, the very project of "inverting the terms" (TI, 47) of fundamental ontology would be meaningless. Thus, Levinas's thought follows the theologic exposed in Derrida's reference to figures of negative theology, and one can say of Levinas what Derrida has said of Eckhart: "this negative theology is still a theology"—despite Levinas's frequent attempts to deny the theological character of ethical metaphysics.

Now, despite suggesting a profound theologic or theological conceptuality at work in Levinas's ethical metaphysics, Derrida nevertheless recognizes that in *Totality and Infinity* the relation with "being beyond the totality" or "the infinity of being" is not presented as a theology or theological relation. "God's name is often mentioned, but this return to experience, and to 'things themselves,' is not theological" (VM, 107–108). How then does Derrida account for the seeming contradiction in his claims? Or, if ethical metaphysics is determined by a theologic, why does it not present itself as a theology; if the absolutely other is theologically determined, why is the metaphysics of the face not a metaphysics of God or the face of God?

Derrida suggests that, contrary to expectations, the absence of any discourse on the face of God indicates the theological project of *Totality and Infinity.*

> The face of God disappears forever in showing itself. Thus are reassembled in the unity of their metaphysical signification, at the very heart of the experience denuded by Levinas, the diverse evocations of the Face of Yahweh, who of course is never named in *Totality and Infinity.* . . . The face of God which commands while hiding itself is at once more and less a face than all faces. (VM, 108)

In other words, if it belongs most essentially to the face of God to disappear in what shows or presents it, then it would not appear in the discourse of the very metaphysics which thinks it. In fact, biblically, the God who is absent from images and idols on earth is present to his people Israel in the commands and imperatives which make up his law. Out of the hiddenness of God in the burning bush issues the law and all the commandments that make it up so that closeness or proximity to God is not articulated in spatial terms as nearness to the center marked by a temple or other image that presents God but in terms of threats and promises and obedience. Thus, in describing the imperative issuing from the face of *Autrui,* ethical metaphysics would be a profoundly theological discourse, to the degree that it responds to a command issued from the essentially hidden face of God.

In order to show the profoundly theological character of ethical metaphysics, Derrida likens this reading of *Totality and Infinity* to the biblical description of Moses speaking face-to-face with God.

> The face of Yahweh is the total person and the total presence of "the Eternal speaking face to face with Moses" [Exodus 33,11] but saying to him also: "thou canst not see my face: for there shall be no man see me and live . . . while my glory passeth by, I will put thee in a clift of the rock, and will cover thee with my hand while I pass by: And I will take away mine hand, and thou shalt see my back parts: but my face shall not be seen" (Exodus 33:20–23). (VM, 108)

In citing this passage from the Bible, Derrida suggests that theology or the description of a theological relation need not make the face of God visible, or visibly apparent. Just as Moses spoke face to face with God without the face of God being visibly apparent to him, so too the ethical metaphysician enters into discourse with God without the face of God being evident to him, seeing instead the face of *autrui.* In other words *Totality and Infinity* is theological, perhaps even biblical, to the degree that the face of God remains invisible in it; for this invisibility responds precisely to the command issuing from this face, the command that it not be seen. "Whence, perhaps, despite all Levinas's precautions, the equivocal complicity of theology and metaphysics in *Totality and Infinity*" (VM, 109).

Naming the Infinitely Other

Derrida's reading shows a theological conceptuality in *Totality and Infinity* not because such a conceptuality points to the inadequate or compromised rigor of such a thought but because this conceptuality indicates the necessity of maintaining the texture of tradition even when Levinas states its before or beyond. If this is the case, this necessity should be reflected in the language of *Totality and Infinity.* That is to say, the language of *Totality and Infinity* should draw on the same and the totality in the very gesture by which it announces the beyond. Thus Derrida will show that "it is necessary to state infinity's excess over totality in the language of totality; that it is necessary to state the other in the language of the Same . . . and that it is necessary still to inhabit the metaphor in ruins, to dress oneself in tradition's shreds" (VM, 112). I therefore want to investigate the conditions for and the effects of Levinas's naming of the infinitely other.

Recalling the logic of the neither . . . nor . . . that marks the progress toward the infinite, Derrida remarks that such a logic implies that it be unspeakable.

> To say that the infinite exteriority of the other . . . is *non*-exteriority and
> *non*-interiority, to be unable to designate it otherwise than negatively—is
> this not to acknowledge that the infinite (also designated negatively in its
> current positivity: in-finite) cannot be stated? Does this not amount to
> acknowledging that the structure "inside-outside," which is language it-
> self, marks the original finitude of speech and what is said in it? (VM, 113)

Approached in the discourse of neither/nor, the infinite, God, is unstated or
unspoken in the very speech that indicates it. The impossibility of finding
language to speak the infinite implies that there is a limit to what speech
can utter, and hence that speech and all that is spoken in it are finite. Thus,
when Levinas declares the infinite beyond the same, uttering it within a
necessarily finite speech, he marks the infinite as finite, as what it is not.
When the infinite or God appears in the discourse of *Totality and Infinity,* it
does not appear unambiguously or without dissimulation; rather, an irreducible equivocation or duplicity infects the declared beyond.

By making it appear as what it is not, Levinas's language partakes of
what Hegel has called "the divine nature of language": namely, "directly
reversing the meaning of what is said, of making it into something else, and
thus not letting what is meant get into words at all." For Hegel, what is
meant does not enter language insofar as language always states universals
whereas what is meant is always a particular: "we do not envisage the universal . . . but we utter the universal; in other words we do not strictly say
what . . . we mean to say." As Hegel describes it, a universal is neither this
nor that and both this and that; it is not the particular but it includes and is
included in the particular. It is thus a "negative in general"—"a simple thing
of this kind which *is* through negation, which is neither this nor that, a *not-
This,* and is with equal indifference this as well as that—such a thing we call
a *universal.*"[17] In thus identifying the sphere of statements and the negative
in general, Hegel defends a position in which negativity is linked indissolu-
bly to language.

The impossibility of maintaining the positivity of the infinite in language
is seen in that as soon as the infinite is uttered it is marked with the negative, with the negation of finitude, in-finite. "Infinity cannot be understood
except in the form of the in-finite . . . the positive plenitude of classical
infinity is translated into language only by betraying itself in a negative
word (in-finite)" (VM, 114). The otherness of the infinite or God is marked
as finite, as what it is not, as soon as it comes into language. As Hegel claims
of every here and now, every presence, the Infinite thus "has vanished and
is converted into its opposite. . . . It has already ceased to be in the act of
pointing to it [designating it]. . . . It is just this: to be no more just when it
is." In designating the infinite as in-finite, language designates it as having
been or being no more, but "what is pointed out, held fast, and abides is a
negative."[18] Language dispels the infinite itself, leaving it to vanish as soon
as it is designated or pointed out, but preserves it as its negative, as what it
is not, in-finite. The infinite thus is preserved, abides, only by negating it,

by keeping it as what it is not. This means that, on Levinas's terms, it has returned to the same. In the very naming of the beyond, in-finite, it returns to this side, the domain where negativity and dissimulation operate. Such an indebtedness to the same suggests that violence is necessary to discourse, even the Messianic eschatology that proclaims the peace of the Infinite.

According to Derrida's notion of the "original finitude of speech and whatever befalls it," one cannot simultaneously save, within a spoken language, the nonnegative infinity and the ethical meaning of infinite alterity. Ethical metaphysics, or Messianic eschatology, is thus confronted with a choice: either, (1) "if one thinks as Levinas does that positive infinity [God] tolerates or even requires infinite alterity, then one must renounce all language, and first of all the words *infinite* and *other*" (VM, 114); or, (2) if one wants to think and speak of the Infinite, God, one must admit the necessity of violence, of negativity, in speech. Ethical metaphysics could thus maintain the Infinite, God, without violating its infinite alterity if it were to divorce speech and thought (the first option). It would then be possible to think the infinitely other as positive infinity or God without subjecting this infinity to the conditions imposed upon it when it enters language (finitude and the violence of dissimulation). In seeming to require a divorce of thought and language, according to Derrida, ethical metaphysics aligns itself much more with the classical framework than with modern philosophy. Such a divorce, however, is rejected by the author of *Totality and Infinity* in that he founds the very possibility of thought on speech with *Autrui*. Faced with the Derridean options, ethical metaphysics must reject the first, for it is incompatible with one of its fundamental claims: "language conditions the functioning of rational thought" (TI, 204). And yet the second option (admitting the necessity of violence in speaking the infinite) is just as incompatible with the central insight of *Totality and Infinity:* the presence of the infinite, God, in the face is the upsurge of both language and peace.

In thus refusing to divorce speech from thought (option 1) and, simultaneously, thinking both the infinite, God, and the ethical meaning of infinite alterity (option 2), *Totality and Infinity* maintains an other that is impossible and unutterable. "As soon as one attempts to think Infinity as a positive plenitude (one pole of Levinas's nonnegative transcendence), the other becomes unthinkable, impossible, unutterable" (VM, 114). On Derrida's reading, Levinas's ethical metaphysics maintains itself in the impossibility, or despite the impossibility, of the other it designates. As it holds to the impossible, Derrida likens ethical metaphysics to a dream: maintaining itself, impossibly and unthinkably, without having confronted the inevitable choice, "it is the *dream* of a purely *heterological* thought at its source. A *pure* thought of *pure* difference" (VM, 151).

It is also a "dream because it must vanish at daybreak, as soon as language awakens" (VM, 151). When language dawns, the (dreamed-of) infinitely other, God, vanishes. As is often the case in Derrida's reading of Levinas, this again recalls the initial stages of Hegel's *Phenomenology of Spirit:* "if they actually wanted to *say* [what] they mean, if they wanted to *say* it, then this is impossible. . . . In the actual attempt to say it, it would therefore crumble away."[19] As impossible to speak, the infinite is ineffable and unutterable, but it is so precisely insofar as there is language, precisely insofar as one attempts to utter it. The infinite is not ineffable, not unutterable, before the awakening of the language which designates it—it crumbles away or is dispelled "in the actual attempt to say it."

As paradoxical as such a statement is by itself, it has an even stranger consequence for Levinas's thought since, for him, the presence of the infinite is the very awakening of language: on the one hand, there is no language without the presentation of the infinitely other in the face; but, on the other hand, as soon as there is language, on Derrida's reading, the infinitely other vanishes, is no longer present, or is present only as a negative. In other words, the awakening of language is the betrayal of the infinite which calls language forth. Language thereby dispels the dream of a purely nonviolent metaphysic of the Infinite. It is for this reason that the very discourse in which Levinas declares the peace of the Infinite, God, negates that peace, for it designates the infinite as having vanished.

Through Derrida's subtle reading, one can see how discourse is not purified of violence if one considers that the face, the upsurge of language, is at once the cause and the end of war. How so? As Levinas insists, the world before the face arises is a world of the worst violence; it is the world of the anonymous or impersonal neutral, the world in which man is deprived of speech, is unable to come to his own defense by attending his manifestation in words. However, Derrida points out, only after the face has arisen does it make sense to speak of murder. Citing Levinas, "violence can aim only at the face."[20] That is to say, it would be meaningless to understand murder or war as an act directed against inanimate-being (a stone) or ideal-being (a concept). There can be war only where there is a face to kill.[21] Derrida summarizes this complication of violence and nonviolence in speech by saying "speech is doubtless the first defeat of violence, but paradoxically, violence did not exist before the possibility of speech" (VM, 117).[22]

If violence arises with the speech that defeats it and if the declaration of peace is inevitably inhabited by war, "the distinction between discourse and violence always will be an inaccessible horizon. Nonviolence would be the telos and not the essence of discourse . . . peace as a *certain* silence, a certain beyond of speech, a certain possibility, a certain silent horizon of speech" (VM, 116). Whereas for Levinas peace arises with the upsurge of language, for Derrida peace is the inaccessible horizon of discourse, silence. Since peace is a certain silence waiting at or beyond the horizon, "here and now (in a present in general), this horizon cannot be stated, an end cannot be stated, eschato*logy* is not possible, except through *violence*" (VM, 130). As a discourse, an *ology*, the messianic eschatology that announces peace and the Infinite, God, is inseparable from violence. This means that messianic eschatology is finally irreducible to the *eschaton*, the peace, it announces: in a simple formula where there is eschato*logy*, there is not *eschaton;* and where there is *eschaton*, there is not eschatology. To avoid the violence inevitable in discourse, this eschato*logy* "would have to have kept its promise already, even to the extent of no longer being able to occur within discourse as eschato*logy*. . . . 'The messianic triumph' 'armed against evil's revenge' would have to have been ushered in" (VM, 130). To escape the complication of violence and discourse, to arrive at the *eschaton* or at pure nonviolence, discourse would have to fall silent.

For Derrida, speaking man finds himself inevitably at war: "there is war only after the opening of discourse, and war dies out only at the end of discourse" (VM, 117). Forever at war, speaking man is inevitably between the inaccessible horizons of pure peace and the purest violence—both of which are silence: the silence of peace ends war, while the silence of the worst violence precedes it. This being between two pure or simple identities—peace and violence—is what Derrida calls history or the world, which is not a totality as Levinas understands it since it tends indefinitely toward a horizon that always waits beyond it, silence.[23] On this reading, the horizon (silence) is not the accomplice of violence because it does not make of the world a totality in the way Levinas understands totality. For Derrida, the horizon at once encloses the world, and because it is inaccessible, "has the form of an indefinite opening" (VM, 120). After all, the horizon is never reached but always retreats from every advance.

To sum up, according to Derrida then, the other must in some way appear within the same if it is to enter discourse. Without such an appearance, the other could never be named in the discourse of *Totality and Infinity.* But, such an appearance entails that the other dissimulate itself, that its appearance be cut to the measure of the same for which it appears. On the one hand, in uttering the infinitely other, God, throughout *Totality and Infinity,* Levinas must in some uncritical, unreflective way have already acquiesced to the violence of appearing. That the infinitely other must have already appeared for the same is, perhaps, the great preliminary to the thought of *Totality and Infinity.* On the other hand, in refusing to acquiesce to the violence in which the other lends itself to language, the violence of appearing, Levinas cannot authorize his own discourse on the infinitely other: "what authorizes him to say infinitely other if the infinitely other does not also appear as such in the zone that he calls the same?" (VM, 125).

Speaking of the Other:
Levinas and Negative Theology

The nature of the predicament in which Levinas, according to Derrida, finds himself can be seen perhaps more clearly by comparing Levinas's naming of the infinitely other with a certain reading of negative theology. According to Derrida's reading of negative theology, God is named or stated not insofar as God is beyond the totality or the same, but insofar as his infinite alterity is also immanent to the totality or the same. Echoing the discourse of negative theologies, Derrida writes,

God is nothing (determined) because he is everything, and therefore is at once all and nothing, Life and Death. [And then shifting to his own terms,] which means that God is or appears, *is named*, within the difference between All and Nothing, Life and Death. Within difference, and at bottom as Difference itself. This difference is what is called history. God is inscribed in it. (VM, 115–16)

The traditions of negative theology to which Derrida refers authorize the naming of God by acknowledging that while God transcends all beings, God is also the immanent cause of all beings and can be named through these, his effects. It is thus possible to name God insofar as God appears in the difference between the beyond and the totality. Negative theology can speak of the infinitely other, God, because it inscribes God within the anterior difference between the same and the other of the same, the difference Derrida calls the world or history.

Likewise, negative theology legitimated its own discourse by recognizing the insufficiency of language to speak adequately of the unspeakable God. This recognition is seen in the co-implication of the cataphatic, or affirmative mode, and the apophatic, or negative mode. The implication of the negative with the positive and the positive with the negative allows the theologian to speak of God (cataphasis) and at once acknowledge that what is said of God does not grasp God (apophasis). Since ethical metaphysics does not practice any negation, unsaying, or renunciation of what it says of the infinite, it is unable to justify any speech about what cannot be spoken.[24] Negative theology also recognized the insufficiency of language in that, according to Derrida, it "traveled through discourse as through a foreign medium" (VM, 116). Most negative theologies aim at silence where the theological itinerary nears the distant and unspeakable, unknowable God. This means that all language is ultimately insufficient and to be renounced. Since its language never pretended to be ultimate, negative theology can justify what it says of the ineffable insofar as all that it says is provisory and to be renounced. In Levinas's ethical metaphysics, on the other hand, language is not to be discarded in the approach precisely because language is both the approach and the realization of the approached. In not acknowledging that it approaches a silence beyond it, ethical metaphysics cannot justify the violence its language inevitably and ultimately does to the Infinite. Unlike negative theology, Levinas "does not give himself the right to speak" (VM, 116). In failing to recognize the infinitely other as appearing within the anterior difference between the same and the infinite, Levinas cannot authorize his discourse on the infinitely other.

Since acquiescence to the violence of appearing opens the possibility of any discourse on the other, Derrida suggests that Levinas's thought "no longer seeks to be a thought of Being and phenomenality" (VM, 82). In aiming at nonphenomenality, Levinas would approach the Infinite that never lends itself to language and hence never suffers the violence of appearing, of dissimulating itself in its appearance as infinite. For Levinas, then, the possibility of thinking a discourse pure of violence entails describing a notion of speech without statement or language. As Derrida writes, "a speech produced without the least violence would determine nothing, would say nothing, would offer nothing to the other; it would not be *history*, and it would *show* nothing: in every sense of the word, and first of all the Greek sense, it would be speech without *phrase*" (VM, 147). That is to say, since the violence of the same infects language insofar as it utters statements about what appears or is present, a speech that says nothing would avoid even the least violence. Such a speech saying nothing, like the mystical moment of theology or the prayer whose invocation opens theology, would speak a "language of pure invocation, pure adoration, proffering only proper nouns, to call the other from afar" (VM, 147). If speech is violent in what it says, then the violence of the phrase might be avoided by a speech that says nothing but the fact of its addressing, invoking, or praying someone.

But, there are two problems, at least, with such a notion of speech without phrase. First, "would such a language still deserve the name? Is [such a] language possible?" A speech without phrase would be indistinguishable from the cry of need or the inarticulate cries of the infant and animal (VM, 147). If there be speech without phrase, how then is it possible to maintain the distinction between this speech, which is ethics, and need, which Levinas claims is closed to the alterity of the other? Second, if speech offers nothing, can it still be gift? For Levinas, speech is ethics because it "offers things which are mine to the Other" (TI, 76). On this reading, ethics is the gift of the world to the other. But, when speech is forbidden to utter the phrase, when it offers nothing but the proper name by which it calls someone, it no longer gives anything to the other. Such an argument makes it appear as if a speech without phrase is incompatible with ethics. On the other hand, according to Derrida, when ethical, speech would be the gift that gives nothing. Though speech becomes violent in the phrase which is offered to the other, insofar as it could be pure offering, an offering purified of anything offered, it would be nonviolent: "in its original possibility as *offer*, in its still silent intention, language is nonviolent (but can it be language, in this pure intention?)" (VM, 148). For Derrida, there is nonviolence only in the silent offer kept by speech. But in keeping silent, is it still language?

Onto-theo-logy and *Totality and Infinity*

In chapter 1, I showed that the goal of *Totality and Infinity* was to reorient metaphysics on the basis of ethics; its author proposed an ethical metaphysics which would join together the aim of thinking the absolutely other and the metaphysical goal of thinking *l'étant* as such. It identified *l'étant*, the aim of metaphysics, with *Autrui*, the aim of ethics. Hence, throughout the text of *Totality and Infinity, Autrui* and *l'étant* are used almost interchangeably to designate the absolutely other being who resists or opposes determinations of metaphysics based on negativity and ontology. It is as if a single being (*Autrui*) subsumed the meaning of beings (*l'étant*) because it was the only being as such, καθ' αὐτό.

The English translation of *Totality and Infinity* seems to understand, perhaps too well, that Levinas intends *l'étant*, the being as such, to refer to the interpersonal situation (that is to *Autrui*), for it almost always renders *l'étant* as "existent," a term that by echoing "existence" evokes the being of man, the being that we ourselves are, what Heidegger calls *Dasein*.[25] While such a rendering, or any other that would equate *l'étant* with *Autrui*, surely captures Levinas's intended meaning, it is perhaps overhasty in reducing an uncertainty and duplicity in the word *étant*: *l'étant* ordinarily designates what is, anything that is, and/or the totality of what is (it is the French translation of Heidegger's *das Seiende*), personal beings (existents) as well as beings other than personal beings (stones, animals, ideas, etc.). If ethics means that *l'étant* as such is welcomed before Being is understood, as Levinas claims in the famous pronouncement, "the terms [ontology, metaphysics; *l'être, l'étant*] must be reversed" (TI, 47), then wouldn't the relation with any being undo the thought of the same? If the "relation with a being [*un étant*] . . . is the ultimate relation in Being" (TI, 48), then wouldn't any being present the absolutely other?

Levinas insists, however, that only the interpersonal relation, the relation with human-being, *Autrui*, presents the absolutely other. As Derrida notes, "ontology would be valid for every being, 'except *Autrui*'" (VM, 135). In promoting an ontology or understanding of Being that is valid for all beings (beings as a whole) except the one being which is matter for (what Derrida shows to be) a theology (a being beyond the totality of beings), the ethical metaphysics of *Totality and Infinity* begins to look as if it were subject to determination by something resembling what Heidegger identified as the onto-theo-logical constitution of metaphysics. I want to conclude this chapter with a brief indication of how an onto-theo-logical constitution might be at work in *Totality and Infinity*. This task is made easier by the fact that Derrida suggests as much in his reading of *Totality and Infinity*.[26]

I should note here that the *locus classicus* for Heidegger's discussion of the onto-theological constitution of metaphysics is an essay with that name in *Identity and Difference*. This work was presented at a seminar in 1959, two years before the French publication of Levinas's *Totality and Infinity* and so was not widely known or extensively commented on at the time of the writing of *Totality and Infinity*. Derrida, on the other hand, wrote his essay about *Totality and Infinity* at a time when "The Onto-theo-logical Constitution of Metaphysics" was more broadly distributed among academics and intellectuals. It therefore bears the stamp of this work and, in all fairness to Levinas, recognizes in several places that the work of Levinas contemporaneous with the writing of "Violence and Metaphysics" has reckoned with many of the issues Heidegger raises.

Now, according to Heidegger's notion of the onto-theo-logical constitution of metaphysics, metaphysics is constituted by its having forgotten the difference between Being and beings. As such, it always and only thinks Being in terms of beings; Being is at once the highest universal, a concept including beings as a whole, and a particular being beyond beings as a whole who nonetheless accounts for beings as a whole. In *Totality and Infinity*, Being is used in precisely this way. In the first place, Being appears as a concept, to be overcome, that seeks to cover the totality of beings or as a horizon which embraces beings as a whole. This is how Being is determined in what Levinas calls ontology; it is the determination of Being which he portrays as complicit with violence against the alterity of the other. In Levinas's thought, ontology or comprehension of Being is violence precisely because Being is generality or a universal or a horizon which embraces the totality of beings and thereby makes possible comprehension of beings as a whole. In short, ontology in *Totality and Infinity* is a vision of Being as totality, beings as a whole. In the second place, Being is *Autrui, l'étant* who is not a being among beings. When Levinas says, "Eschatology institutes a relation with Being [*l'être*] beyond the totality" or "Exteriority is the essence of Being [*l'être*]," it is clear that this exteriority or beyond wherein the essence of Being resides is *Autrui,* that is, the being broached in ethical metaphysics. To cite Levinas, "the ethical relation [that is, the relation with *l'étant* called *Autrui*] . . . goes towards Being [*l'être*] in its absolute exteriority" (TI, 47). Does it not seem clear here that Being is thought as a being (*l'étant* called Autrui) beyond the totality of beings—that is, as a highest being or a being par excellence?

Here it might be objected, however, that whereas for Heidegger the being par excellence relates to beings as a whole by grounding them, for Levinas, the absolutely other being, *Autrui,* is by no means the ground of the totality of beings, what Levinas calls Being. This is true—but on condition that one thinks of grounding solely in terms of causal relation. To be sure, *Autrui* does not cause beings as a whole in the way that a cause causes effects formally, efficiently, materially, or teleologically. I will grant that this qualification does in fact hold; but if *Autrui* is not the cause of beings as a whole, it certainly is the source or origin of signification and thus, in a certain way, accounts for (*begründen* is Heidegger's word) beings as a whole. This is precisely what Levinas means when he says that there is no comprehension of Being, the all-embracing horizon or concept, without the relation to *Autrui.* And, furthermore, if universals arise in and through the relation to *Autrui,* the claim could again be defended that for Levinas, as for onto-theo-logically constituted metaphysics, beings as a whole are accounted for in terms of a being par excellence.

Now, according to Heidegger, this determination of Being arises precisely from having forgotten the difference between Being and beings. The Heideggerian "step back" out of the onto-theo-logical tradition of metaphysics was therefore a step in the direction of Being as such, that is Being thought in its difference from beings where Being would no longer be understood either as the highest being or as the highest generality or concept. For Heidegger, Being was not a predicate which marked the transition of a particular subject to a universal predicate, ultimately the most universal predicate. As Derrida observes,

> If Being is taken as essence or existence (as Being-such or Being-there) . . . then the Being of the existent does not belong to the realm of predication, because it is already implied in all predication in general, and makes predication possible. . . . It is beyond genre and categories, transcendental in the scholastic sense, before scholasticism had made of the transcendental a supreme and infinite existent, God himself. (VM, 136)

Not the highest category or most universal predicate, Being is not the ally of totality. This is why the Heideggerian understanding of Being might not be violence, not a suppression of the alterity of the absolutely other being. Furthermore, without this understanding of Being, one would be forbidden every, predicative or otherwise, determination of beings. There would be no predication without the presupposition that the determined being already belonged to Being. Being is presupposed both in the copula which predicates attributes distinguishing beings and in the "is" which posits determinate existence. In fact, it is only in this verb of a statement that Being has any meaning at all.[27]

Can such a forgetting of Being as such in its difference be seen in Levinas? If Being is not the totality but the verb of a proposition, when Levinas determines *l'étant* as *Autrui*, hasn't he already understood Being, and done so in a way which is nonviolent? In order to determine *l'étant* as *Autrui*, to distinguish it from other beings among beings [*l'étant*], even if this difference does not depend on any predicated difference, must not Levinas let this being be as it itself is? And what else is this than to understand its difference from other beings as a different way to be? *Autrui* differs from stones and animals, for example, in that, among *l'étant*, it "is" in a different way—namely by presenting the face which, unlike natural objects, absolves itself from every manifestation. How else could it be maintained that both the face and stones and animals are *l'étant*? Finally, when he claims "exteriority is the essence of Being," doesn't Levinas indicate that he has already thought and understood Being?

What I am trying to suggest here is twofold: there is a presupposed and undiscussed understanding of Being at work in *Totality and Infinity*, and this meaning of Being is not the same as that which Levinas says is grasped in ontology. The author of *Totality and Infinity* has determined the meaning of Being as, on one hand, a generality that embraces the totality of beings (Being in its violent determination) and, on the other, the one being who presents *l'étant* as such (Being as *Autrui* met in ethical metaphysics). Comparison with Heidegger's reading of the onto-theo-logical constitution of metaphysics shows that what is omitted from this discussion is any consideration of Being in its difference from beings. In determining Being in this way, the author of *Totality and Infinity* gives an almost perfect indication of onto-theo-logical constitution. As Derrida writes,

> By refusing, in *Totality and Infinity*, to accord any dignity to the ontico-ontological difference, by seeing in it only a ruse of war, and by calling the intra-ontic movement of ethical transcendence . . . *metaphysics*, Levinas confirms Heidegger in his discourse: for does not the latter see in metaphysics (in metaphysical ontology) the forgetting of Being and the dissimulation of the ontico-ontological difference? (VM, 142)

The ethical metaphysics of *Totality and Infinity* thus illustrates Heidegger's conceptualization of metaphysics. Constituted by having forgotten the difference between Being and beings, metaphysics always dissimulates Being. Always determined as a being and so nothing outside beings, Being never appears as such in metaphysics. As Derrida writes,

> Being, since it is always, in fact, determined as an existent and is nothing outside the existent, is always dissimulated. Levinas's phrase—the preexistence of the relation to a being—is the very formula of this initial concealment. Being not existing before beings . . . begins by hiding itself beneath its determination. This determination as the revelation of beings themselves (metaphysics) is the very veiling of Being. . . . Without this dissimulation of Being by beings, there would be nothing. (VM, 144)

On this reading, then, it belongs to the onto-theo-logical forgetfulness of the difference to propose the priority of beings—exactly in the way that ethical metaphysics does: beings assume priority to the degree that metaphysics fails to see in them the dissimulation of Being.

More, this forgetfulness belongs to Being itself: as nothing outside beings and yet different from beings, Being "is" only by being the beings it is not; that is to say, it "is" only by not being itself. "Since Being is nothing (determined), it is necessarily produced in difference (as difference)" (VM, 150). If there is no Being before there are beings, then Being begins by hiding itself. This is the very reason why one who fails to see this differing in Being, or Being in this differing, says that beings precede Being.[28] Hence, Levinas's claim (metaphysics precedes ontology; the relation to beings precedes the relation to Being) becomes an effect of Being itself. It is evidence of the Being which "is" by hiding itself. In claiming that the relation to beings precedes ontology, ethical metaphysics would be an example of this concealment of Being: beings are revealed to the degree that Being is concealed. Ethical metaphysics has forgotten the very Being whose forgottenness Heidegger, in taking a step back and as this step back, will attempt to remember by thinking its necessary dissimulation—by thinking it as dissimulation or by remembering it as necessarily forgotten.

3

Reduction to
Responsibility

Chapter 2 concluded by showing that the ethics of *Totality and Infinity* is still part and parcel of the tradition whose violence it intends to surpass. Like metaphysics as Heidegger understands it, *Totality and Infinity* has forgotten the ontological difference, and so its descriptions of the absolute are relativized or determined by this unthought forgetting. *Totality and Infinity,* that is, would still presuppose an unasked question of Being, wherein Being is no longer the matter of ontology but of a *Seinsfrage* that thinks it in its difference from beings.

It is not surprising, therefore, that in the 1977 preface to the second edition of *De l'existence à l'existant* Levinas comments as follows on the "philosophical progress going from *Totality and Infinity* to *Otherwise than Being, or, Beyond Essence*":

> To glimpse in the "existant," in the human being, and in what Heidegger will call "the beingness of beings," not an occultation and a "dissimulation" of Being, but a step towards the Good and towards the relation to God and, in the relation between beings, something other than "an ending of metaphysics"—this does not mean that one simply inverts the terms of the famous Heideggerian difference by privileging beings to the detriment of Being. This reversal will have been only the first step of a movement which, being open to an ethics older than ontology, will allow the signifying of significations beyond the ontological difference, which, without a doubt, is, in the end, the very signifying of the Infinite. (EE, 12)

This passage claims that the progress to *Otherwise than Being, or, Beyond Essence* is made with respect to the ontological difference. Whereas *Totality and*

Infinity was only a reversal of the difference, in Levinas's subsequent work it is a question of passing to significations beyond or on the hither side of the ontological difference.

In making such a passage, ethics is no longer a relation in which the relation between two beings simply precedes and in this way dissimulates the relation to Being; it is instead one in which there is "an exception putting out of order the conjunction of essence, entities, and the 'difference'" (OBBE, xli). Disqualifying the difference which holds together and apart Being (what Levinas calls "essence") and beings, ethics introduces a disjunction of beings and Being such that the "beings" involved in the ethical situation are not joined to Being and therefore are not, so to speak, beings. "The hither side or the beyond being is not an entity on the hither side of or beyond being" as it appeared to be in *Totality and Infinity* (OBBE, 45). Thus, in *Otherwise than Being, or, Beyond Essence,* when it is a task of surpassing the ontological difference, Levinas will speak of an "ontological indifference" (OBBE, 178). The task of Levinas's later book is to achieve this indifference by articulating an order of signifying in which the ontological difference is rendered indifferent.

The Ontological Difference Ignored

This "ontological indifference" sounds strikingly similar to the "forgetting" which Heidegger stigmatized throughout his writings on metaphysics, a forgetting which seems to have determined *Totality and Infinity.* As Levinas admits, the ontological in-difference does indeed entail "a forgetting of being and non-being" (OBBE, 177). However, according to Levinas, in this indifference, forgetting is not "an 'unregulated' forgetting. . . . [b]ut a forgetting that would be an ignorance in the sense that nobility ignores what is not noble, and in the sense that certain monotheists do not recognize, while knowing, what is not the highest. Such ignorance is beyond consciousness; it is an open-eyed ignorance" (OBBE, 177). The ontological in-difference is reached not by forgetting that one has forgotten the ontological difference but by seeing it with open eyes and at once seeing through it in the way that one sees through an impostor impersonating the king or through the emperor's proverbial new clothes. In a way that strangely evokes Nietzschean nobility (though reversed) and monotheism together, Levinas sees the ontological difference only to ignore it. As nobility passes by the pitiful, Levinas passes by the ontological difference without being troubled by it; as monotheism sees idols of the divine only to reject their claim to divinity, Levinas sees the ontological difference only to see through it and thereby disqualify its claim to ultimacy.

Such an ontological in-difference is achieved by envisioning the ontological difference from the perspective of a different difference, a difference with respect to the ontological difference itself. Without achieving this perspective, one can deny the ultimacy of the ontological difference only in a reactive, nay-saying, way, and worse yet a way that is void of reasons and defenses. From the perspective of this second difference, however, the ontological difference is rendered indifferent. The doubling of difference appears in the phrase "non-indifference," as when Levinas writes "this indifference is not purely negative, for in another sense it is non-indifference" (OBBE, 178). To render indifferent the ontological difference is a task not simply of negating this difference but of ignoring it in the name of another difference—the difference of nonindifference. By describing the order and the effects of this redoubled difference, *Otherwise than Being, or, Beyond Essence* distinguishes itself from *Totality and Infinity;* for in seeking to articulate the sense of a different difference, this work does not simply reverse the ontological difference but transcends it. This attempt leads to the audacious title *Otherwise than Being*—a title which is substituted for a more proper title, one appropriate to the ultimacy of the *Seinsfrage,* such as "Being otherwise" or "Non-being."

Since the ontological difference is not merely forgotten, it does appear in *Otherwise than Being, or, Beyond Essence;* but it appears only as seen from a perspective higher than it. Thus, it appears as revoked or ignored, as indifferent. The effects of its appearance are seen in that Levinas adopts terminological distinctions that reflect its operation. For instance, Levinas uses the term "essence" to designate Being thought in its difference from beings: "the term essence here expresses being different from beings, the German *Sein* distinguished from *Seiendes,* the Latin *esse* distinguished from the scholastic *ens*" (OBBE, xli); "in this work, the term *essence* designates being as differentiated from entities" (OBBE, 187). As it is to be thought in its difference from each and every being, essence must *not* be understood by reference to beings—it does not designate a being, nor does it designate the totality of beings, nor does it designate what is most general in beings. For this reason, Levinas does not "write *essance* as would be required by the history of language, where the suffix *-ance,* deriving from *-antia* or *-entia,* gave birth to abstract nouns of action" (OBBE, xli). "Essence" is meant to evoke the purely verbal sense of being. "The term *essence,* which we do not dare spell *essance,* designates the *esse,* the process or event of being, distinguished from the *ens,* the *Sein* differentiated from the *Seiendes*" (OBBE, 187). "Essence" is thus the name for the event or happening of Being, the event in which Being is deployed in beings or in which each is appropriated to the other. As such, the name "essence" marks the effects of the ontological difference in *Otherwise than Being, or, Beyond Essence.*

Though the ontological difference is operative in what essence names, this difference is nonetheless ignored by the thought of *Otherwise than Being, or, Beyond Essence.* Ignored or rendered indifferent, the difference does not appear as such (as difference) even if its effects are recorded in the name "essence." Having rendered indifferent the difference named in "essence," Levinas sees in essence not so much a difference to be determined, remembered, or achieved as what he will call "the amphibology of *being* and *beings*—in which beings dissimulate being" (OBBE, 7). In *Otherwise than Being, or, Beyond Essence*, the ontological difference appears not as such but as an amphibology—that is, the difference appears only in and as the dissimulation of Being in beings. In commenting on the ambiguous sense in which being is said, Levinas asks,

> Does the mystery of being and entities, their difference, concern us already? The distinction and the amphibology of being and beings will turn out from the start to be important and to be determinant for truth, but this distinction is also an amphibology and does not signify the ultimate. (OBBE, 23)

For Levinas, the amphibology of Being and beings does not offer the starting point for a hermeneutic or recollective thinking that aims to wrest the difference from it and so to think Being in its difference from the beings in which it always is. This is so because, for Levinas, the difference between Being and beings is not forgotten but rendered indifferent or amphibological in light of a different ultimate. The definition or description of this "ultimate" and the means of arriving at it will thus be a crucial task of *Otherwise than Being, or, Beyond Essence*.

The Relativization of the Difference, the Said

If the *Seinsfrage* is not ultimate, then it must be possible to explain "essence" without reference to the ontological difference. Where and how do "essence" and the distinction between Being and beings emerge? Levinas gives a short and simple answer to this question: "it can be shown that even the distinction between Being and entities is borne by the amphibology of the said" (OBBE, 6). The source of the difference, and hence of "essence" and the amphibology, is thus located within a particular interpretation of language, one in which language is understood primarily and exhaustively in what Levinas calls the said: "the logos as said, a revelation of Being in its amphibology of Being and entities" (OBBE, 27). In claiming that the difference between being and beings is borne by an amphibology in the said or in the logos as said, Levinas stigmatizes the conditions under which this difference is first evoked: it arises only insofar as the revelation of beings happens in the said of language.

In the term "said," Levinas captures what is called the apophantic function of the logos, its function of showing a being by making a predicative statement about it. But, according to Levinas, who here follows Heidegger, when stated in the said or the proposition, not only does the entity appear or is it shown in the nouns that designate it but essence also resounds: "In a predicative proposition, an apophansis, an entity can make itself be understood verbally, as a way of essence, . . . a modality of this essence or temporalization"; "it is the verbalness of the verb that first resounds in the predicative proposition" (OBBE, 38, 39).[1] In order that essence (the verbality of Being/beings) might resound, the being must be stated in the said or the proposition because it is in the said that the verb is heard at the heart of the statement of beings. The distinction between Being (verbal) and beings (nominal) is thus situated in the said; it arises only when beings are said in the apophantic proposition. Without hearing the apophantic logos, the distinction between Being and beings, essence and entities, would not and could not be sought: "the birthplace of ontology is in the said" (OBBE, 42).

But, the fact that essence is born and is heard in the said or the apophantic proposition means that it is forever "on the verge of becoming a noun" or identified as a being (OBBE, 41). In the said, even verbs have a nominal function, according to Levinas, insofar as they are taken as words designating actions; the verbality of a verb is lost when it appears in the said where the function of signs is to designate. "It is probably this function of signs, designation (which words incontestably exercise within the said), that is implicitly ascribed to a verb when one tries to reduce the function of the verb to the 'expression' of events, actions, or alterations" (OBBE, 39). When stated in the said, then, "essence" appears only in order to disappear or to become hidden. In this way, Levinas gives his own account of the onto-theo-logical constitution; the onto-theo-logy (or at least the theo-logy of onto-theo-logy) in which the verbal sense of Being is confused with a being par excellence arises not because the difference between Being and beings has been forgotten but because Being appears in the said of the apophantic logos.

Fundamental ontology, or the *Seinsfrage,* is born from the determination of language as said and the restriction of Being's appearance to such language. Since the appearance of "essence" (verbality) is at once its disappearance (the verb taken as a said that designates), philosophy adopts a special procedure to uncover and make heard the hidden verbality of the verb. This need for a hermeneutic which can wrest the verbality of Being or "essence" from its appearance in the amphibology of Being and beings creates the space where fundamental ontology (the *Seinsfrage*) can operate.

Importantly, in Levinas's rendering of the birth of the *Seinsfrage,* "essence" hovers in the ambiguousness of Being and beings (the ambiguity which gives cause for the quest) *not* because philosophy has forgotten the difference between being and entities. Rather, it does so because of an ambiguity inherent to the logos in which it is born. "Logos is the ambiguousness of being and entities, the primordial amphibology" (OBBE, 42). In insisting that the amphibology of being and entities is based in the primordial ambiguity of the logos as said, Levinas is not playing some unimportant game with language. Rather, in locating the origin of the distinction between Being and beings, Levinas makes its privilege (and hence the privilege of the ontological quest) depend on a more fundamental decision in the history of philosophy; namely, the decision to start philosophizing by an analysis or description of the apophantic logos.

That this start is indeed the result of a decision and not of a necessity can be seen in the introduction to *Being and Time* when Heidegger writes,

> This mode of making something manifest in the sense of letting something be seen by pointing out [apophansis] does not go with all kinds of discourse [logos]. Requesting (*euchē*), for instance also makes manifest, but in a different way. (BT, 56 [32])

In a similar passage in *The History of the Concept of Time*, Heidegger makes the decision even more evident as a decision when he writes,

> The apophansis, letting the spoken be seen in itself, is a particular meaning of discourse. Not every proposition is a theoretical proposition, an assertion about something. None of the following is an apophantic logos, in which something is communicated: an exclamation, a request, a wish, a prayer. But each is a [*semantikos*], each signifies something. In these instances, however, signifying does not mean the theoretical apprehension of something. (HCT, 85 [116])[2]

Heidegger here suggests that the determination of philosophy as *Seinsfrage* is not opened by a consideration of all forms of signifying or ways of appearing but by starting from only one particular form of manifestation or signification—that of the apophantic logos. The search for Being thus achieves its privilege only by excluding other forms of signifying, only by eliminating nonapophantic forms of signification from the field of philosophical questioning. What would it mean for philosophy to explore these other fields, those ruled out or left aside by the decision to start with the apophantic? Is there a way to figure philosophical intelligibility such that these other forms of signifying or modes of appearing are allowed to signify and appear?

The Saying

In these two passages, Heidegger offers the fact whose significance Levinas will take as his point of departure: if the search for essence depends on a decision to consider only one particular form in which discourse signifies, this search does not exhaust the possibilities of signifying or appearing. Levinas names this broader possibility of signifying "saying." Located in the said, the amphibology of Being/beings is always spoken, which means that it is delivered in a saying.

> To affirm that the mutation in the amphibology of being and entities is an amphibology of the logos, that it is due to the status of the said . . . is to measure the pre-ontological weight of language. . . . But also, by interpreting the fact that essence exposes and is exposed, that temporalization [verbalness] is stated, resounds, is said, it is not to give priority to the said over the saying. (OBBE, 43)

Housed in the said, the amphibology of being and entities is not ultimate but is borne or carried by the saying which precedes it: "the said, the appearing, arises in the saying"; "the apophansis is a modality of saying. . . . It refers to a saying on the hither side of the amphibology of being and entities"; "saying states and thematizes the said" (OBBE, 46, 47; 46). In other words, according to Levinas, there would be no said, hence no amphibology of being and entities to motivate the question of Being, if this said were not first stated by the saying which delivers it.

As it delivers the said, the saying is not interpretable in terms of Being or the said. Not offering an alternative form of the said or a said saying something else, the saying is the signifying of the very signification stated in the said—the fact of signification itself. Saying, then, does not signify in the way that words of the said signify either by difference from other words or by reference to things designated. The signifyingness of saying precedes all signification and hence all language. It is a "pre-original language" or a "foreword preceding all language" in the sense that it opens all language and signification by delivering the said (OBBE, 5, 6). Nothing would ever be said if a saying did not say it.

It is important here to distinguish saying from the act of speaking or the speech act. Saying is not the act of speaking if the act of speaking, as act, implies decisions taken by a subject who has thought out what he wants to say, who has consciously considered his words before speaking and then chosen the words that best suit the meaning he intends to communicate externally. Similarly, saying is not a speech act insofar as the primary function of a speech act is to effect a change, to bring something about, in a particular context. A speech act, or performative, is effective because it takes place in a particular setting within a particular context of rules governing its utterance. The words "I do," after all, only effect a marriage when they are said in a particular setting—the church, temple, house of justice, or other authorized location—and in the presence of officials whose power to recognize and effect a marriage is granted by the authority of the state, church, or other body politic. These acts of speaking, or speech acts, still presuppose the saying: "Saying is communication, to be sure, but as a condition for all communication, as exposure"; "saying is a denuding of denuding, a giving a sign of its very signifyingness, an expression of exposure, a hyperbolic passivity"; "it is to exhaust oneself in exposing oneself, to make signs by making oneself a sign" (OBBE, 48, 49, 49). In other words, the saying precedes and opens the signification of the Said in the sense that there would be no opening for the said to arise without the antecedent exposure of the subject to the other. "Saying prolongs this extreme passivity, despite its apparent activity" (OBBE, 153). This exposure, this passivity, does not signify, Levinas argues, by exposing a signification that I intend to give in and through a sign; it exposes me passively—or, as saying, I am exposed passively as the very giving of signs, as a sign that exposes the giving of signs, that in fact signs are being given.

Saying means the exposure of the subject not in the sense that I actively hold myself ready to hear the words of the other but in that if there is to be a statement of the said I must first be exposed, passively, to the other. This notion of exposure is more radical than that which Martin Buber, Franz

Rosenzweig, and others—including Karl Rahner in his notion of a "hearer of the word"—designate by the term "readiness," religious man's readiness for revelation. Exposure must not be understood in terms of readiness insofar as readiness implies a certain preparedness of the subject. As ready or prepared, the subject has provided for the other's arrival; he has made preparations which diminish the surprise of the other's advent or which measure this appearance to the ready or prepared subject's capacity for receiving.[3] Receptivity would thus imply a residue of activity, the activity of taking up or assuming, that is not operative in exposure.

In claiming that saying signifies the extreme passivity of a subject exposed to the Other, Levinas suggests the terms in which saying will signify outside of or before the signification possible in an apophantic language. The saying which bears the said does not have an ontological sense but the ethical sense of responsibility. "Saying states and thematizes the said, but signifies it to the other, a neighbor, with a signification that has to be distinguished from that borne by words in the said"; "the act of saying will turn out to have been introduced here from the start as the supreme passivity of exposure to another, which is responsibility for the free initiatives of the other"; "responsibility for another is precisely a saying prior to anything said" (OBBE, 46, 47, 45). These examples make it quite clear that for Levinas saying means responsibility; it is in terms of the ethical relation with an other that saying signifies. Ethics is the order of signifying that exceeds that of the apophansis; it is the order of meaning excluded, arbitrarily and decisively, at the outset of ontology. Whether it is *the* order or *an* order of signifying is a question that remains to be decided, one that I will broach below in chapters 5 and 6.

In *Otherwise than Being, or, Beyond Essence,* therefore, the description of the responsible self is meant to fulfill the stated aim of "showing the signification proper to the saying on the hither side of the thematization of the said" (OBBE, 43). This is an important point because it will prove integral to Levinas's claim that "ethics is first philosophy." Without noting these arguments, it remains unclear just at what point and why ethics intervenes in the course of philosophy, why philosophy is ethics, and why ethics is philosophy. As I have already begun to suggest, however, a crucial ambiguity haunts these arguments: to what extent is ethics a "region" or an order of signifying excluded from a philosophy that starts with the logos as said; and to what extent is ethics the source or possibility, the signifying, of all signification?

From the Said Back to the Saying—a Reduction

In evoking the saying that carries the said, Levinas is able to explain both why the *Seinsfrage* is not ultimate and how it might be mistaken for the ultimate. "Is not the inescapable fate in which being immediately includes the statement of being's other not due to the hold the said has over the saying?" (OBBE, 5). In other words, philosophy will take the question of Being to be both first and ultimate when the signifyingness of saying is taken to be exhausted in, correlative with, or reducible to the signification of what is said—that is, to an apophantic logos.

As prior to language or the signification of the said, Saying "has to be reached in its existence antecedent to the said, or else the said has to be reduced to it. We must fix this antecedence. What does saying signify before signifying a said" (OBBE, 46)? This passage identifies two problems: (1) what does saying signify? and (2) how is philosophy supposed to gain access to this order of signifying? With respect to the first point, I have already suggested that saying signifies in terms of ethics or responsibility. This observation only makes it more pressing that the second point be addressed.

Against the tendency to let the saying die and be absorbed in the said, Levinas proposes that "from the amphibology of being and entities in the said, we must go back to the saying which signifies prior to essence, prior to identification, on the hither side of this amphibology" (OBBE, 45–46). To take this movement back to the saying, Levinas has recourse to a philosophical operation that was absolutely central to phenomenology as it was methodically articulated by Husserl: the reduction. In Levinas, the reduction leads back to what is prior to the correlation of the saying and the said, that is, to the saying without the said: "one has to go back to that hither side, starting from the trace retained by the said, in which everything shows itself. The movement back to the saying is the phenomenological reduction"; "the reduction is reduction of the said to the saying beyond the logos, beyond being and non-being, beyond essence, beyond true and non-true. It is the reduction to signification, to the one for the other involved in responsibility" (OBBE, 53, 45). According to Levinas, the reduction suspends or puts in parentheses the content of what is said in order to consider the saying without the said, as if the said counted for nothing. After the reduction has suspended the said, saying can be seen to "deliver itself without saying anything said. . . . No said equals the sincerity of the saying. . . . Sincerity would be saying without said, apparently a speaking so as to say nothing" (OBBE, 143). By treating the said as if it were nothing, the reduction isolates the saying—considers it in relation to nothing—and thereby removes from its consideration the cause of this saying being interpreted in terms of the said.

In adopting the reduction, Levinas adopts one of Husserlian phenomenology's key techniques—in fact the technique that, according to Husserl, is the key to his phenomenology: "those who set aside the phenomenological reduction as a philosophically irrelevant eccentricity . . . destroy the whole meaning of the work and of my phenomenology."[4] The reduction is the method which discovers a terrain for phenomenological philosophy, which brings philosophy back to the appearing of phenomena. In practicing a reduction, then, Levinas positions his work within the phenomenological tradition of Husserl. Unlike Husserl, however, Levinas claims that the point to which the phenomenological reduction leads is not subjectivity in the form of consciousness or intentionality but "subjectivity in the form of saying," which means, as we saw above, subjectivity as responsibility (OBBE, 45). This explains why Levinas says that the work of *Otherwise than Being, or, Beyond Essence* is "built around chapter four [entitled "Substitution"] which is its centerpiece" (OBBE, xli). For it is in this chapter that Levinas offers the most detailed and also most concentrated description of that to which the reduction leads back: subjectivity in terms of responsibility. Chapter 4, "Substitution," is the centerpiece of the work because it is in this chapter that, the reduction having been acquired, Levinas is able to describe subjectivity as responsibility which expresses the very signifyingness of all signification stated in ontology and the said. It is thus the reduction to the saying which permits philosophy to describe the ultimate (the subject as responsibility) from which the difference between being and beings, a difference of the said, can be ignored, rendered indifferent, with eyes that see through it.

An Ethical Supplement to Phenomenology

Though merely claiming a name from one's master does not suffice to identify one as a disciple, when Levinas claims to practice the reduction, he indicates, at the very least, his conviction that the possibility of appearing that exceeds the field circumscribed by the said can be reached through phenomenology.[5] Or phenomenology can provide, by means of its methodical practice of the reduction, a figure of the subject in which phenomena appear outside the limits set by the said. Part 2 of this book is therefore presented as something like a comparison of the three major claimants to the office of phenomenological subject—Husserl's transcendental I, Levinas's responsibility, and Heidegger's *Dasein*.

If the phenomena of phenomenology give themselves to an I, or alternatively are given by an I, then assessing the place and function of this I in the appearing of phenomena seems absolutely essential to understanding the limits or limitlessness of appearing in each case. The fact that in Husserl the appearing of phenomena to the I always drifts and becomes the appearing of phenomena by or from the I suggests that here the possibilities of appearing are in fact measured not from the phenomena themselves but from the I. The intentional activity of the I establishes the conditions and the limits by which the possibilities of appearing can be measured in Husserlian phenomenology. The fact that both Heidegger and Levinas prefer to relinquish the name "I" when determining the subject (Heidegger displacing it in favor of an analytic of Dasein; Levinas dismissing it in the face of the oneself or me) already gives a preliminary clue to what could be construed as the central issue of this comparison. Heidegger and Levinas will endeavor to open possibilities of appearing for phenomena other than those that can be constituted by the intentional activity of an I. This entails construing the subject in an essential passivity (thrownness in Heidegger, responsibility in Levinas) such that the I does not submit the appearing of phenomena to conditions that are set and measured by its own activity (intentionality, horizonality, temporal modification). The passive subject "constitutes" phenomena passively—that is, by bearing, supporting, or perhaps receiving their appearance before the subject has time to generate their possibility on its own accord.

This manner of discussing responsibility in Levinas leads to what I believe is one of the crucial uncertainties in interpreting Levinas. To what extent is the description of ethics and the responsible self meant to be a phenomenological account of one particular "region" or one particular phenomenon ruled out by the Husserlian manner of construing phenomenality, and to what extent is the description of the subject as responsibility meant to open the possibility of appearing as such? When Levinas claims that "ethics is first philosophy" or that responsibility is "the signifying of all signification," he seems to be undertaking a much more vast project than simply the task of describing one particular field of appearing. This more vast project could not be described better than it has been by Adriaan Peperzak. Adopting such a project, Adriaan Peperzak suggests that "ethics" be taken in its broadest sense so that it "covers everything that is appropriate to do or desire in relation to what shows itself. . . . Every phenomenon requires that I respect its mode of Being and that I respond to it in an appropriate manner. . . . Every description which does justice to the phenomena, every concrete phenomenology, is *ipso facto* ethical."[6]

This complicated relation between ethics and phenomenology can, I believe, be understood in terms of the logic of the supplement that Derrida sketches in *Of Grammatology*. In the chapters making up Part 2 of this book, I will claim that ethics is added to Husserlian phenomenology as a sort of "originary supplement": it is an addition from outside a strictly Husserlian phenomenology but an addition which Levinas shows to be constitutive of the phenomenological reduction and one which eventually substitutes itself for the thing it supplements.[7]

PART 2
Ethical Phenomenology

4

Insight and Drift

Husserl

After metaphysics came to an end (positively in Hegel, negatively in Nietz-sche), it was Edmund Husserl and phenomenology which inspired a new beginning of philosophy. For better or worse, this fact cannot be denied, and the twentieth century has again and again borne witness to the phi-losophical inspiration to be found in Husserl's phenomenological insight. Many of the most well-known thinkers of the past hundred years began their careers with work on Husserl, the founding figure of phenomenol-ogy—Maurice Merleau-Ponty, Paul Ricoeur, and Jean-Paul Sartre, to name just a few. Even Jacques Derrida's earliest works were confrontations with Husserl, and it was in and through readings of Husserl that Derrida worked out his earliest critiques of metaphysics and presence. Looking at this list of names, therefore, it would not be extravagant to suggest that, throughout the twentieth century, it has been the reception of Husserl and phenom-enology that has stimulated and fertilized new advances in continental phi-losophy—even if these authors eventually left phenomenology for Marxist engagement, literary theory, or perhaps more generally the structuralist/poststructuralist debates.

Recently, at the end of the twentieth century, philosophy has seen an-other return to phenomenology that has brought it back to the forefront of philosophical debate. Some have even hailed this retrieval of phenomenol-ogy as a counter to the dominance of the structuralist discourse that has so thoroughly expelled philosophy from the philosophical discipline—or swal-lowed it up. Like all returns, however, this return enacts a difference. Many previously central phenomenological concepts have been displaced or re-vised, no longer assuming the importance they once had; and many previ-ously overlooked or marginalized concepts and passages have assumed central importance. It is as if the return to phenomenology claimed that it was going back to the idea, or ideal, of phenomenology glimpsed by Husserl but lost or suppressed by each of its historical manifestations—Husserl's own phenomenology included. My reading of phenomenology will follow the readings of Husserl put forward by the leaders of this movement. For my purposes, Jean-Luc Marion and Michel Henry offer the most powerful interpretation of the idea of phenomenology; and it is to their readings of Husserl that I will make reference in seeking to understand the phenomenological notion of phenomenon and subjectivity.

The Appearing of Appearance

Phenomenology has been able to initiate this new beginning because of its pretense to lay bare not simply a new region of beings or objects of experience but the necessary beginning of any and all experience. As opposed to particular regional sciences, phenomenology, and the reduction which was its royal road, claimed to lay bare the appearing of all that appears—beings, objects, or whatever else one wants to call what appears in experience. As such, the phenomenological breakthrough represented a radical attempt to extend the possibility of appearing to all beings. According to Jean-Luc Marion, the question motivating phenomenology was this: "Can the conditions of presence be extended to the point that all beings reach it, beyond the limits set by previous states of metaphysics, or even by any metaphysics at all? Can the givenness in presence of each thing be realized without any condition or restriction?"[1] This attempt to embrace the appearing of each and every implies a radical redefinition of possibility (and eventually of presence) such that the possibility of appearing is extended to all that appears, even what appears as the impossible, without regard for prior conditions or limits.

As Marion has argued, the phenomenological redefinition of possibility marks a radical departure from previous figures in the history of philosophy. In Kant, for instance, "that which agrees with the formal conditions of experience, that is, with the conditions of intuition and of concepts, is possible."[2] In this definition, possibility is determined not simply by the appearing of phenomena but by the conditions for experience. The field of phenomenality or appearing is thus limited to what is embraced by these conditions, and only those phenomena which admit these conditions are allowed the right to appear. More specifically, these conditions are the forms of the intuition and the concepts of the understanding, conditions which are identified precisely with the power of knowing in and through a finite, that is limited, mind. In Kant, at the least, what appears owes the possibility of its appearance to the power of knowing, which alone can legitimate, justify, grant that appearance. Thus, anything is possible, so long as it submits to the conditions of knowing.

But one might well wonder: doesn't the meaning of appearance imply appearing with or without justification, indeed before there is any question of conforming to conditions which would justify its possibility? Wouldn't demonstrative procedures that impose a conclusion as evident through methodical procedures of argumentation be thoroughly opposed to what is meant by appearing? Wouldn't an appearance appear at its own initiative before being demonstrated or justified by prior conditions?

This question gives voice to the insight driving the phenomenological breakthrough. It motivates the most famous of the principles put forth by the inaugural figures of phenomenology—Husserl and Heidegger. First, Husserl's principle of principles: "every originarily donating intuition is a source of right for cognition, that everything that offers itself to us originarily in intuition is to be taken quite simply as it gives itself out to be" (Id, §24).[3] All that appears has the right to appear. The appearing of phenomena is no longer justified by submitting to the conditions imposed by the concepts of the finite understanding active in knowledge or experience but simply by appearing in intuition. This appearing needs no a priori or background to justify, legitimate, or make it possible insofar as the intuition in which it arises is not determined by pure forms but is itself originary. This corresponds to the declaration thirteen years earlier in the *Logical Investigations* of "the principle of the absence of presupposition," and it reappears fourteen years later in Heidegger's famous definition of the phenomenon as *"that which shows itself in itself from itself"* (BT, §7). Read in this light, the phenomenological dictum "To the things themselves!" would therefore mean going back to the appearing that is decisive in the appearance of phenomena. "The things themselves" would be precisely the things seen in light of their own appearing such that the dictum could be read as saying "the right to determine appearing belongs 'to the things themselves!'"[4]

Phenomenologically speaking, then, for a phenomenon to be possible, it has only to appear; and this appearing arises at the initiative of the phenomenon, without regard for the determinations that knowing might impose on it. Put otherwise, for a phenomenon to appear, it has only to be possible; and this possibility is determined by the phenomenon insofar as it shows itself originarily—that is, without presupposition or prior a priori—in lived experience (*Erlebnis*). If phenomena appear for phenomenology without submitting to conditions, the possibility of appearing will have been extended to each and every phenomenon.

That phenomenology seeks to understand the appearance of phenomena as unrestricted and unlimited by conditions other than their own appearance can be seen in how Husserl understands "phenomenon" in one of his earliest texts, *The Idea of Phenomenology*: "The word 'phenomenon' is ambiguous in virtue of an essential correlation between *appearing and that which appears*. [Phenomenon] in its proper sense means that which appears, and yet it is by preference used for the appearing itself" (IP, 11 [modified]). Phenomenologically understood, the phenomenon is an appearance which appears in its own appearing. That is to say, for a phenomenon to appear,

the appearance does not need to be traced back to prior conditions identified with the forms and categories of the knowing mind but to the appearing of that appearance. Appearing, by contrast, is not something which a
knowing mind operates, regulates, or determines but something which is
handed over to or correlated with the appearance itself. Well before Husserl
proposed the correlation of noesis and noema, and contrary to the drift
announced in the correlation of intention and intuition, "the correlation
between *appearing and that which appears as such*" occupied his attention and
provoked the wonder which he himself admitted would sustain his investigations for the remainder of his career.[5] As Jean-Luc Marion has commented, "there is never an appearing without something that appears, and there
is never something that appears (something appearable, if we might risk
the neologism) without an apparition."[6] What is quite noticeably absent
from this correlation of appearing and what appears is, of course, the limits,
conditions, or justificatory role played by the finite subject or knowledge.
No such third term here intervenes to operate this correlation. Knowledge
has been displaced, at the very least, from its prior (metaphysical) position
as a priori determinant of phenomenality and appearing.

The Disappearing of Appearing

The phenomenological "breakthrough and the broadening"[7] consists in the
correlation of appearing and appearance such that the possibility of appearing is given over to the appearance, not to finite knowledge or the knowing
subject. The advance of this breakthrough will nevertheless be stymied by
Husserl himself and his fascination with the correlation of intuition and
intention or noesis and noema, intention and object. This drift or veering
from the paths opened by the breakthrough will recur again and again.

To anticipate what I will be developing at greater length below, when the
phenomenon is understood as the correlation between noesis and noema
or intentionality and its object, the focus of phenomenology shifts *from* an
appearing determined by what appears and an appearance given in its appearing *to* a mental or intentional object, including the subjective acts that
constitute or determine it, and its secondary correlation with a thing. The
role of noetic acts in the constitution of the noematic object marks one of
the most obvious moments in the drift whereby the appearing of the phenomenon *to* the I slips into a constitution of the phenomenon *by* the I. This
drift reaches its consummation, of course, in the *Cartesian Meditations,* where
Husserl claims that "the Objective world, the world that exists for me (*für
mich*), that always has and always will exist for me, the only world that ever
can exist for me—this world, with all its objects, I said, derives its whole
sense and the existential status which it has for me (*für mich*) from me
myself (*aus mir selbst*), from me as the transcendental Ego" (CM, 26). In
setting its sight on the correlation of objects and the transcendental Ego,
phenomenology will experience what Paul Ricoeur has called "Husserl's

rather disconcerting glide from the 'for me' (*für mich*) into the 'from me' (*aus mir*)."[8] Ricoeur, here, is pointing out that in Husserlian phenomenology the world that exists *for* me turns out to be equivalent to the world that gets its being *from* me such that the correlation of object and I, noema and noesis, has replaced the correlation of appearing and appearance.

In a similar vein, when the correlation of intuition and intention occupies center stage in phenomenological investigation, what appears in intuition no longer appears of itself or in its own appearing but as the appearance of an intention, an appearance appearing as the eventual fulfillment of the intentional meaning previously established. Appearing only as the fulfillment of what can thus welcome it, appearance in intuition is cut to the measure of what an intention can contain or accept. This is stated by the highest ideal of Husserlian phenomenology, the ideal of adequation: the fullest or most perfect phenomena are those where what appears in intuition equals what I intend. This ideal is rarely met, almost always fallen short of, and never exceeded. The fact that the phenomenological ideal should be adequation testifies to the limit within which intuition and so the possibility of appearing is confined: it is not possible for more to appear in intuition than an intentionally constituted meaning can contain. Even the principle of principles, in which Husserl glimpsed the determination of the possibility of appearing in terms of appearance itself, already betrays a shying away from this limitless possibility when it adds, almost as an afterthought ("on second thought" or "upon reflection"), the important qualifier "within the limits in which it is given there": "Every originarily donating intuition is a source of right for cognition, that everything that offers itself to us originarily in intuition is to be taken quite simply as it gives itself out to be, *but also only within the limits in which it is given there*" (Id, §24 [italics mine]). These limits are operative in correlating the glimpsed limitlessness of appearing in intuition with intentions; that is, they arise when the correlation shifts from appearing/appearance to intuition/intention.

For Husserl, access to the appearing of what appears is granted in the reduction. Put simply, the reduction does not reduce the appearing; it reduces all that blocks or interferes with the appearing of what appears. The reduction thereby lays bare the correlation appearing/what appears, which is constitutive of the phenomenon, so that phenomenology can therefore state the following equivalence: "The truly absolute datum is the *pure phenomenon*, that which is reduced" (IP, 5). The reduction is a leading-back *from* the natural attitude which considers the already given or already accomplished appearance of beings or objects *to* the appearing of these beings or objects as phenomena. As Husserl was to remind his audience again and again, the prototype for the phenomenological reduction is Cartesian doubt. Even before the full expression of his phenomenology in the *Cartesian Meditations,* where the claim to Cartesianism is evident in the title, Husserl's first outline of phenomenology, *The Idea of Phenomenology,* laid claim to a certain Cartesianism: "Here the *Cartesian method of doubt* provides a starting point. Without doubt there is *cogitatio,* there is namely the lived experience [*Erlebnis*] during our living of it and in a simple reflection upon it. The seeing, direct grasping and having of the *cogitatio* is already a cognition. The *cogitationes* are the first absolute data" (IP, 2 [modified]). Following the path of Cartesian doubt, the reduction leads back to *cogitatio,* which designates the phenomena of phenomenology. *Cogitatio,* Husserl continues, is given in an immanence which is the "genuinely immanent (*reell Immanente*) [and] is taken as indubitable just on account of the fact that it presents nothing else, 'points' to nothing 'outside' itself" (IP, 3). Presenting nothing other than itself, *cogitatio* would name the correlation of appearance and appearing, seeing the appearance in the appearing, which is nothing outside it. The indubitability of the Cartesian *cogitatio* would be the model for the self-appearing of phenomena, something which Husserl expresses in the equivalency: "the *cogitatio,* the appearing itself" (IP, 11).

The *cogitatio* that remains at the end of Cartesian doubt is accomplished in the *videre videor* [it seems that I see], the seeming or appearing that remains even if what is seen does not exist and in fact even if I do not exist.[9] Reached after Cartesian doubt or the phenomenological reduction has bracketed or suspended all foreign or transcendent considerations, the *cogitatio* which remains appears solely by itself and of itself, needing nothing else to appear since it indeed appears precisely when everything else has been suspended. In its indubitability, *cogitatio,* in other words, would be another name for the appearing of what appears, and the fact that it is reached only after doubt or the reduction has suspended the existence of the world and even of the I means that this appearing admits no other conditions but those set by the appearance itself.

The same text which states the absolute self-givenness and indubitablity of *cogitatio* also attests the drift or displacement whereby Husserl substitutes for the appearing of what appears something else: namely, consideration of the gaze or sight which makes an object appear out of this appearing. "Without doubt there is *cogitatio,* there is namely the lived experience [*Erlebnis*] during our living of it *and in a simple reflection upon it*" [emphasis mine]. The *cogitatio* is now divided between the actual living of the lived experience and the second order, reflective sight that sees and grasps this *cogitatio.* It is this second, reflective gaze on the *cogitatio* that will come to occupy Husserl each time he arrives at the *cogitatio* throughout his work. For it is in this second order, reflective cognition of the *cogitatio* that phenomenology is able to constitute objects and so earn its scientific status. Again, the same text which states the phenomenological breakthrough will state its foreclosure: "In reflection, the *cogitatio,* the appearing itself, becomes an object" (IP, 11). What is lost in this becoming, however, is nothing other than the appearing itself or the determination of phenomena in terms of appearance correlated with appearing. In its place, Husserl has put the determination of appearing in terms of objectness, that is, in terms of the subjective conditions for the constitution of objects.

This drift is evident in another crucial passage. When Husserl writes, "I can, while I am perceiving, direct towards this perception the gaze of pure sight: towards the perception such as it is already there" (IP, 23), he acknowledges that the perception received or impressed upon me, that is, the *cogitatio*, precedes the gaze that I direct upon it. Phenomenologically, the *cogitatio* accomplishes itself on its own without its appearance being measured by the I or the gaze directed upon it. This is what it means for the *cogitatio* to be already there when I direct my gaze upon it. The whole of Husserl's phenomenological enterprise, however, unfolds as if it were an attempt to revoke this unconditional appearing by replacing it with the reflective gaze on the *cogitatio,* whereby the transcendental I becomes the operator of the phenomenality of phenomena. "Cognition itself is a name for a manifold sphere of being which can be given to us absolutely, and which can be given absolutely each time in the particular case. The thought processes which I really perform are given to me insofar as I reflect upon them, receive them and set them up in a pure seeing" (IP, 23). The absolute givenness of the *cogitatio* is here transformed into an effect of the I casting its reflective gaze on its own lived experience of *cogitatio.* The power of making appear has been handed from the *cogitatio* to this reflective sight which now establishes the prior condition for the appearance of objects in *cogitatio.*

The mistaking of the appearing of appearances for an appearing made by the I could not be more palpable. The lived experience or *cogitatio* is already there accomplishing itself when the gaze of the transcendental I comes on the scene, seeing it and making it into an object absolutely given. The appearing has already accomplished itself on its own or left its impression when the I directs its gaze upon it. This gaze, however, interprets "the 'there' of this 'already there' . . . as a 'there' for it and from it, while it can in fact no longer claim anything more than the being-seen of the *cogitatio,* in no way the existence which it presupposes as already accomplished or accomplishing itself without it."[10] It is for this reason that Jean-Luc Marion and Michel Henry will, in their penetrating readings, apply Husserl's judgment of Descartes to Husserl himself and show that "for [Husserl] to discover and to abandon were the same thing" (see IP, 7).

Phenomenology then, from its very inception, finds itself at a crossroads where it must choose between, on the one hand, the gaze by which I make of the *cogitatio* an objective phenomenon constituted by me and, on the other hand, the unconditional self-appearing, self-accomplishing of the *cogitatio* itself. The development of Husserl's phenomenology is clearly based on a choice in favor of the reflective I whose gaze then becomes equivalent to the power of making appear. In doing so, he loses sight—precisely because he sees—of the unconditional possibility of appearing that phenomenology sought. A final text from *The Idea of Phenomenology* again states the drift from an unconditioned possibility of phenomena, where appearance is correlated with its own appearing, to a possibility subjected to the limits of a gaze which looks at them: "*Every lived experience* [*Erlebnis*], while being enacted, *can become the object of a pure seeing and understanding, and is something absolutely given in this seeing*" (IP, 24 [modified]). The absolute given mentioned in this text does not come up simply because the phenomenon accomplishes itself or appears without any conditions besides itself but because it *becomes* an object of *the gaze* where I look at it. In this becoming, one could see the whole difficulty of Husserlian phenomenology. If a phenomenon must become a phenomenon over and above its appearing as such, then the phenomenality of the phenomenon is not determined by the "things themselves," by the phenomenon itself, but by another instance under whose authority and subject to whose conditions and activity a phenomenon becomes such. If the phenomenon has to become a phenomenon, it does not give itself as such, but as an object of the gaze or the transcendental I entrusted with the power of making phenomena appear. From here on out, phenomenality will be determined as objectness, being the object of a gaze or of an I such that all that appears appears as object and what does not appear as object is nothing at all, indeed is less than nothing.

One of phenomenology's leading and most radical interpreters, Michel Henry, has described this loss of the original sense of appearing to the benefit of the constitution of objects as a sort of neurotic obsessiveness. "Analyses which were not part of the program suddenly unfold their implications with the sole aim of permitting access to new objects that substitute for the lost reality."[11] Almost as if he were echoing Freud, Henry argues that the fascination with new and multiple objects both denies and presupposes the loss of this primal reality of the *cogitatio*. The substitution of the objective phenomenon for the original *cogitatio*, Henry continues, carries with it a perversion or reduplication of the fundamental categories of phenomenology—most significantly, the categories of immanence and transcendence. Thought as the unconditional appearing of phenomena, the *cogitatio* is referred to the category of immanence, where immanence is taken literally as a remaining-in-self such that appearance and appearing coincide, leaving nothing of the appearing to the operation of anything outside the appearance. For this radical concept of immanence, in which the possibility of appearing is determined strictly from the appearance itself, Husserl substitutes another form of immanence: the immanence of consciousness reflecting on itself, that is, the immanence of the gaze seeing its own passing flow of *cogitationes*. The *cogitatio* thus becomes the object of a transcendental I, a *cogito*, such that the immanence of the gaze includes within it the transcendence of the *cogitatio*.

It is at this point that it then becomes possible for Husserl to substitute for the phenomenological determination of appearance in terms of its own appearing the determination of appearance in terms of the power of the gaze that sees. "In a gaze bearing on the pure phenomenon, the object is not found outside knowledge or outside 'consciousness,' and at the same time it is given in the sense of the absolute self-givenness of an object of the pure gaze" (IP, 31 [modified]). This passage completes the displacement which inaugurates Husserlian phenomenology. The phenomenon is now determined as an object seen by a gaze that looks at knowledge or consciousness so that consciousness has become the locus or stage for the absolute self-givenness of phenomena. Self-givenness or phenomenality is not determined unconditionally in terms of the phenomenon itself but in terms of consciousness and the gaze of an I seeing its own thought. Husserl makes explicit this decision to understand phenomenology in terms of a seeing I: "inquiry must concern itself always with *pure 'seeing'* and therefore not with the genuinely immanent. . . . The root of the matter, however, is *to grasp the meaning of the absolutely given, the absolute clarity of the given,* . . . in a word, to grasp the absolutely 'seeing' evidence which gets hold of itself" (IP, 7). The genuine immanence of the *cogitatio* is no longer the scene of appearing; instead, the transcendence of the gaze and the objects of its reflection on thought have become the place where appearances find the possibility of appearing. This comes to expression in the *Ideas,* where Husserl claims, "In reflection, every cogitatio effected takes on the explicit form, cogito. . . . In Kant's words, 'The *"I think" must be capable of accompanying all my presentations'"* (Id, 132–33). *Cogitatio* having been formulated explicitly and completely as *cogito,* phenomenality is now determined as objective being in and through the I think.

This reduplication of immanence so that it stands for not just the originary *cogitatio* but the gaze of an I and its object goes hand in hand with another decision that proves decisive for the development of Husserlian phenomenology, namely, the choice to restrict the radicality of the reduction and Cartesian doubt. Doubt and the reduction had, I noted, the potential of suspending not just the existence of the world but the existence of the I as well such that even the seeing was suspended in the *videre videor* [it seems that I see] which remains. Husserl, however, admits that such a reduction proves too radical and chooses instead to limit its practice when in §32 of the *Ideas* he introduces what he calls a "limiting consideration," claiming "on good grounds we *limit* the universality of this epoché" (Id, 110). In claiming that its universality must be limited, Husserl seems to acknowledge that the reduction is more powerful than such limits will allow it to be, that it is able to operate beyond the limits that "we" will allow it. To keep this power in check, the reduction must be reined in—and "on good grounds." What are these good grounds? Husserl specifies them:

> Since we are completely free . . . to parenthesize every objectivity which can be judged about if [the reduction] were as comprehensive as possible, then no province would be left for unmodified judgments, to say nothing of a province for science. But our purpose is to discover a new scientific domain, one that is to be gained *by the method of parenthesizing* which, therefore, must be a definitely restricted one. (Id, 60)

If the power of the reduction must be reined in, this is because "we" seek not merely the phenomenality or unconditional appearing of phenomena but an objectivity that can be the province of science and scientific judgments.[12] Reduction is now no longer a reduction to genuine immanence but a reduction to transcendence—the immanent transcendence of the object and the I. The reduction is practiced in this limited form for the very good reason that, if unlimited, it would suspend even the objects of the gaze in its radical progress to the immanence of *cogitatio*. Husserl has made a choice, and the consequence of this choice is that the reduction leads not to the appearing of appearance in immanence but to the gaze of an I. The transcendental I is thus set up as the condition for the appearance of phenomena.

The Intentional A Priori

The notions of transcendence and immanence having been thus perverted or transformed, Husserl can ask a question which seems absurd from the point of view of the original insight into the absolute or genuinely immanent self-givenness of appearance in their own appearing: "The truly absolute datum is the *pure phenomenon,* that which is reduced. . . . How can the pure phenomenon of cognition reach something which is not immanent to it? How can the absolute self-givenness of cognition reach something not self-given and how is this reaching to be understood?" (IP, 5). The phenomenon is here submitted to a demand to be correlated with something which is not it itself, something which would transcend the genuine immanence of what has appeared in its appearing. From the perspective of this demand, phenomenality would no longer mean the appearing of appearance but the outlook for a gaze looking out through and beyond the phenomenon it sees (immanent transcendence) toward a horizon of the unseen and not-given (transcendent transcendence). The "marvelous correlation," before which wonder gives birth to philosophy, can therefore be rephrased as "this marvelous correlation between *the phenomenon of cognition* and the *object of cognition*" (IP, 10).

From this point on, phenomenology will present itself in an inseparably twofold way: "[If we] confine ourselves purely to the task of *clarifying the essence of cognition and of being an object of cognition, then this will be phenomenology of cognition and of being an object of cognition*" (IP, 18). Husserl has thus formulated the phenomenological project in such a way that two tasks— phenomenology of cognition, phenomenology of being an object of cognition—are articulated together; but by doing so, he eliminates consideration of the *cogitatio* which, giving itself in genuine immanence, would not need to correlate appearance in cognition and being an object of cognition since its appearing is in fact the appearance itself. Indeed, it has been noted that as Husserl's work progressed, the second aspect of the twofold task was in fact the one which determined the whole of the phenomenological project: the phenomenology of cognition was precisely the phenomenology of that *cogitatio* which provided objects for thought such that the model of objective perception proved decisive in determining the meaning of phenomenality.

With this decision orienting phenomenology in the direction of objects of cognition, a particular theme is designated for it: "intentionality, which one can designate as the general theme of 'Objectively' oriented phenomenology" (Id, 199). It is in fact the doctrine of intentionality which states the correlation of the two transcendences in phenomenological practice, the (immanent) transcendence of the *cogitatio* made into an object of the reflective gaze and the (transcendent) transcendence of the object of that objectified *cogitatio*. Henry has described the relation of these two transcendences: "The first transcendence is a departure from the reality of the *cogitatio*. The second transcendence is a departure from the seeing of sight. But the second transcendence presupposes the first. Passing beyond the seeing of sight toward the intended or the presumed is possible only for an intentional aim which has already accomplished the departure from the reality of the *cogitatio*."[13] *Cogitatio* having already been taken as *cogito*, the reflective I gazing at its thought sees these thoughts fully present to its gaze (first transcendence); but beyond what is seen, a second transcendence is intended: the intentional object which is not seen fully but is only meant as the object implied in such thoughts. The only transcendence that appears absolutely to the gaze of the I is its thoughts, but these thoughts intend or mean objects which are not contained in thought or consciousness. The reality of the transcendent or objective world is thus broached through the reality of thought or consciousness which can be subject to or object of a reflective gaze.

What appears appears in the conscious processes directed toward it, that is in intentional acts. Consciousness or intentionality has become a stage where appearing is correlated with what appears. This can be seen by returning to Husserl's description of the marvel which gives rise to philosophy: "The things are and are given in appearance and in virtue of the appearance itself. . . . This marvelous correlation between the *phenomenon of cognition* and the *object of cognition* reveals itself everywhere" (IP, 10).

Intentionality describes how it is possible for consciousness to have an object. "Under intentionality, we understand the own peculiarity of mental processes 'to be consciousness *of* something.' We first of all encounter this marvelous ownness, back to which all rational-theoretical and metaphysical enigmas lead, in the explicit *cogito*" (Id, 200). Always consciousness of . . . , consciousness is marvelous, a marvel worthy of serving as the basis of philosophy because it does not refer to itself what occurs to it; it is the being which makes the experience of something other than itself. It is important to emphasize that intentionality is a characteristic of the mind, not of the sense data which the mind receives or of the appearance understood in its own appearing. Intentionality is the act by which the mind refers some of its *cogitationes* to something else besides itself. This something else, the intentional object, is in fact not a preexisting source of appearing but the result of the intentional leap from consciousness to an object. As intentional, consciousness is in this way "an A priori of a completely novel kind, namely the A priori of constitution" (CM, 137), where "constitution" does not mean making an objective being, effecting the actuality of a being where before there was none, but seeing this object in the intentional acts in and through which it appears.

The fact that Husserl reduplicates not only immanence but transcendence, keeping the term to designate the object found in thought or consciousness when previously it referred to being or the world outside consciousness, serves as the basis for understanding how consciousness will serve as such an a priori. Heidegger, in his interpretation of Husserl, called this "the intentional a priori" and claimed that it alone constitutes the subject of phenomenology. The priority of this a priori does not consist in its being a firmly established and certainly known point from which a series of deductions demonstrating all beings can begin—this is what Husserl reproached Descartes for—nor does it consist in the temporal or causal priority that a cause has over its effects. Likewise the priority of the intentional a priori does not have a solely subjective sense as it does in Kant, where the a priori is specifically epistemological and concerns only the critique of knowledge and objects known. Rather, intentionality is an a priori in the sense that it is the possibility for a meaningful world of beings or objects. For anything to be it must first be possible, and this possibility is found in the appearance a thing has in the intentional acts whereby consciousness constitutes it. As the study of such an a priori, phenomenology "confines itself to the realm of pure possibility and instead of judging about actualities of transcendental being, judges about its a priori possibilities, and thus at the same time prescribes rules a priori for its actualities" (CM, 28). These possibilities "belong to the total constitution accomplished in my own ego—the constitution as whose correlate the Objectively existing world for me and for any ego whatsoever is continually given beforehand" (CM, 137). Phenomenology, therefore, is a description of objective beings considered as possibilities of consciousness.

Intentionality arises when it is a matter of inserting consciousness into the world, of explaining how it is not just a separate sphere but is in fact the a priori where the objective world itself is "given beforehand." As intending objects, the *cogito* is not confined to a specific region, the region of pure thought, but is instead outside itself, directed toward objects, "its correlates." Thus, for Husserl the phenomenology of consciousness is the way back to the original appearing, where objects are given beforehand as pure possibilities constituted in the conscious ego. This means: everything that befalls consciousness from the "outside" finds its possibility given beforehand in the ego. Intentionality means precisely this rigorous correlation between what appears and the acts of consciousness wherein it first appears as a possibility. Robert Sokolowski, in *The Formation of Husserl's Concept of Constitution*, has put forward a useful distinction that can help us understand the sense of the Husserlian a priori. Sokolowski claims that beginning in Husserl's *Ideas*, after the definitive drift, the phenomenological ultimate has a twofold sense: (1) our experiences of consciousness are indubitable and absolutely certain; this gives rise to phenomenology as the exploration of a particular sphere of experience; and (2) a meaningful world cannot be thought without consciousness; this gives rise to a phenomenology that explicates the experience of all other objects as well.[14] Therefore, in making the reduction, Husserl writes, "we have not lost anything but rather have gained the whole of absolute being which, rightly understood, contains within itself, constitutes within itself, all transcendencies" (Id, 113).

In its role as constitutional a priori, consciousness, or *cogito*, is not qualified as a priori because of any temporal priority. The priority of the *cogito* is seen instead in that consciousness is the possibility for a meaningful world: the world is preceded by consciousness in the sense that possibility precedes actuality. Here, possibility should not be construed in the Kantian sense of prior conditions for the possibility of existence. Such an understanding thoroughly misses the sense in which for Husserl the description of consciousness is itself a description of the things themselves in their appearing, where such appearing is understood as *cogito*. For Kant, claims about beings were to be subject to correction and limitation by a critical theory of how consciousness operates; epistemology was clearly distinguished from "ontology," and metaphysics had to abandon the latter in order to find the security offered by operating within the limits set by the former. For Husserl, in contrast, the theory of consciousness was itself an inquiry into the appearance of objective beings. Husserl's phenomenological critique of consciousness describes not only the conditions for the possibility of objects; it describes objects—though not as they are actual but as they are possible.

The Determination of Phenomenality in Terms of Thought

The doctrine of intentionality having inserted consciousness into the world, the appearance of the thing-itself is reconnected with its appearing in the *cogito* such that the phenomenological description of the *cogito*, that is the reflective gaze of consciousness on its own contents, is in fact the unfolding of the objective world. When Husserl writes, "the things are and are given in appearing and in virtue of the appearing itself," he seems to bespeak one idea of phenomenology, an idea in which the phenomena determine their own manner of appearing and the possibility of appearing is determined in accordance with appearance. When, however, he immediately glosses this passage by remarking, "this marvelous correlation between the *phenomenon of cognition* and the *object of cognition* reveals itself everywhere," he seems to evidence the drift whereby phenomenality and the possibilities of appearing are determined by thought (IP, 10 [12]). For if the phenomenon is correlated with an object, this correlation happens through the operation or mediation of cognition. That is to say, the determination of phenomenality in terms of the binary appearing/appearance is surrendered in favor of a determination in three terms: phenomenon or appearing/object or what appears/cognition or intentionality where the correlation is put into operation. "The transcendental heading *ego cogito* must therefore be broadened by adding one more member. Each *cogito*, each conscious process [*Erlebnis*], we may also say '*Means' something or other* and bears in itself, in this manner peculiar the *meant*, its particular *cogitatum*" (CM, 33).

Let me recall the passage which Henry cites as marking the consummation of the Husserlian turn in phenomenology: "In a gaze bearing on the pure phenomenon, the object is not found outside knowledge or outside 'consciousness,' and at the same time it is given in the sense of the absolute self-givenness of an object of the pure gaze" (IP, 31 [modified]). In other words, objective appearance has its appearing in intentional conscious processes (*Erlebnisse*) such that it is thought or consciousness that determines the structure and guides the genesis of appearance. To appear as an object is to appear as part of the conscious processes (*Erlebnisse*) submitted to the reflective gaze of a pure ego such that objectivity has primarily the kind or mode of being of consciousness. The primacy of consciousness or thought of consciousness in the determination of phenomenality has been well-described by Jean-Luc Marion in his commentary on passages from volume 3 of Husserl's *Ideas*.

> "In the phenomenology of the consciousness of the thing [*Dingbewusst-sein*], the question is not [to know] how things in general *are*, not what in truth belongs to them as such, but how the consciousness of things is made. . . ." Thing-consciousness is not equivalent to the consciousness of the thing itself; thing-consciousness is accented according to the consciousness and envisages the thing only between quotation marks, as an "object of research" . . . the phenomenologist, for his part, does *not* orient himself toward objects (as things by full right) but "exclusively toward lived experiences and the correlates of lived experiences."[15]

Thing-consciousness, or the thing in thought, receives its primacy, for Husserl, precisely because consciousness, unlike the external thing, is essentially capable of being perceived in reflection. Having been reached at the end of the reduction, the reflective regard on consciousness offers in each moment something absolute and indubitable and will therefore be the place where Husserl's phenomenology will look to find objects, now exhaustive of the meaning of the things themselves.

This then establishes the series of related questions that can guide inquiry to an understanding of the Husserlian determination of phenomenality, a determination which I have strongly suggested represents an arbitrary and contingent limitation or conditioning of the possibility of appearing. How are the objects of thought constituted? What does it mean to appear when all appearance happens in consciousness? When consciousness determines appearance, what appears or how is what appeared structured? What are the categories and limits of appearance when appearing happens in consciousness? Put most generally and articulated in terms of thought thinking its own consciousness, phenomenality means objectivity, to be an object. What then does it mean to be an object? Two points can be noted: (1) objects appearing in the stream of consciousness appear within a horizon, the horizon of appearings yet to come and those just past; and (2) objects appear in the present of consciousness, a present which stretches ecstatically beyond the immediacy of the instantaneous now to make a space for objects to be present.

First, according to Husserl, the phenomenon of consciousness differs from the ontical being encountered in natural perception in that whereas ontically the thing is an undifferentiated unity, the phenomenon of consciousness is a synthesis of appearings. The phenomenon, Husserl writes, "is given continuously as an objective unity in a multiform and changeable multiplicity of manners of appearing" (CM, 39). In order, then, for these multiple manners of appearing to constitute a phenomenon, they must be combined in such a way that they "belong together inseparably. The sort of combination uniting consciousness with consciousness can be characterized as a synthesis, a mode of combination exclusively peculiar to consciousness" (CM, 39). Given in a multiplicity of appearings or in combination with other lived experiences, what appears appears only by appearing within a horizon, the horizon of appearances to come and those already past.

This is the very ordinary experience made every moment of every day. In any given moment what appears is only a surface or facet of the thing. The screen before which I sit typing, for instance, is not the whole of my monitor. Other surfaces or facets can be added by rotating the thing, moving around it, imagining it from other perspectives, or opening it up; but I will never see the thing itself in its entirety, each of its facets all at once— excepting of course if I adopt the standpoint of cubism![16] And yet, with only a surface (the screen) actually appearing, I nevertheless know or have a full object (my monitor). The object thus implies a horizon of unfulfilled intuitions. In the absence or lack of such intuitive fulfillment, this object is meant or intended. In this way, the intentional object is greater than what is given in each moment of appearing.

> Intentional analysis is guided by the fundamental cognition that, as a consciousness, every cogito is indeed (in the broadest sense) a meaning of its meant [*Meinung seines Gemeinten*], but that, at any moment, this something meant [*dieses Vermeinte*] is more—something meant with something more—than what is meant at that moment 'explicitly.' In our example, each phase of perception was a mere side of 'the' object, as what was perceptually meant. The *intending-beyond-itself* which is implicit in any consciousness must be considered an essential moment of it. (CM, 46)

Moments of appearing become a phenomenon only on account of intentionality and the gaze reaching beyond and setting them against a horizon where the profile stands out and is perhaps eventually filled in. Failing this intentional transcendence and its opening to a horizon, appearing would offer no objects—only evanescent flashes and fragments in "the realm of a Heraclitean flux" (CM, 49).

The promotion of a horizon or context, then, is the first and necessary preliminary to the appearance of phenomena constituted in and through consciousness. "The multiplicity of the intentionality belonging to any cogito . . . is a theme not exhausted with the consideration of cogitationes as *actual* subjective processes. On the contrary, *every actuality involves its potentialities,* which are not empty possibilities, but rather possibilities intentionally predelineated. . . . With that *[a] fundamental trait of intentionality* is indicated. Every subjective process has a 'horizon'" (CM, 44). The phenomenologist directs his gaze beyond the appearing *cogitatio* toward the horizon of not-yet or already past appearing appearances and uncovers the object in and through the explication of what is found there. This means that the object is construed in advance of its ever being met in person or in its own presence and that many other determinations remain unfulfilled in the constitution of the object. As such, the object "is never present to actual consciousness as a finished datum" but is always something meant. "The object is so to speak *a pole of identity,* always meant expectantly as having a sense yet to be actualized" (CM, 45–46).

Second, once appearing has been reduced to the gaze on consciousness, an indication of the second determinant of appearance is provided by those instances where Husserl betrays the drift from the appearing of appearance to the appearance of phenomena in the gaze that makes them an object: "the *cogitatio,* the appearing itself, becomes an object" (IP, 11) or the *cogitatio* can *"become the object of a pure seeing and understanding, and is something absolutely given in this seeing"* (IP, 24 [modified]). The fact that this becoming is necessary to the appearance of phenomenon in consciousness implies a gap between the appearing of the *cogitatio* and the eventual appearance of the object. Thought in terms of consciousness, "the *cogitatio* meets the conditions for phenomenality, in the gaze of a reflective sight, only on the basis of this first gap which is Time."[17] In other words, the becoming implies time, but time understood in a particular way appropriate to consciousness, namely, the ecstatic present of consciousness. How so?

For phenomena to appear across a multiplicity of appearings, they must appear by diverging from themselves without this divergence implying any lack. Such a divergence or getting out of phase with itself happens only in time—time of a particular sort, the temporal flux of consciousness. "Looking straightforwardly, we have perhaps the one unchanging shape or color; in the reflective [that is, phenomenological] attitude, we have its manners of appearance . . . following one another in the continuous sequence" of their temporal flow" (CM, 40). In Henry's words, Husserl's phenomenology "results from substituting for the original immanence of the *cogitatio* the 'immanence' of the *Erlebnis* that constitutes itself in ecstatic temporality. Truthfully speaking, [Husserl's] reduction is just that: *the passage from im-*

manence I to immanence II, the entry of the real *cogitatio* into the gaze of phenomenological reflection and thus into flux," the flux of the temporal stream of consciousness.[18] What should be fully apparent in its own appearing (*cogitatio*) is no longer the matter of phenomenological investigation when the *cogitatio* becomes *cogito*. Having entered the temporal flux constitutive of consciousness, the *cogitatio* exceeds this moment of its own appearing and is dispersed in the time of consciousness. The time of phenomena is now determined by the time of consciousness.

Making the Present

For the immanent, absolute appearing of the *cogitatio* to fall under sight, it must be seen in a reflective gaze—which means that the instant of its appearing must be held from passing away. This act of holding fast the instant that passes away is retention. Retention is the condition for the phenomenological reduction practiced by Husserl, according to Henry, because retention keeps the *cogitatio* available for the reflective gaze of the transcendental I. Without retaining the appearance, I would have no time to reflect on it. As "a unity belonging to a passing flow of multiplicities," the phenomenon is not only a flowing or passing away in time; for such passing away would mean that an appearance never appears but vanishes in the instant it presents itself. In and through consciousness, however, the dispersed appearings "are not an incoherent sequence of subjective processes. Rather they flow away in the unity of a synthesis, such that in them 'one and the same' is *intended* as appearing" (CM, 39). In other words, the presence of what appears in this dispersion or disaggregation is rediscovered in a present where the synthetic unity of this flow is established as the object of an intentionality which reaches beyond each momentary appearing toward the object intended. The presence of the phenomenon is thus determined according to the temporality of consciousness. This presence finds its place only in the ecstatic present of consciousness which extends or stands outside itself.[19]

In this time of consciousness, the passing or flowing away of appearance is not a pure loss but a modification of the instantaneous now. Reached through a reduction to consciousness and made in the gaze of a transcendental I reflecting on this consciousness (*cogitatio* having become *cogito*), appearing does not happen simply in the moment of an appearance but in a present that is ecstatically open to what has just been and what is about to come. This present is the present of internal time consciousness. "In this sinking back, I still 'hold' it fast, have it in retention, and as long as the retention persists the [object] has its temporality" (PIT, 44). The object then endures or appears or comes to presence only so long as its passing away is retained or held in a present that therefore persists longer than the blink of an eye.[20] The presence of appearance is thoroughly determined by the present of consciousness. As Paul Ricoeur has observed, "Husserl, crushing this last prestige of the in-itself which might still insinuate itself into presence, decides that the presence *of* the thing itself is *my* present. The radical otherness attaching to presence is reduced to the nowness of the present."[21] Losing the presence of the thing itself, phenomenology recovers it when it sees things in the present of consciousness, only this recovered presence is determined in terms of thought thinking itself, reflective consciousness. This is so because appearances appear in and through the modifications whereby consciousness makes objects in the present. In and through retention, consciousness allows appearing to persist in the present without vanishing as soon as it appears in a moment that would otherwise last only as long as the blink of an eye.

Presence is thus given, for the phenomenologist, as a stretch of time, a stretch which is called the present. Such a present clearly is not a punctual moment or slice of time but is in a certain way ecstatic, reaching beyond itself into what has just been and what is about to come. As Husserl says, "It belongs to the essence of lived experiences that they must be extended in this fashion, that a punctual phase can never be for itself" (PIT, 70). Appearing on the stage of consciousness, phenomena submit to the operations of consciousness where the present is stretched and space is made for phenomena to appear. This space is accomplished through retention of the just having been. As Husserl writes, "Intuition of time . . . is the consciousness of *what has just been* and not mere consciousness of the now-point of the objective thing. . . . In every point there is an extension and in the extension there is the 'appearance'" (PIT, 53–54). In other words, the present is not intuited as an instantaneous now but as a stretch of time that extends back to what has just been. The paradox of how phenomenality can be at once a lived experience of appearing (*cogitatio*) and second order reflection on these *Erlebnisse* can thus be explained, or at least accounted for, by the fact that the present of *Erlebnis* includes within it an element of the not-present or just-past subject to reflection. Ultimately, this accounting betrays the drift or loss of the original essence of the appearing *cogitatio;* but within the framework of Husserlian phenomenology, the ecstatic present does account for this multiplication of immanence.

Making the duration of time endure is the spontaneous work of consciousness. In and through acts of retention, it makes the fleeting now harden into the present. "The unique quality of the spontaneity of consciousness is that it merely brings about the growth, the development of the primally generated" (PIT, 131). In other words, the spontaneous operation of consciousness is responsible for the modification of an original impression, an impression that marks the instant or now. Through the modifications of consciousness (protention and retention), the ecstatic present in which beings appear is generated from this impression. Although Husserl asserts quite clearly that the primal impression is not generated by consciousness but received passively, he dismisses consideration of this primal impression and instead concentrates on the conscious work of generating a present through the continuous modification of this impression by consciousness. That is to say, he sees in the passively received primal impression only a beginning point that can be taken up by the conscious modifications that generate objects in their presence.[22] This means that when Husserl describes the conscious modifications as a passive genesis or passive synthesis, he is describing a passivity that is nonetheless active. The active sense of the passive genesis is seen when Husserl writes, "Temporal Objects, and this belongs to their essence, spread their contents over an interval of time, and such Objects can be constituted only in acts which likewise constitute temporal distinctions" (PIT, 61); it is even more evident when he speaks of "retention as proper intentionality" (PIT, 52). If retention is an intentional act, and if it is only through retention that presence as duration in the present is possible, then one must conclude that the so-called passive genesis of present beings happens because of the acts of consciousness.[23]

As the inquiry into the field where the present is made, Husserl's phenomenology uncovers nothing but the present in consciousness; to put it another way, the inquiry into consciousness is an inquiry into the present. This is true even when it analyzes the past. When retention stops, the object slips into the remoteness of consciousness, recesses which are the past. But as a remoteness of consciousness, this past is still conscious, still able to be presented in a memory. "The same duration is present, actual, self-generating duration and then is past, 'expired,' duration, still known or produced in recollection 'as if' it were new. . . . The sound [the object used in Husserl's example] vanishes into the remoteness of consciousness. . . . The sound itself is the same, but in the way that it appears, it is continually different" (PIT, 45, §8). This means that, for consciousness, the past differs from the present only in how it is made to appear to my gaze, in recollection as a past present or in perception as a present present. Differing only in terms of the act which presents it, the past is a duration that was once present but now is no longer given in connection with an impression.

Thus, for consciousness, objects are temporal, but this temporality is always in terms of the temporality of consciousness and so a present; even if the object is past, it is past as a present past, as a past that was once present but has now faded into the remoteness of consciousness. All of consciousness is present—if not actually present, then potentially present in a representifying act of memory.[24] Nothing enters consciousness without being detected by the consciousness that makes the present; nothing appears without announcing itself in the present of consciousness. Conversely, nothing that appears in consciousness ever leaves it insofar as the present being merely fades into a past present, never a perfect past. "Consciousness, considered in its purity, must be reckoned as a self-contained system of being, as a system of Absolute Being, into which nothing can penetrate, and from which nothing can escape" (Id, 153, §49). This means furthermore that "it [consciousness] is 'consciousness' through and through" (Id, 251, §86). That is to say, nothing appears in consciousness without consciousness being conscious of it, and all that is in consciousness is conscious. All experience is conscious experience, even if, for the moment, my ego does not direct its attention to it; as consciousness through and through, all that appears to consciousness can become, at least in potential, the object of its gaze.[25]

Conclusion

Phenomenality having been determined as thought thinking itself, the reflective gaze of the ego on its own thoughts becomes the unfolding of the objective world. This has the significant consequence that not only is the *cogito* related to its objects ecstatically, through the ecstasy of intentionality, but the I too relates to itself ecstatically, or intentionally, in reflection. Husserl is quite clear that "phenomenological method operates exclusively in acts of reflection" where the Ego is a "'non-participant onlooker' at himself" such that the transcendence of intentionality directed at objects is repeated within consciousness itself in the gaze of this spectator ego (Id, 174; CM, 37). In a gesture that has to be understood as a form of schizophrenia, the Ego is exiled from itself or split off from itself in what Husserl will call a "splitting of the Ego (*Ichspaltung*)" (CM, 35) that results in it being excluded from the sphere of consciousness all the while haunting it as the operator whose gaze directs manifestation. It therefore must be admitted that what the Ego sees with its intentional gaze is not itself since the ego itself is the seeing or thinking, the intending, which makes appearances appear. There is, in other words, no sight of the seeing Ego itself, no intending of intentionality itself; for what seeing sees and what intentionality intends are their objects; and objects are precisely what seeing and intending, as acts, are not. The pure ego would be, in the words of the *Ideas*, "a transcendency of a peculiar kind—one which is not constituted—*a transcendency within immanence*" (Id, 133).

Everything in Husserlian phenomenology seems to happen therefore as if, together with the drift from unconditional appearing, the subjective Ego itself disappears. *Cogitatio* and ego disappear from this phenomenology precisely insofar as it seeks to found the possibility of appearing on thought thinking itself in the form of intentionality. This twofold disappearance has the paradoxical consequence that the appearing of appearance constituting itself, the very phenomenality sought by phenomenology, has vanished. According to Henry, for phenomenology the question is "how does phenomenality manifest itself. The fact that the solution will be sought in intentionality, that the self-revelation of absolute subjectivity [where appearing occurs] will be understood from the start as self-constitution, is what makes manifest phenomenology's incapacity, from its inception, to provide a response to its own question. The ultimate constituent is deprived of any and all phenomenological status."[26] The loss of this ultimate sense of phenomenality (*cogitatio*), the very constituting of phenomenon themselves, can be seen both from the side of the subject and the side of appearance. In terms of the subject, the vanishing of an absolute appearing and the ultimate constituent is seen in the disappearance of the pure Ego from phenomenology. In terms of appearance, this vanishing is seen in the disappearance of appearing itself, the *cogitatio*. Both on the side of the appearance and on the side of the Ego, phenomenology has failed to recover phenomenality itself.

These remarks lead to one conclusion: if phenomenology is to think phenomenality in terms of the appearing phenomena themselves, it must set forth a phenomenology of a nonintentional ego which would have as its "correlate" an unconditional or self-giving appearance. The *cogitatio* in which appearing would appear would imply a subject no longer thought on the basis of intentionality. Can there be a relation between *cogitatio* and the ego where the I does not direct this appearing by thinking it but is in fact constituted by the appearing of the phenomenon? It would seem that phenomenology itself demands it; for not only would this correspond to the ideal articulated at the outset of this chapter, it would also give or constitute the very ego on which Husserlian phenomenology depends but for which it itself can give no account except to note it.

5

The De-posited Subject

Levinas

Levinas's work is often treated as if it belonged solely and only to a post-modern morality. He is read as a philosopher who, running contrary to the main currents of postmodern thought, admonishes us to be more moral, to think first of the Other before ourselves. On the other hand, philosophers often treat his work as a phenomenological description of a particular, here-tofore neglected region within the phenomenological terrain: namely, eth-ics. In both cases, it seems to me Levinas's claim that "ethics is first philoso-phy" or that responsibility is "the signification of all signification" is not being heard with all its resonance. If responsibility is not meant to describe just a particular dimension of subjective life but the very meaning of sub-jectivity (as Levinas claims), then his so-called ethics is far more than a morality or description of moral experience. When Levinas's work is treated solely as the demand to be more responsible, the sense in which ethics is philosophy or the sense in which philosophy needs an appeal to ethics re-mains unexplained. When Levinas's work is read as a phenomenology of a particular sphere of phenomena, the sense in which ethics is first, not just a first part but a part on which the rest rests remains unexplained.

These two interpretations are in fact invited by Levinas's own manner of presentation. Levinas presents us with dazzling descriptions of the ethical encounter itself, descriptions of the self obsessed by responsibility for the neighbor. The awful beauty and the sheer volume of these descriptions invite us to appropriate Levinas's project to some sort of postmodern mo-rality calling us to action. In this chapter, building on discussions in chap-ters 3 and 4, I intend to investigate Levinas's ethics as at once an addition to phenomenological philosophy and a replacement for it. In this way, ethics could be considered according to the logic of the supplement presented by Derrida in his *Of Grammatology:* "The supplement supplements. It adds only to replace. It intervenes or insinuates itself *in-the-place-of.*"[1] Ethics is added to phenomenology in the sense that, as those who never tire of criticizing phenomenology as unethical remind us, it comes seemingly from the outside of Husserl's practice of the discipline; and it puts itself in the place of Husserlian phenomenology insofar as responsibility, not consciousness, is the subject to which the reduction ultimately leads and which constitutes the ultimate sense of the subjectivity of the subject. Though ethics is added to phenomenology from a strictly Husserlian nonphenomenological perspective, it also substitutes its own aims and figures for those of Husserlian phenomenology. According to the irresistible logic of the supplement, the addition is also a replacement, substituting itself for the deficient thing to which it is added.

Hence, not only does the phenomenology of consciousness presuppose ethical descriptions but these presupposed ethical descriptions result in a quite different figuring of the subject and of the relation between the responsible self and the phenomena which it "grounds." The responsible self, like Husserlian consciousness, plays on the stage of an originary appearing; but this appearing appears in a manner of phenomenalizing itself that is quite different from that which appears in consciousness. As responsibility, the phenomenological subject is ultimate or a priori in a new way: it is not first in itself, not first by being sufficient to itself, but is in itself affected by others before affecting itself.

The Constitution of Nonconstituted Transcendence

From the perspectives opened by Husserl's reduction, the being of each and every being becomes comprehensible to the philosopher in its appearing as an object of the intentional acts of consciousness. Consciousness bears the limits of all that appears: what is not discovered as an object intended by consciousness has no being, is less than nothing. Consciousness, then, is equal to thinking or to assuming everything that appears since everything that befalls it *is* according to it. Within such a determination of being as an object, as Levinas has said, "the reduction of subjectivity to consciousness dominates philosophical thought" (OBBE, 103).

Contrary to Husserl's phenomenology, Levinas claims that "the appearing of being is not the ultimate legitimization of subjectivity. It is here that the present labor [*Otherwise than Being, or, Beyond Essence*] ventures beyond [Husserlian] phenomenology" (OBBE, 183). The subject is not, finally, reducible to the field or the event wherein beings are deployed in their being. There would be more to subjectivity than the role it plays as consciousness, and the reduction would reach an ultimate beyond or on the hither side of the subject's role in the apparition of objective beings. Levinas therefore asks,

> Is signifying exhausted in manifesting itself, in offering itself to knowl-
> edge? . . . Does the psyche exhaust itself in deploying the "energy" of
> ess*a*nce, of the positing of beings? To state such a question is not to expect
> that the *in itself* of beings might have a sense stronger than that which it
> obtains from the identifying consciousness. It is to ask oneself whether the
> psyche does not signify *otherwise* than by this "epic" of ess*a*nce which ex-
> alts in it and lives. It is to ask whether the positivity of *being*, of identity, of
> presence are the ultimate affair of the soul—and consequently whether
> knowledge is such an affair. (GCM, 104)

If the subject of phenomenology were to include more than consciousness,
it would open an order of meaning or intelligibility beyond that measured
by the description of consciousness; and "phenomena" that did not appear
when consciousness was the subject of phenomenology would "appear" in
such a philosophy. This something more than consciousness in subjectivity
suggests that the ultimate, or *archē* reached by Husserl's phenomenology is
already a restriction of meaning, a limitation of a broader and more vast
order of signification than that measured by the reflection of consciousness. In this order of signification, the possibilities of appearing are no longer measured by the field of objectivity, a field determined by the knowing
intentions of consciousness.

Levinas suggests that this something more than consciousness in the subject might be approached in terms of a certain notion of the one-self, where
the oneness or uniqueness of the self testifies to its noninclusion in consciousness. Since consciousness is the field where every content has been
generalized, either by means of eidetic abstraction (Husserl) or the labor of
the negative (Hegel), and since generalization annuls singularity, this oneself would not belong to the consciousness it nevertheless haunts. "In the
traditional teaching of idealism, subject and consciousness are equivalent
concepts without even suspecting the *who* or the *one* (*le qui ou l'un*). This
one is a nonrelation but absolutely a term" (OBBE, 103). In other words,
the subject of phenomenology bears a hidden point—the *who*, the *one*, or
the *oneself*—which remains hidden to philosophy insofar as the subject is
thought to be exhausted in consciousness. In but not of consciousness, the
oneself is antecedent to the self's knowledge of itself; it is a point outside and
even before the play of reflection, the play—underlying every relation to
beings—in which consciousness affects itself. The oneself "is already constituted when the act of constitution first originates" (OBBE, 105). In the very
heart of the subject, therefore, is found a point which the subject itself did
not constitute, did not intend, and which is not interpretable in terms of
consciousness—a transcendence in immanence.

In this way, Levinas's discussion of the oneself would echo Husserl's discussion of the pure ego, "a transcendency of a particular kind—one which
is not constituted—a *transcendency within immanency*" (Id, 133). As nonconstituted, the pure ego remains inaccessible and indescribable to Husserlian
phenomenology insofar as this is precisely a phenomenology of intention-

ality and constitution. Even if phenomenological reflection, precisely as reflection, is unable to constitute the transcendence in immanence of the pure ego, it remains that it cannot do without it; for the pure ego is that which in consciousness sees what is seen, intends what is intended, and so directs the appearing of what appears.

> We shall not encounter the pure Ego anywhere in the flux of manifold mental processes which remains. . . . The Ego belongs to each coming and going mental process; its "regard" is directed "through" each actional cogito to the objective something. This ray of regard changes from one cogito to the next. . . . The Ego, however, is something identical. At least, considered eidetically, any cogito can change. . . . The pure Ego would, however, seem to be something essentially *necessary;* and as something absolutely identical throughout every actual or possible change in mental processes, it *cannot in any sense be a really inherent part or moment* of the mental processes themselves. In every actional cogito the ego lives out its life in a special sense. (Id, 132)

As that which remains "absolutely identical in the flux of passing experiences," the pure ego bears the identity of consciousness; it is because the ego remains identical that every lived experience flashing in the evanescent flux of *cogitatio* is said to be mine. But at the same time, it is precisely because the ego remains self-identical that it is not part of the flux of consciousness where objects spread out their identity over time.

This is precisely what Levinas thematizes as the oneself or me. On it, there rests the very possibility that consciousness might accomplish its play of reflection; for consciousness could not return to its self without having been already given the meaning of its self: "The oneself (*se*) involved in maintaining oneself, losing oneself or finding oneself again (*se maintenir, se perdre, se retrouver*) is not a result but the very matrix of the relations or events that these pronominal verbs express" (OBBE, 104). This oneself can be compared to the pure ego not in that it looks on in consciousness, but in that it too is the prior condition for the identity of the subject, an identity which is not itself constituted by the consciousness whose identity it confers. Preceding consciousness and the origin or *archē* that consciousness marks, this oneself, like the pure Ego, is an an-archy, defecting from the very consciousness which rests on it and, in so defecting, undoing or defeating the pretense of consciousness to exhaust the field of phenomenality.

If for Husserl the pure ego is a nonconstituted transcendence in immanence and so "in itself and for itself indescribable," then, says Levinas, "the movement back to the saying [that is, responsibility] is the phenomenological reduction. In it, the indescribable is described" (OBBE, 53). The identity of the ego, an identity prior to its sending out a ray of intentionality toward the phenomena it constitutes, can itself be constituted in a phenomenology of responsibility where the initiative of appearing resides with the Other whose appearance summons the self in and as a response. To constitute the Ego, however, entails that this Ego be not the source of intentionality but its recipient. This would be an ego without "an intentional aim, implicit and purely of accompaniment. Non-intentional to be distinguished from the inner perception into which it is apt to be converted. . . . What goes on then in this non-reflexive consciousness which is taken as merely pre-reflexive, and which, implicit, accompanies intentional consciousness as the latter intentionally focuses in reflection on its own self?" (EN, 128). Levinas's answer is responsibility—responsibility happens in this nonreflexive, nonintentional Ego which bears the identity and very possibility of consciousness and its reflective gaze on itself. Instead of trying to dispel the nonconstituted transcendence of the pure Ego, Levinas's phenomenology will in fact broach it under the figure of a nonintentional Ego (who might therefore no longer merit the name Ego, but self or oneself or me) constituted in responsibility.

When Husserl discusses the splitting of the Ego that results in the establishment of the transcendental spectator who gazes on in acts of reflection, he writes that "the phenomenological Ego establishes himself [*sich etablieren*] as '*disinterested onlooker*'" (CM, 35). It is precisely the reflexivity or self-referentiality of the verb that betrays phenomenology's inability to constitute the transcendental power. For Levinas, however, the phenomenological ego does not so much establish itself as it is established by another in an "inversion of intentionality" (OBBE, 47). Subject to an intention, the act by which the ego establishes itself (*sich etablieren*) does not remain within the reflexivity of an auto-constitution but is taken in a passive sense, *sich etablieren*, according to an ambiguity that inheres in both German and French pronominal verbs. The difference between consciousness and the pure ego that looks upon it, the difference which constitutes the possibility of phenomenological attitude for Husserl, is therefore established in and through the consideration of a prereflective passivity in which the pronoun (*sich, se,* self) is first an accusative: "The reflexive pronoun *se* . . . raises a problem. . . . The originally accusative sense of this pronoun is hardly perceptible when it is joined to verbs and used to confer on them a passive form in the said" (OBBE, 43). For Levinas, then, the attempt to describe the passivity in which the ego is established (*le Je s'établit*) amounts to treating the reflexive pronoun *se, sich,* self as if it had the sense of an accusative; as an accusative, the ego would be an "object," the "object" of another's gaze or the object of an inverted intentionality. This inverted intentionality would point to the fundamentally ethical scene on which the establishing of the pure ego or oneself is staged; for if the ego is to be the object of an intention, there must be another to exercise this intention, and this other is met in the interpersonal dimension of ethics.

In short, consideration of the Ego as nonintentional or as recipient of an intention must precede consideration of the intentional a priori for phenomenology to constitute its ownmost possibility by constituting the very transcendental itself; but in this supplemental constitution of its origin, phenomenology itself is altered to the core.

Responsibility, Unconditional Affection

In what follows, I want to outline the other order of "meaning" or "intelligibility" (nonmeaning and unintelligibility for consciousness), which might be opened by a phenomenology that goes in the direction of the stage where the one-self is constituted. According to Levinas, this other order, this stage, signifies ethically; the subject to which the reduction leads, for Levinas, is ultimately not consciousness but responsibility. In terms of responsibility, Levinas argues, it is possible to philosophically articulate the meaning of an affection that does not rest on consciousness giving objects to itself. By returning initiative to the phenomenon, the affectedness broached by a phenomenology of responsibility frees appearing from the conditions set for it by the Husserlian practice.

Not only is there something more than consciousness in the subject, but according to Levinas this something more is also the ultimate meaning of the subject. When the subject is taken to be equivalent to consciousness, philosophy forgets the very subjecthood of the subject, the very fact of being a subject. Levinas writes, "consciousness, knowing of the self by the self [*savoir de soi par soi*], is not all there is to the notion of subjectivity. It already rests on a 'subjective condition,' an identity that one calls ego [*Moi*] or I" (OBBE, 102).[2] This subjective condition of the I is what Levinas describes in terms of the responsible self: "the subjectivity or the very sub-jection of the subject is due to my being obsessed with responsibility for the oppressed who is other than myself" (OBBE, 55). For Levinas, subjectivity does not signify first as the ego that knows itself in conscious reflection on its own consciousness but as an I subjected to responsibility for others; the subject is first subjected to. . . . According to Levinas, responsibility, being subjected to the demands of the other, is the meaning of the very fact that I am a subject. It is the unthought and forgotten "underside of a fabric woven where there is consciousness," an underside which is the meaning of the subjective—sub-jective, or thrown under (OBBE, 103).

In responsibility, Levinas hears a meaning of subjectivity that is not that of the consciousness which precedes beings and in which beings first appear but that of what rests underneath, bearing, responsibly, what presses down on it. He writes, "the self is a sub-jectum; it is under the weight of the universe, responsible for all" (OBBE, 116). The sub-jectivity of the subject is its having been thrown under (sub-jected) the world that lies upon it (as Levinas says, "is incumbent upon it"). Subjectivity bears the world in the way that what is thrown under supports what comes, anachronistically, before it. What Levinas calls "the nobility of pure supporting" is the meaning of the subjectivity of the subject (GCM, 68 [modified]). As what supports or lies under, responsibility is thus a sort of "ground" or condition for "beings"—which are no longer beings insofar as they stand not in Being but on responsibility. As sub-jectum, the responsible self anachronistically "grounds" "beings"—if such language can be retained—without preceding them, without generating them, and without limiting their possibility to its own measure.

In this way, Levinas is "trying to express the unconditionality of a subject, which does not have the status of a principle. This unconditionality confers meaning on being itself and welcomes its gravity. It is as resting on a self, supporting all being, that being is assembled into the unity of the universe and essence into an event" (OBBE, 116). As responsible-for-all, the responsible self is the unconditioned condition on which there ultimately rests not only consciousness but all the beings whose being consciousness is. Importantly, this unconditional responsibility is not an *archē* or principle. It does not precede and ground beings in the a priori acts constituting them, nor is it sufficient to itself. Instead, responsibility is an "anteriority 'older' than the apriori. . . . The relationship with exteriority is prior to the act that would effect it" (OBBE, 101). As responsibility, the self is first affected by others or by exteriority without finding the possibility of this affection as an intentional meaning constituted in itself. The responsible self is 'first' or 'ultimate' not in that it precedes and prepares the possibility of its being affected but in that it is the first to be affected by or to respond to what precedes it. When Levinas writes that "to understand intelligibility does not consist in going back to the beginning" (OBBE, 122), he suggests that philosophy is a reduction not to the a priori of consciousness but to what precedes the principle, what comes before the beginning— affection in responsibility. In a paradox that is essential to grasping Levinas's thought, the responsible self joins the phenomenological aim of reaching an unconditioned condition of appearing with the affectedness in which this ultimate is articulated. The condition of all, yet affected by all, such is the responsible self, "a subject supporting everything, subject to everything, that is, suffering for everyone, but charged with everything" (OBBE, 148).

This strange "inversion of consciousness" (OBBE, 101)—whereby the 'first' precedes the *archē* and is not, therefore, a principle—leads Levinas to speak of responsibility as an anarchy: "it undoes thematization, and escapes any *principle,* origin, will, or *archē* which are put forth in every ray of consciousness. This movement is in the original sense of the term, an-archical" (OBBE, 101). As an anarchy, preceding and undoing consciousness, responsibility will be ordered according to a strange temporality whose effects I have already begun to broach here: a temporality in which the self can be first person, can be anachronistically the ultimate source of sense, while nonetheless being affected by what precedes it, by what comes before the first. "This anachronism attests to a temporality different from that which scans consciousness" (OBBE, 88).

As first or ultimate without being *archē,* the responsible self is first without being the origin of itself or sufficient to itself. Whereas for the phenomenology of consciousness the I appears either by constituting itself (as in Husserl's *Cartesian Meditations*) or is not constituted and so does not appear (as in the *Ideas*), for Levinas the I appears through "an inversion of intentionality" (OBBE, 47).[3] In this inversion, it is no longer the case that others appear for me through my intentional acts; rather, it is I who appear or am constituted in response to the summons of another. "The way I appear is a summons. I am placed in the passivity of an undeclinable assignation, in the accusative, a self" (OBBE, 139). In responsibility, the I is first person but comes after its summons. As itself an appearance placed in its position by a summons from the other, the I is no longer the privileged place where beings appear, the prior place whose limits measure what can appear. In responsibility, I am not the place or stage of appearing but the first to appear on the stage. This is why Levinas speaks of a "responsibility ordered to the first one on the scene" (OBBE, 144).

Responsibility "is thus the latent birth of the subject. Latent birth for prior to an origin, an initiative, a present designatable and assumable, even if by memory. It is an anachronous birth, prior to its own present, a non-beginning, an anarchy. As a latent birth it is never a presence" (OBBE, 139). Happening before consciousness in which everything finds its beginning, the birth of the I does not happen in a time with a beginning or an origin. The I, born in this an-archic past, cannot recall its having been born in affection since this origin is not found in consciousness where everything is present—either in the present now perceived or the present past remembered. The an-archy of responsibility means that the responsible subject is ultimate without this ultimacy implying that, like a principle standing on itself, it is sufficient to itself.

Insofar as this summons is the way in which I appear, the responsible self "cannot slip away from this call. The subject is inseparable from this appeal or this election which cannot be declined" (OBBE, 53). Responsibility is ultimate insofar as it cannot be declined, cannot be refused or turned away, without nonsensically denying the very subject who refuses it. This undeclinability is thought in terms of an ineluctable accusation. "The undeclinability of the ego is the irremissability of the accusation, from which it can no longer take a distance, which it cannot evade" (OBBE, 112). The accusation or responsibility in which I am summoned to appear is absolute or unconditioned because even if I refuse to heed the summons, even if I flee or evade it, I have still responded. Once the summons summons me, a response is inevitable inasmuch as refusing to respond acknowledges the ego that has been summoned, if only for it to reject the summons.

In its undeclinability, responsibility meets in a certain way the phenomenological (and the Cartesian) demand that first philosophy be a philosophy of apodictic or indubitable evidence: in responsibility, I am summoned to appear as an apodictic evidence, as an evidence that cannot be declined without confirming the summons that posits it. This undeniability of the summons has its correlate in the undeniability of the phrase which figures its response: *me voici/here I am*. This phrase, like the summons, cannot be denied without the one making the denial immediately testifying to the impossibility of his denial—one cannot say "I am not here" without testifying that one is here.

If responsibility marks a figure of the apodictic, however, it does so in such a way that the apodicticity of the apodictic is not thought in terms of science or knowing, where apodicticity means the indubitable existence and certain knowledge of a principle. The apodicticity of responsibility differs from the evidence of consciousness in that, for Levinas, apodicticity resides not in a subject sufficient to itself, one that finds apodicticity by acts and experiences that reflect on its own experiences and acts, but in the affection of the subject by an other. "In divesting the ego of its imperialism, the hetero-affection establishes a new undeclinability" (OBBE, 121). Unlike the auto-affection of consciousness, the apodicticity of responsibility requires an other, another intentionality which issues the undeclinable summons to appear. Like the apodicticity of a principle, the responsible self is the first; but whereas principles "can be seen to be themselves apodictic . . . as 'first in themselves'" (CM, §6), the responsible self is not first on its own, not first in itself (nor even first for itself), since the summons calling it to answer for another precedes it and reaches it in a hetero-affection.

Haunted by the insufficiency of its not having constituted its own origin, the apodicticity of responsibility therefore occurs "in an evidence that is inadequate" because not given in reflective immanence (CM, §6). Such inadequacy, however, in no way compromises the apodicticity of responsibility; for, even in Husserl's phenomenology, "adequacy and apodicticity of evidence need not go hand in hand" (CM, §9). Though Husserl here suggests that apodicticity extends beyond what is given in adequate evidence, he nevertheless holds his own phenomenology to the description of those evidences which can be known adequately. In doing so, he maintains phenomenology as a field of science, a science which secures the presence of objects by passing from the less adequate evidence furnished by natural perception to the more perfectly adequate evidences found in the intuition of consciousness itself. But, such a security is purchased at the cost of limiting the phenomenological insight; it turns the gaze away from the far wider horizons it was capable of investigating.

Levinas, on the other hand, takes the insight into an apodictic sphere beyond that of adequate evidence as a point of departure. It suggests to him that the description of the phenomenological subject might proceed into the margins where apodicticity exceeds the possibility of adequate evidence or intuitive fulfillment.[4] His description does not, and will never, yield adequate knowledge since it describes the birth of a subject in response to a summons which called before there was a consciousness to intend it. Adequate evidence will always be lacking for the very fact that the responsible self is structured in such a way that it is constituted in the absence of its own beginning. The apodicticity of responsibility in no way derives from the certainty or indubitability with which it is known or undergone, since, by definition, responsibility is undergone in the face of absence. This means that one cannot argue against the apodicticity of responsibility by claiming that since I am not always in a situation which calls for responsibility, that is since the face does not always face me, responsibility is not the absolute, unconditional subjectivity of the subject but a contingent happening that befalls the subject from time to time. Such an argument misses responsibility; for responsibility means just that: I am always absent from the instant in which responsibility summons me; the face never appears in my present since it disappears, passes, in the moment I appear.

The Subject as Responsibility

If responsibility as the phenomenological ultimate means that even the I, the subjectivity of the subject or the self, appears or is constituted as a phenomenon, it becomes possible for a phenomenology of responsibility to account for the genesis and structure of the I. As appearing in responsibility, the subjectivity of the subject means, for Levinas, that, from the moment I am, I am concerned not for myself but first for the other who summons me in the face. Maintaining that responsibility precedes any concern of a subject for itself, Levinas claims that responsibility is so enormous as to go to the extreme point of being responsible for every other, even for what the other is responsible for. Responsibility, in this way, is less an active engagement or commitment that I undertake at my own initiative than it is a passive supporting of the world that, from the first, is impressed on me. For such a self, what is at stake is not being but the good: "the self is goodness, or under the exigency of an abandon of all having, of all one's own and all for oneself, to the point of substitution" (OBBE, 118). Required to abandon itself in responsibility for the other, the responsible self, as goodness, is thus "despite itself," a phrase which suggests both that I have (and receive) no interest in my responsibility and that I undergo responsibility before intending to assume it.

In such a notion of responsibility, at least four characteristics of the responsible self can be distinguished: Uniqueness, Passivity, Belatedness, and Accusedness.

1. *Uniqueness.* The responsible self is absolutely unique or singular, for no one can take responsibility for me. As Levinas writes, the responsible self is "one inasmuch as irreplaceable in responsibility," or "no one can substitute himself for me who substitutes for all" (OBBE, 103, 126). In other words, the responsible self is unique in that only it is subjected to or substituted for others. "Its exceptional uniqueness . . . is the incessant event of subjection to everything, of substitution. It is a being divesting itself, emptying itself of its being" (OBBE, 117). In responsibility, I am unique and irreplaceable, but unique and irreplaceable not in that I alone appropriate my own being or become my own self but rather in that only I am substituted for others and thereby dispossess or divest myself of my own. Thus, the very uniqueness of the self, in responsibility, is at once its renunciation or emptying of all self: "the more I return to myself, the more I divest myself . . . the more I discover myself to be responsible" (OBBE, 112).[5]

This means that subjectivity is authentically itself in "an authenticity that, precisely, is not measured by what is proper to me [*ce qui m'est propre:* what is mine], by *Eigentlichkeit,* by what has already touched me, but rather by pure gratuity towards alterity" (GCM, 165). As the pure gratuity of sub-stitution, authenticity is produced at the very same moment that I am dis-possessed of all that would be authentically my own being.[6] Such an au-thenticity is purely gratuitous in two senses: first, it rests on no prior cause, motive, or reason; second, it is not done in exchange for anything. Insofar as its authenticity is measured not by its own being but by substitution, the responsible self does not first have its being to itself and then give itself over; rather, it is from the first devoted to the other. Gratuitously abandon-ing its being before it has it, the responsible self is not first a being exist-ing for itself, one whose mode of being would be substitution. As Levinas writes, "we do not mean to reduce an entity that would be the ego to the act of substituting itself that would be the being of this entity" (OBBE, 117). In responsibility, the uniqueness of the self is thought not in terms of Being but in terms of gratuity or goodness: "the self is goodness, or under the exigency for an abandon of all having, of all *one's own* and all *for oneself,* to the point of substitution" (OBBE, 118).

Not only does the singularity of the self mean that it is dispossessed of its own being, it also means that the responsible self is unable to double itself or set itself at a distance from itself. In this vein, Levinas writes of the "atom-ic, that is in-dividual [graphically emphasizing the sense of not divisible], unity of the self," or of the self as a "oneness without duality" (OBBE, 107, 104). To describe such a singularity, Levinas introduces the term "recur-rence," implying that the responsible self does not develop or grow beyond itself but repeats itself. "The term in recurrence will be sought here beyond or on the hither side of consciousness and its play, beyond or on the hither side of being which it thematizes, outside of being, and thus in itself as in exile" (OBBE, 103). Not part of the stream of consciousness just as Hus-serl's pure ego does not participate in the passing flow on which it gazes, the recurrence of the oneself designates a temporality that is not that of consciousness, not that of a flux in which impressions are grown in and through conscious modification and then fade into the recesses of con-sciousness where they are always available for recall. Rather, as recurring, the responsible self begins again in each instant such that its birth or ap-pearance never has the status of a beginning or origin on which a history would rest.[7] Happening in a "dead time or meanwhile," the oneself recurs in a sort of eternity that does not grow or modify itself in the time of con-sciousness (OBBE, 109).

As a term in recurrence, the responsible self does not bear its identity as do beings. Always recurring and so unable to double itself or disperse itself into distinct moments, the oneself does not appear in or for conscious-ness, Levinas argues, by multiplying itself in images spread out in time and gathered together in a present made in and through the synthetic activities of identification. The identity of the singularity is no identity at all; for it does not gather together and identify any dispersion. As singular, it is iden-tical to nothing, not even itself since it happens uniquely each time it re-curs. Moreover, the singularity of the self does not appear by putting on a mask or a semblance so as to show itself as something it is not. Such an appearing would introduce a duality (the distinction of the manifest and the latent) into the oneness of the self. "The oneself does not enter into that play of exposing and dissimulations which we call a phenomenon (or a phenomenology, for the appearing of a phenomenon is already a discourse)" (OBBE, 104).

Unable to double itself and so set itself at a distance from itself, the responsible self cannot autonomously realize its own identity by reflecting upon itself. It is so much in itself that it cannot see itself and so cannot realize itself; it is thus in itself like an exile who is not at home in the place he finds himself.[8] "Exiled in its own fullness" (OBBE, 104), the oneself is not in itself in the way that consciousness is: at home with itself and satisfied with itself since it is equal to all that is in it. The oneself is a "self that has never been able to diverge from itself, to then enter into its limits, and identify itself by recognizing itself in its past. Its recurrence is the contracting of an ego" (OBBE, 114). Like an exile, the responsible self does not realize its identity by venturing away from home so as to discover itself in adventures on the far reaches of its own frontier before returning home in full knowledge of itself and the homeland it inhabits. Instead, it contracts its identity in the contraction by which it enters so deeply into itself that it loses sight of all history and any others in which it might be able to recognize itself.[9]

Since it is so singular as to be unable to realize or conceive itself, to present itself to itself, the identity of the oneself must be assigned to it. Hence, the second characteristic of this responsible self.

2. *Irreversible Passivity.* The "oneself cannot form itself; it is already formed with an absolute passivity" (OBBE, 104). For Levinas, subjectivity does not constitute itself or identify itself in reflection upon its own consciousness but is instead "a point already identified from the outside, not having to identify itself in the present nor to state its identity, already older than the time of consciousness" (OBBE, 107). Since the responsible self was summoned to itself in responsibility, it has already been identified from the outside before the ego generates itself in a reflective act. This means the responsible self "is not an objectification of the self by the ego" but an identity already constituted by the summons of an other, a summons which strikes me before the ego arrives on the scene (OBBE, 121). In responding to its summons to appear, the responsible self is affected by a "command that is not the recollection of a disposition belonging to the constitution of the ego" (EN, 172). The responsible self is "already constituted when the act of constitution first originates" and so is not itself constituted in the acts of consciousness (OBBE, 105).

Unable to generate itself or even to reflect on itself in and through the act of consciousness, subjectivity, as responsibility, is not its own ground or the condition of its own identity. Instead, it is assigned to itself. According to Levinas, this happens in the "one-way, irreversible being affected" of responsibility (OBBE, 84). Affected irreversibly, the responsible self is affected by the other before it is conscious of the other, and so before it is able to assume or be conscious of what affects it. The summons to responsibility assigns me to myself in an irreversible passivity such that I have no time for conscious deliberation and a measured response to the summons. It is a "responsibility that does not leave me time" (GCM, 71). Paradoxically, then, the passive self marries a pure patience or passivity with an "extreme urgency" wherein "I have no time to face it" (OBBE, 88). Always lacking time, the responsible self is affected with urgency in the midst of its very passivity.

In its passivity, the responsible self is not at liberty to judge the summons or summoner so as to accept or reject them accordingly. "I am as it were ordered from the outside . . . without asking myself: What then is it to me? Where does he get his right to command? What have I done to be from the start in debt?" (OBBE, 87). The responsible self is not conscious of itself or of the other who summons it and so does not know why or to whom he responds. In fact, where there is consciousness, according to Levinas, responsibility is no longer. "Consciousness . . . would have already lost [the] proximity [of the other in responsibility]. . . . Proximity is no longer in knowing in which these relationships with the neighbor show themselves" (OBBE, 83). In place of the passive urgency and urgent passivity of responsibility, consciousness pauses to deliberate—taking or making the time to know or become familiar with the situation in which it finds itself so as to then reason and decide whether or not, and if so how, it might best respond. According to Levinas, however, "consciousness is not interposed between me and my neighbor" (OBBE, 87). The affection of the self in responsibility cannot be reversed by my coming to know the source of my affection; for if consciousness were to reverse the passivity of my affection by coming to know who calls, the affection is lost and responsibility vanishes.

Being assigned in an irreversible affection, the responsible self is "compelled before commencing" or is responsible for the other before having been present to freely commit itself to the other (OBBE, 103). In this sense, "substitution is not an act; it is a passivity inconvertible into act, the hither side of the act-passivity alternative" (OBBE, 117). On the one hand, responsibility is not the act of a conscious ego which first exists for itself then chooses or decides to act responsibly by substituting itself. On the other hand, responsibility is not the sort of passivity belonging to a conscious ego, a passivity which is able to receive or assume through the modifications of protention and retention what leaves an impression on it, but "a passivity that does not revert into an assumption" (OBBE, 113). In rejecting the language of reception and assumption, the analyses of *Otherwise than Being, or, Beyond Essence* depart not only from the phenomenology of consciousness and the temporality of the ecstatic now but also from those of Levinas's own *Totality and Infinity*, where ethics is interpreted as a sort of receptivity, a reception of the Other: "This book [*Totality and Infinity*] will present subjectivity as welcoming the Other, as hospitality" (TI, 27). In *Otherwise than Being, or, Beyond Essence,* however, "the leisure necessary for a welcome" is a leisure enjoyed only by consciousness (OBBE, 102). Having no time and no intentionality in and through which it could generate what affects it, the responsible self is unable or powerless to receive or welcome the Other and so is traumatized by responsibility. Such a shift makes it even more clear that the appearing of the Other is in no way conditioned by the responsible self; for this appearing happens even when the self is unable to welcome or receive the appearance.

Lacking the capacity for a welcome, reception, or assumption of what affects it, the passivity of the responsible self implies that I swallow my own intentions and intentional activity. In responsibility, I hold back my expectations of what might come and forget my memories of what has been in order to respond gratuitously and generously without consideration for what has been my relation with this other or what might come of it. The responsible self is a "psyche holding its own intentionality as one holds one's breath, and, by consequence, a pure patience" (GCM, 118). To appreciate the difficulty of what Levinas here describes, one need only imagine the very significant conflict between his position and that of Nietzsche (and Freud) on the question of holding back one's own intentionality. For Nietzsche, the forces which drive man seek above all to discharge themselves in an act that responds to the stimulus which excites them. When this discharge is blocked and the forces are unable to act out the reaction to which they are driven, these forces will find a way to express themselves through alternate means. In Nietzsche's thought, a pure patience, pure withholding of all my intentions, is impossible. It is undertaken only by *ressentiment,* which *professes* such pure patience only to hide its desire for revenge against the intentions of those who have supposedly caused its pathos and which in fact achieves a sort of imaginary triumph over its oppressors in the form of religious and moral righteousness and the promise of a future reward: heaven, "the meek shall inherit the earth," etc. Nietzsche would no doubt suspect that the responsible self resents the obligations which command it to hold back its own intentions. The sacrifice and dispossession of the responsible self would have to be read in terms of Nietzsche's notion of asceticism to appreciate the challenge posed by Levinas's notion of holding back one's own intentions. Seen in this way, the self-abandon of the responsible self would be a means for this self to save its own will by willing its own destruction since it was blocked from discharging its will against the true source of its pathos. Levinas of course means to resist Nietzsche's objection by claiming: (1) the sacrifice of the self does not save the self, does not preserve a self who could receive a return on this self-abasement; the sacrifice of the self is not a sacrifice undertaken as part of a plan for salvation of the self but a pure loss; and (2) the self does not willfully sacrifice itself but is itself sacrificed, passively as it were, in a pure patience.

Levinas's attempt to evade objections of the Nietzschean sort can be seen in the radical depth of passivity he attempts to broach. This passivity could be called, following the formulations adopted in mystical theologies, a hyperpassivity in order to capture the sense in which responsibility happens in a passivity beyond the alternative activity-passivity. This term is suggested by Levinas's frequent use of the phrase "more passive than passive" and what he at least once calls a "hyperbolic passivity" (OBBE, 49).[10] This hyperpassivity of the responsible self issues from the fact that it is affected even before being and so before being free to choose. "As chosen without choosing its election, absent from the investiture received, the oneself is a passivity more passive still than all the passivity of undergoing. The passivity of the one, its responsibility or its pain, do not begin in consciousness" (OBBE, 57). In the hyperpassivity of a nonchosen responsibility, the other regards me—gazes on me, concerns me—before I am conscious of him and so before his gaze appears as the correlate of my intention. Appearing without my intending it, the summons affects me without finding a beginning in me and so without my being able to assume or undergo the affection.

Struck in a passivity that does not choose or intend to be so affected, "the subject then cannot be described on the basis of intentionality, representational activity, objectification, freedom and will; it has to be described on the basis of the passivity of time" (OBBE, 53). A certain notion of time thus proves crucial to understanding the passivity of affectivity in which the responsible self appears. In the patience in which I passively suffer the passage of time, Levinas finds an "event" that happens despite me, one that concerns me without my intending it. Reached before intentionality and representational activity have the time to operate, time is temporalized, according to Levinas, in a way quite different from what the phenomenology of consciousness sees. In the latter, temporalization happens in a series of consciousness's own retentions and protentions which gather time passed or to come, or—better—which gather the temporal modifications of an originary impression into a being present in and for consciousness. When the intuition of the present ceases, the present does not pass so much as it is modified while it slips into ever deeper, but always illuminable, recesses of consciousness.

The notion of time that is discovered in the description of the responsible self is quite different. It is a notion of time understood as a "lapse" or "loss" that happens without the activity of a subject intending beings:

> Temporalization as lapse, the loss of time, is neither an initiative of an ego, nor a movement toward some telos or action. The loss of time is not the work of a subject. . . . The temporalization of time, the lapse irrecuperable outside of all will, is quite the contrary of intentionality. . . . In it what is a subject is the inverse of a thematizing subject. (OBBE, 51)

In order to describe the passivity of the subject, a subject without intentionality, Levinas looks to the temporalization of time, but he does so only insofar as such temporalization is understood not as the gathering or recuperation of temporal modifications in and through the intentional acts of consciousness, but as a lapse in which time is lost irrecuperably without my intending it to so pass. The instantaneous now of the present is not held or stretched in its passing away; it is lost.

Analyzed in terms of a lapse of time, the hyperpassivity of the subject summoned to respond before it begins to be leads to the third characteristic of the responsible self.

3. *Belatedness.* As identified from the outside before it is present to respond to this assignation, the responsible self is "anachronously delayed behind its present moment, and unable to recuperate this delay" (OBBE, 101). The an-archy in which the other affects me issues in my lateness, my lagging behind the present in which I would begin. Since the assignation "assigns me before I show myself, before I set myself up" (OBBE, 103), I am never present, fully, to assume my responsibility. I am always late responding to the other for whom I am responsible. "My reaction misses a present which is already the past of itself. . . . The delay is irrecuperable" (OBBE, 88). In responsibility, the other, therefore, affects me without this affection having a present or without this present of the affection ever being present to me.

Since the self was assigned its identity by an assignation that precedes it, that came before it was, the responsible self is unable to catch up with its origin and so is never fully present to itself. This lateness, or lagging behind its own origin, is the very meaning of the diachrony of time: "The diachrony by which the uniqueness of the one has been designated, is the fact that one is required, on the hither side of essence, by responsibility, and is always lacking with respect to itself" (OBBE, 57). This lack of the self is not due to some missing piece or some recess of consciousness as yet unilluminated by the light of reflection; it is due instead to the lateness in which the self appears. Always lagging behind itself, the diachrony of responsibility is a "disjunction of identity where the same does not rejoin the same" because the lapse of time which separates them cannot be recuperated (OBBE, 52). Thought as irrecuperable loss or lapse, the diachrony of time also undoes the Hegelian notion of a time which can be gathered into the unity of a complete and coherent history. In its diachrony, time is not the history where spirit or being enters into dispersion and otherness so as to return to itself in the plenitude of self-consciousness or absolute spirit.

Since responsibility affects me before I am there to be conscious of it, it affects me without ever entering the present that is found in and through consciousness. The belatedness of the responsible self means that it does not share a present with that which affects it. As never having been present, the summons cannot be recalled or remembered. It is instead an-archical, coming from an immemorial past that never began in a present. This is why the belatedness of the self cannot be redeemed by an act of consciousness which would remember the event of the summons in order to make amends for its tardiness. The passivity of the self is irreversible in precisely this way: it cannot reverse the lapse of time which passes between it and its summons. The other is lost in the lapse of time without this loss being held in a synthesis; responsibility entails "a diachrony without synthesis" (OBBE, 183). "This diachrony of time is not due to the length of the interval" or stretch of time that consciousness measures (OBBE, 52). Time is *not* diachronous insofar as it measures a stretch of time, a comet's tail having the present as its nucleus or head (see Husserl, PIT §11). Rather, the diachrony of time is the irreducible divergence (the two times of a responsibility that Levinas says happens in "several times" [OBBE, 183]) of my appearance and the anarchic past in which the other summoned me to responsibility before I was there to have a present.

Not able to reduce the diachrony of time to a present, the responsible self always arrives on the scene too late and so is unable to be conscious of that which affects it. Inversely, that which affects it is always already past, has always already departed, before the self is present to respond to it. This lateness, the diachrony of time, means, therefore, that "my presence does not respond to the extreme urgency of the assignation. I am accused of having delayed" (OBBE, 89). This leads to the fourth characteristic of the subjectivity of the subject.

4. *Accusedness.* Since it is forever late, the responsible self stands irremissibly—and unjustly—accused of failing to meet its duty. This accusation marks the origin of the self. Levinas writes, "in responsibility for another, subjectivity is only this unlimited passivity of an accusative which does not issue out of a declension it would have undergone starting with the nominative. . . . Everything is from the start in the accusative" (OBBE, 112). That is to say, before I am I, I am first assigned to be me; the assignation summons me in the accusative, as accused, before I am there to hear the summons. Hence, "in responsibility, the same, the ego, is me, summoned, provoked as irreplaceable" (OBBE, 135). The first meaning of the person, the meaning of the first person, would not be found in the position of the active subject (the I of I think) but in the passivity of a me, affected in responsibility.

The undeclinability of this accusative me would articulate the irreversible passivity of the responsible self: "Such is the exceptional condition or unconditionality of the self, signification of the pronoun *se* for which our Latin grammars themselves know no nominative form" (OBBE, 112). Expressed by a pronoun which has no nominative form, the responsible self is posited in a passivity that cannot be converted into the activity of a subject. It is a passivity which does not form the basis on which an active subject, I, might emerge. The subjectivity, or the subjected, is thus posed as deposed; in responsibility, the subject is de-posited. "The subject posed as deposed is me [*posé en tant que déposé—moi*]. . . . Already the position of the subject is a deposition [*la position du sujet est dé-position*]" (OBBE, 126–27).

Because the assignation to responsibility accuses me before I could be there, freely or willfully, to assume responsibility, it assigns me with an "accusation without foundation" (OBBE, 110). The accusation (and therefore the responsible self which it summons) lacks foundation or is unconditional precisely because it accuses me without considering what I might possibly have done. The self is responsible even though, as nonintentional, it does not intend anything at all.[11] Accused before being, the responsible self is accused without this accusation in any way being conditioned by what it freely or willfully (intentionally) might have done or been able to do. In other words, the accusation, me, is unconditional or without foundation precisely because it precedes the origin or *archē* which consciousness is in being.

Lacking grounds, being without foundation, the accusation is an "accusation preceding the fault, borne against oneself despite one's innocence" (OBBE, 113). Accused in its innocence, the responsible self, me, cannot acquit itself of its accusation; it is innocent, but nonetheless accused. Such an accusation is the very meaning of injustice—but, Levinas responds, who ever said responsibility was just? In the preface to the German edition of *Totality and Infinity*, a preface written in 1987, well after *Otherwise than Being, or, Beyond Essence* had been published, Levinas suggests that one of the main advances made by the later work was a sharper distinction between ethics and justice. *Totality and Infinity*, by not making a distinction between "mercy or charity, the source of a right of the other person coming before mine, in the first case, and justice, in the second, where the right of the other person [is] obtained after inquest and judgment," used the notion of justice and ethics indifferently in both situations (EN, 198). However, in *Otherwise than Being, or, Beyond Essence*, ethics or responsibility means precisely to be affected by an unjust accusation. The realms of justice and ethics could not be more sharply divided.

De-posited as me, the responsible self cannot acquit itself of its accusation by taking refuge in the concept of an "I" or "selfhood." Such a concept, indeed any concept to which the me would be granted access, would annul my singularity in a general or a universal. Under the concept I, responsibilities (and hence the justice of an accusation) are measured by what "I" have committed freely and willfully or by what I have chosen to do. Under this concept, "I" can reverse the accusation, turn it against the others, and hide from its undeclinability since, according to the concept of an "I," we are all equally I and so equally responsible to each other. The accusation of responsibility, however, strikes me despite my innocence, even casts me out of the concept "I" which would allow me to defend myself, and thus bears on me without my being able to defend myself or to take shelter from it by stating my innocence. It therefore takes on the characteristics of a persecution: "I have not done anything, and I have always been under accusation—persecuted" (OBBE, 114).

Affected in an unconditional accusation, an accusation without foundation, "the self, the persecuted one, is accused beyond his fault before his freedom and thus in an unavowable innocence" (OBBE, 121). The persecuted innocence of the responsible self is "unavowable" insofar as the accused "cannot defend himself by language, for the persecution is a disqualification of the apology. Persecution is the precise moment in which the subject is reached or touched without the mediation of the logos" (OBBE, 121).[12] As a singularity without concept or universal, the self is summoned in responsibility by a "wordless accusation" that "leaves it speechless," and so without any of the mediations that language or logic (the logos) might offer to the violence of a persecution (OBBE, 127, 101). Bearing on me outside language and logos, responsibility entails that this self remain absolutely foreign to the order of concepts and universals wherein it would be possible to measure and pass judgment on the enormity of the demand that befalls me. Such measures would allow the self to evade or decline the enormity of its responsibility by permitting it to excuse itself from responding to a demand that is judged to be put forth without regard for what an I should justly be asked to do.

In the unconditional accusation of responsibility, however, these measures are unavailable; for the persecution "undoes the logos in which the apology by which consciousness always regains its self-control, and commands, is inserted" (OBBE, 102). The possibility of the apology constitutes another evident difference between *Totality and Infinity* and *Otherwise than Being, or, Beyond Essence*. Whereas, in the later work, the responsible self is denied the possibility of apologizing, in the earlier work, the apology is the ethical essence of language: "The very fact of being in a conversation consists in recognizing in *Autrui* a *right* over this egoism, and hence in justifying oneself. Apology, in which the I at the same time asserts itself and inclines before the transcendent, belongs to the essence of language" (TI, 40). Unlike the I of interiority in *Totality and Infinity*, the responsible self of *Otherwise than Being, or, Beyond Essence* is touched without the mediation of the logos and so without having the means to make an apo-logy for its irremissible lateness. It therefore remains accused without being able to make amends or offer compensations which would, logically, acquit it and so is persecuted with a "responsibility over and beyond the logos of response" (OBBE, 102).[13] The accusation of responsibility is one to which, contrary to logic, no amount of responsibility responds sufficiently. Without the logos by which apology or compensation is possible, the responsible self cannot have done with its accusation, cannot pay back the debt which it is accused of having incurred. "The accusation is in this sense persecuting; the persecuted one can no longer answer it. More exactly, it is an accusation which I cannot answer but for which I cannot decline responsibility" (OBBE, 127).

As proceeding to the extreme of a persecution, the irreversible accusation of the singular self happens without regard for what metaphysics or the phenomenology of consciousness has considered the transcendental conditions for the possibility of experience. In its extreme accusation, the responsible self is affected irreversibly by "an exigency without regard to oneself where what is possible is not measured by reflection on oneself. . . .

This extreme accusation excludes the declinability of the self, which would have consisted in measuring the possibilities in oneself, so as to accuse it of this or that, of something committed" (OBBE, 112–13). Whereas the critical project of modern metaphysics (inaugurated by Kant and even Descartes, then consummated in Husserl) seeks the limits and conditions of the possible by reflecting on the conscious subject, Levinas finds that in responsibility the self is accused of what it was never present to have committed and thus for what it is impossible to account for by starting from reflection on consciousness. Responsibility "would be an exigency with regard to oneself where what is possible is not measured by a reflection on the self, as in the for-itself" (OBBE, 112). Rather, it befalls me without its having to be submitted to or conditioned by the limits set by what a conscious I can experience. In the enormity of responsibility, Levinas thus finds an event that happens beyond the limits set by modern metaphysics and its consummation in the phenomenology of consciousness.

Is the Ethical Horizon Necessary?

Levinas insists that the supplement of phenomenology be carried out in explicitly ethical terms; only ethical language suffices for the description of the subject that emerges in the course of practicing a phenomenology that proceeds beyond consciousness: "No language other than ethics could be equal to the paradox which phenomenological description enters" when describing the affected subject (OBBE, 193, n. 35). "The ethical language we have resorted to does not arise out of a special moral experience, independent of the description hitherto elaborated. . . . The tropes of ethical language are found to be adequate for certain structures of the description" (OBBE, 120).[14] The aim of phenomenological description leads it inevitably to ethical language. When put this way, one is immediately struck by questions like: Why no language but ethics? Are other languages adequate? Might they be more or less adequate?

These questions seem to have been presupposed in readings of Levinas by at least two commentators. In a reading of Levinas that, most will agree, captured something essential in his thought, Mark C. Taylor avoids giving the subjectivity of the subject a specifically ethical cast.[15] A similar reading was offered by Simon Critchley at a Loyola University conference on Levinas in the summer of 1993. These readings, precisely because they are compelling renderings of Levinas, lead me to wonder if the structure of subjectivity sought by Levinas's phenomenology could be articulated without the specifically ethical terms in which Levinas insists it must be described. One might also point to the almost indiscernible difference between the subject in Levinas and Blanchot as evidence for such a claim.

In asking this question, I have immediately contested the privileged place of ethics in phenomenological philosophy. It seems that Taylor and Critchley, as convincing as their readings are, have presupposed an answer to this question without really asking it in a way that is rigorous or even explicit. To make their readings more penetrating, they would have to ask, first, why Levinas believes that the subject of phenomenology is essentially responsibility, and, then, if there are phenomenological reasons necessitating this conclusion. I hope to have addressed the first part of this question in chapters 4 and 5. It is to the second part of this question that I now want to turn through a reading of Heidegger's existential analytic.

6

The Affected Subject: Responsibility or *Dasein?*

If the same structure of subjectivity can be found outside ethics, then phenomenological philosophy would not necessarily call for an *ethical* supplement. Though Levinas claims that ethical language alone can guide phenomenology to the ultimate meaning of subjectivity, one might very well contest the privilege granted to ethics and attempt to articulate a meaning of subjectivity which accomplishes for phenomenological philosophy all that Levinas sought to accomplish for it without recourse to specifically ethical language. In this chapter, I want to suggest that Heidegger's existential analytic provides one such alternative articulation of the phenomenological subject.

In Heidegger, phenomenological philosophy develops a philosophical meaning of subjectivity that is quite similar to that developed by Levinas; but it proceeds in existential rather than ethical terms. By means of phenomenological philosophy, Heidegger's existential analytic of *Dasein* entails a similar subversion of the I by an analysis of what precedes and undoes it. This alternative figure of the ultimate is structured in a way that is quite similar to that of the responsible subject in Levinas. In short, for Heidegger as well as Levinas, phenomenological phenomenology finds its ultimate figure in the investigation of a subject which is first without being origin of itself or sufficient to itself and which is so precisely in terms of a certain understanding of its uniqueness, the passivity of affectivity, and its lagging behind itself.

These similarities challenge the privilege which Levinas grants to ethics in the phenomenological search for subjectivity. They suggest that the presentation of the subject as ethical depends less on a philosophical necessity than it does on an interpretive choice. In this way, my presentation will help make clear the point at which ethics breaks from philosophy: if Levinas decides that the subject is ethical and not existential, this decision depends not so much on a phenomenological necessity as it does on a prephilosophical experience or interpretation—which explains why a work which is so concerned with (first) philosophy will say in its preface, "No doubt [the movement of this work] is not completely disengaged from pre-philosophical experiences" (OBBE, 20).

The Phenomenological Necessity for a *Dasein* Analytic

The continuity of the *Dasein* analytic with the phenomenological project is not immediately evident from *Being and Time* since this work begins not by exercising a reduction but with the attempt "to reawaken an understanding for [the question of the meaning of Being]" (BT, 19). In what sense is this a phenomenological question? Isn't this the very question which the phenomenological reduction put out of play when it suspended all consideration of being? In fact, the question of Being and the existential analytic in *Being and Time* might not appear to belong to Husserlian phenomenology precisely because they presuppose an immanent critique of such a phenomenology that can be found in the lecture courses of 1925, published in English under the title *History of the Concept of Time: Prolegomena*. In this work, Heidegger showed that the very principle of phenomenology, and so the very possibility that phenomenology might be phenomenological, required that it ask the question of the meaning of Being.

According to Heidegger, the phenomenological field is consciousness understood as intentionality; "the field of phenomenological research is *intentionality in its apriori*" (HCT, 78). Whereas Kant "joined the question of the apriori with his specific epistemological inquiry" and thereby limited the a priori to the sphere of a subject cut off from beings, phenomenology claims that the a priori is not a feature specific to such a subject (HCT, 74). Instead, it locates the a priori in intentionality which, by definition, overcomes the simple distinction between the immanence of the subject and the beings of the transcendent world. Overcoming the (Kantian) distinction between an immanent subject and transcendent beings, the a priori is "a feature of the being of entities and not a feature of entities themselves"; it is a "title for being" (HCT, 75, 74). On Heidegger's reading, phenomenological philosophy aims not only at beings but at their being, or at beings in their being, a being which it describes in and through intentionality. Seeing beings in their being, it thus goes back "to the things themselves." As such, these things are found in the description of intentionality: "intentionality now is nothing other than *the basic field* in which these objects are found. [As *intentio* and *intentum*, it is] the totality of comportments and the totality of entities in their being" (HCT, 78). Since phenomenology thus has a field of its own (intentionality, where beings in their being are found, or the things in themselves), it is not simply a "propaedeutic science for the traditional philosophical disciplines" but is itself philosophy (HCT, 79). And since this field includes consideration of any being in its a priori, phenomenological philosophy is "philosophy properly named—that is to say, first philosophy."[1]

Thus, Heidegger argues, the very possibility of phenomenological philosophy depends on its singling out and securing the field of intentionality, and "this securing of the sphere of acts and its objects in the uniformity of a specific sphere is called reduction" (HCT, 100). The reduction is absolutely essential to progress in phenomenology since it is the reduction which distinguishes the field of intentionality or consciousness, the a priori, from other fields and thereby discovers the terrain wherein phenomenology operates. The reduction thus makes a difference, distinguishing consciousness and its intentional acts from transcendent beings, and thereby leads to what Husserl calls "the most fundamental and pivotal difference between ways of Being, that between Consciousness and Reality" (Id, §42). In making this difference, the reduction brings phenomenology to its own terrain: the sphere of intentionality in its a priori or consciousness as "the original category of Being generally (or as we would put it, the original region), in which all other regions of Being have their root" (Id, §78). Having performed the reduction, phenomenology is now prepared to enter and describe what it sees in the a priori of intentionality.

According to Heidegger, however, if the Husserlian reduction makes this crucial difference, it is unable to cross the line and enter its promised land. The reduction discovers every being in its being—with the exception of one, the being which is its most proper: intentionality. This means that precisely when phenomenology seeks to enter its own field, it becomes unphenomenological: phenomenology "denies the original leap to the entity which is thematically intended. In the basic task of determining its ownmost field, phenomenology is *unphenomenological!*—that is to say, *purportedly phenomenological!*" (HCT, 128). This is so because, according to Heidegger, the field of intentionality, consciousness, is not determined in its Being or its a priori, a determination which marks a philosophy as phenomenological or first philosophy.

Instead of grasping consciousness in its Being or a priori, Heidegger argues, Husserl determines it according to the traditional idea of an absolute science. The traditional determination of the phenomenological field is seen, according to Heidegger, in that the four determinations which Husserl gives to consciousness (immanent, absolute, self-sufficient, and pure) all aim to determine it as a region for scientific consideration. These determinations do not arise from the thing-itself (consciousness) but only to the extent that it is

> placed under scrutiny as apprehended, given, constituting, and ideating.
> . . . In point of fact all of these determinations of being are derived with a

view to working out the context of lived experience as a region for absolute scientific consideration. . . . This idea, that consciousness is to be the
region of an absolute science, is not simply invented; it is the idea which
has occupied modern philosophy ever since Descartes. The elaboration of
pure consciousness as the thematic field of phenomenology is *not derived
phenomenologically by going back to the matters themselves* but by going back to
a traditional idea of philosophy. (HCT, 106–107)

Instead of elaborating the being of intentionality or consciousness, Husserl
has recourse to a traditional, metaphysical definition of consciousness: when
it is apprehended, it is said to be immanent; when its mode of givenness is
considered, it is absolute; when its role of constituting being is considered it
is self-sufficient; when its essence is considered, it is pure. Each determination of consciousness arises, according to Heidegger, not from consciousness itself but from the scientific perspective under which it is considered.
This means that the field of intentionality is not grasped in its a priori (since
the a priori is a "title for Being"), is not grasped in accord with the maxim
"to the things themselves" (since it is understood according to a traditional
idea of it), and so is not grasped phenomenologically. Therefore, when Heidegger claims that phenomenology has not determined the being of the
intentional, he does not accuse it of a mere neglect but in fact accuses it of
betraying itself, of denying itself the power to phenomenologically determine the field which it laid bare as its ownmost.

In addition to neglecting the being of the intentional, phenomenology
also neglects to ask the question of the meaning of being itself. But, again, is
such a question necessary for phenomenology? According to Heidegger, it
is—because only by asking this question can phenomenology secure for
itself what it claimed to have accomplished with its reduction: namely, "the
most radical of all distinctions of being" (Id, §76; cited in HCT, 114). By
failing to ask the question of the meaning of Being, this fundamental and
radical distinction falls into indifference or is rendered inconsequential: if
the question of the meaning of being is not asked, then being appears indifferently each time it is said; and consequently, the being of consciousness
and the being of reality are said in the same way. According to Heidegger,
this leads Husserl to treat consciousness as if it had the same being as a
being in the natural world. Such treatment is evident, first, in that both the
being of consciousness and the being of the natural world are determined
as essential being, that is to say are regarded solely in terms of their "what-
content" (HCT, 110). After bracketing the existence of beings, the reduction, as eidetic reduction, also brackets the existence of conscious acts in
order to reach their essence or what-content.

To protect itself against the insecurity of this distinction in being, Heidegger argues that phenomenology must ask "what it is which directs the
entire process of making this distinction of being, in short what the sense of
being is" (HCT, 115). For how can the most fundamental and radical distinction in being be drawn without inquiring into what being means such

that it might be so distinguished? Heidegger thus objects not to the making of such a distinction but to the failure to demarcate it clearly and securely enough: "From this it becomes clear that *the question of being is not an optional and merely possible question, but the most urgent question* inherent in the very sense of phenomenology itself" (HCT, 115).

In summary, then, Heidegger stigmatizes two fundamental neglects in Husserl's phenomenology: (1) neglect of the question of the being of the intentional; and (2) neglect of the question of the meaning of Being. These two neglects "go hand in hand. It is precisely because it was postulated that there is no other meaning of Being than occurring as a thing in the world understood as nature . . . that the question of the meaning of the Being of the intentional being is avoided."[2] Inversely, I would add, because Husserl overlooked the being of the intentional, he failed to realize the phenomenological necessity of asking the question of the meaning of Being itself. These two neglects must be addressed because (1) they "deny the original leap to the entity" which the phenomenological reduction has discovered, thus leaving phenomenology only at the edge of its ownmost terrain, and because (2) they leave insecure the fundamental distinction by which phenomenology demarcates intentionality or consciousness from natural being or objects of nature, thus threatening to dissolve phenomenological terrain itself. Hence, the question of Being as it is posed and addressed in *Being and Time* appears as a phenomenological necessity.[3]

Before addressing Heidegger's proposed cure, it is appropriate, as any doctor knows, to ask after a diagnosis: Why is phenomenology not able to ask the questions which alone will bring it into phenomenological terrain; from what affliction does it suffer? According to Heidegger, the deficiency is rooted in the Husserlian practice of the reduction. "In its methodological sense as a disregarding, then, the reduction is in principle inappropriate for determining the being of consciousness positively. The sense of the reduction involves precisely giving up the ground upon which the question of the being of the intentional could be based" (HCT, 109). In other words, the Husserlian reduction bars phenomenology from asking about the being of the intentional because, by definition, it suspends consideration of the being of the intentional in order to focus on the intentional constitution of beings in their being, a constitution which is wholly ideal or essential.

> In the consideration and elaboration of pure consciousness, merely the *what-content* is brought to the fore, without any inquiry into the being of the acts in the sense of their existence. Not only is this question not raised in the reductions, the transcendental as well as the eidetic; it *gets lost precisely through them.* From the what I never experience anything about the sense and the manner of the that. . . . [In the reduction,] the what of any entity is to be defined by disregarding its existence. (HCT, 110)

The reduction cannot inquire into the being of the intentional because this sphere is entered only by disregarding questions of existence in order to arrive at a definition of the essence or whatness of a being. It thus loses the specificity of the intentional sphere by ranging its being along with the being of other beings which belong to the world of objects. Since the practice of the reduction is at once the way to phenomenology's founding discovery and the cause of its ills, Heidegger will correct its practice without abandoning it. Just how this correction is worked out will appear in the course of my commentary on *Being and Time*.

Heidegger takes this oversight of the Husserlian reduction as a negative indication of the direction in which phenomenology ought to proceed. The neglected being of the intentional can be found precisely there where the phenomenological reductions exclude being: namely, in existence. This means that the subject of phenomenology should not be consciousness and its intentional acts—for these have solely essential being—but a being whose essence is to exist: "if there were an entity *whose what is precisely to be and nothing but to be,* then this ideative regard of such an entity would be the most fundamental misunderstanding" (HCT, 110). According to Heidegger, then, the question of the being of the intentional requires not an ideative regard but an existential analytic, a descriptive analysis of existential being. The phenomenological necessity of an existential analytic, then, explains why the question of the sense of being is also necessary for phenomenology: if the being of consciousness is found in existence, then in order to arrive at this being one must first consider the meaning of being, the different ways in which being is said, since without heeding the meaning of being one will never see the sense in which the being of consciousness (existence) differs from the being of beings or objects (essential being).[4]

At this point, it becomes phenomenologically comprehensible why Heidegger chooses *Dasein,* not consciousness, as the being to be interrogated in *Being and Time:* "the first priority is an ontical one: Dasein is an entity whose Being has the determinate character of existence; the second priority is an ontological one: Dasein in itself is 'ontologically' [*ontologisch*]" (BT, 34). *Dasein* is the subject of phenomenological inquiry because, according to its ontical priority, its mode of being is that which Heidegger suggests belongs to the being of the intentional—existence. Since "we cannot define Dasein's essence by citing a 'what' of the kind that pertains to a subject-matter" (BT, 32), *Dasein* designates a mode of being, existence, which is distinct from that of other beings. This leads to the second, ontological reason why Heidegger identifies *Dasein* as the being proper to phenomenological inquiry: "Dasein is an entity which does not just occur among other entities. . . . It is peculiar to this entity that with and through its Being, this Being is disclosed to it. *Understanding of Being is itself a definite characteristic of Dasein's Being*" (BT, 32). Since *Dasein*'s very way to be is to understand Being, *Dasein* emerges as the entity who understands the meaning of Being and so is suited to the phenomenological necessity of asking the question of the meaning of Being. "If to interpret the meaning of Being becomes our task, Dasein is not only the primary entity to be interrogated; it is also that entity which already comports itself, in its Being, towards what we are asking about when we ask this question" (BT, 35). Thus, as the being who exists and as the being who exists by understanding the meaning of Being, *Dasein* replaces consciousness as the entity that provides phenomenology its proper subject.[5]

If *Dasein* replaces consciousness as the subject of phenomenology, one might now wonder how this replacement compares with that effected by the responsible self. What I want to suggest in and through the following explication of *Being and Time* is that *Dasein* offers a phenomenological subject that is structured quite similarly to the responsible self. That is to say, the "mineness" which characterizes *Dasein*'s being parallels the substitution which names the responsible self: both name a figure of the subject which is, ultimately, absolutely unique and unsurpassable yet not sufficient to itself, not able to generate itself, but in some way affected by what it cannot master—a nonoriginary origin. For Heidegger, *Dasein*'s ownmost being, the "mineness" of its being, is de-posited in a certain passivity that is revealed in a privileged mode of being affected—anxiety—and that cannot be declined since it is given to *Dasein* in the inescapability of its death.

Mineness vs. the Seductiveness of the I

The mineness of *Dasein*'s Being is stated in a variety of formulae repeated throughout *Being and Time*, but it is first named in paragraph §9: "We are ourselves the entities to be analyzed. The Being of any such entity is *in each case mine.* . . . Being is that which is an issue for every such entity." Though such a definition might appear at first glance as an affirmation of the self and the securing of being as its property, in fact it proves to be a radical deposition of the sovereign I. The I is no longer a principle which explains and justifies itself autonomously in reflection but is relativized by an anterior instance upon which it depends (its own Being): "Because Dasein has *in each case mineness* [*Jemeinigkeit*], one must always use a personal pronoun when one addresses it: 'I am', 'you are'" (BT, 68). Relativized in this way, the I loses the privilege of the first person, being ranged alongside the second person as (posterior) determinations of (anterior) mineness.

The definition of mineness echoes others that do not name mineness though it is clear that mineness is operative therein. *Dasein* is that being which "in its very Being, has that Being at issue for it" (BT, 32); "Dasein is an entity which, in its very Being, comports itself understandingly towards that Being" (BT, 78). *Dasein* in its Being is not concerned with an essential thing or object called its self, a thing which it would be a matter of knowing, comprehending, or even autonomously constituting in acts of reflection; it is concerned with its Being which precedes itself, and even more radically with Being in general. Always having its Being at issue, *Dasein* is not first master of this Being; rather, Being is at stake or in play for *Dasein* such that it is its own to win or to lose in each case as long as *Dasein* exists.

As Heidegger claims, "in each case [*Dasein*] has its Being to be, and has it as its own" (BT, 32–33). Having its own Being to be, *Dasein* is always ahead of itself looking not to be the essential self it is but to become the being whose task it is for *Dasein* to be. "Delivered over to the Being which, in existing, it has to be," *Dasein* can neither evade or decline its Being nor can it constitute this Being to which it is already delivered over (BT, 173).

Though mineness and being-at-issue offer a preliminary sketch of *Dasein*'s Being, it is for Heidegger only a prelude to the more complete thematization which follows. In filling in this sketch, the existential analytic must find a way of access to this Being: "The right way of presenting it is so far from self-evident that to determine what form it shall take is itself an essential part of the ontological analytic of this entity" (BT, 69). This concern with method, "the right way of presenting it," arises insofar as Heidegger remains faithful to the phenomenological principle, "to the things themselves." The task for the existential analytic then is to find a method that will let the Being of this being "be seen from itself in the very way in which it shows itself from itself" (Heidegger's definition of phenomenology in BT, §7). In *Being and Time,* Heidegger will ever be on the lookout for such a disclosure of *Dasein* in its own Being.

Heidegger contends, in a series of rhetorical questions whose implied answer is clear, that the givenness of the I in reflective awareness, a givenness which gives an indubitable and apodictically certain evidence, is not the proper starting point for an existential analytic of *Dasein*. Even though the definition of *Dasein* as mineness might lead us to believe that it is I myself who is *Dasein*, Heidegger contends that the evidence of the I is seductive—it leads the existential analytic astray by offering a phenomenon in which *Dasein* itself does not attest its own Being from this Being.

> Is it then obvious apriori that access to Dasein must be gained only by mere reflective awareness of the 'I' of acts? What if this kind of 'giving-itself' on the part of Dasein should lead our existential analytic astray [*eine Verführung wäre* (Courtine translates, in French, *fût pour l'analytique existentiale une séduction* [should be seductive])][6] and do so, indeed, in a manner grounded in the Being of Dasein itself. Dasein is in each case mine, and this is its constitution; but what if this should be the reason why Dasein, proximally and for the most part, *is not itself.* What if the aforementioned approach starting with the givenness of the I to Dasein itself, and with a rather patent self interpretation of Dasein, should lead the existential analytic, as it were, into a pitfall? (BT, 151)

According to Heidegger, the evidence of the I gained in reflection and self-interpretation is seductive. What is given in and as the I of reflection, a givenness where the I ultimately gives itself to itself, is not the Being to which Dasein has been delivered over but a being which it itself constitutes. When phenomenology takes self-reflection as its method and its theme, it falls, precisely, into the trap laid for it by a certain tranquilizing and seductive understanding of *Dasein* as disinterested spectator of itself, a being for whom its Being is not at issue but at-hand, available for observation. A disinterested onlooker, the I of reflection does not care about what it sees in itself, does not find itself at stake in what it sees, so much as it makes sense of what happens to it and thereby constructs objects.

The seductiveness for which reflective phenomenology falls entails over-looking or forgetting *Dasein*'s Being-at-issue-for-itself. In straying from *Dasein*'s ownmost Being, reflective phenomenology falls into an average inter-pretation of *Dasein* such that what is reflected upon can be read in light of what Heidegger calls the they-self. The self or I is not one that is authenti-cally my own but one that has been given in the opinions that others have about what it means to be a self. Because *Dasein*'s being includes being-with-others, who *Dasein* is happens to be not itself.

> It itself is not [*Nicht es selbst ist*]; its Being has been taken away by the Others. Dasein's everyday possibilities are for the Others to dispose of as they please. . . . One belongs to the Others oneself [*Man selbst gehört zu den Anderen*]. . . . The who is not this one, not that one, not oneself, not some people, and not the sum of them all. The who is the neuter, *the they* [*das Man*]. (BT, 164)

Because *Dasein*'s Being includes being-with-others or publicness, what it means to be a self gets determined by the ways in which the public under-stands self-hood. One's self belongs to the others, the public, who have determined the ways in which a self is; and the transcendental I is not uniquely my own since it is one that we all are. Because this self, or tran-scendental ego, belongs just as well to others, it is therefore not its own to be. "Proximally, it is not 'I,' in the sense of my own self, that 'am,' but rather the Others, whose way is that of the 'they.' In terms of the 'they,' and as the 'they,' I am 'given' proximally to myself [*mir selbst*]" (BT, 164, 167). Disclosing its 'I' by reflecting on itself does not at all attest to the mineness of *Dasein*'s own being; for this I is one that is said in an average way, equally by everyone else and so by no one in particular—we are all I, and so no one has his own Being.

For the existential analytic not to be seduced and led astray it must there-fore isolate *Dasein*, securing it in the care it has for its ownmost being by detaching it from its subjection to them—the others. Husserl's error lay in not practicing a reduction that isolated the self before reflecting upon the contents of consciousness; this error led him to take the phenomenological subject to be an I that was determined not on the basis of itself but on the basis of what 'they' say an I is. The pretended evidence of the *ego cogito* must be secured against this possibility of seduction if the subject of phenom-enology is to be disclosed in its ownmost Being. To anticipate subsequent developments, *Dasein* is isolated, for Heidegger, not in reflection which clos-es it up like a monad but in anxiety which brings it, passively, before noth-ing—thereby at once opening it and isolating it.

Dasein as Affectedness

If reflection does not reveal *Dasein*'s being as it shows itself in and from itself, does this mean that *Dasein* is forever inaccessible to phenomeno-logical sight? According to Heidegger, this is not the case because *Dasein* "carries in its ownmost Being the character of not being closed off. In the expression 'there' [the *Da* of *Da-sein*], we have in view this essential disclos-edness. By reason of this disclosedness, this entity (Dasein) . . . is there for itself" (BT, 171). The seductiveness of self-reflection does not mean that access to *Dasein*'s being is forever barred, forever closed to sight; for this being is, in its very being, disclosed and so there for itself in a nonreflective manner: "*Dasein is its disclosedness.* . . . [This means] that the Being which is an issue for this entity in its very Being is to be its 'there'" (BT, 171). The phenomenological task of describing *Dasein*'s own being thus becomes a matter of going back to a primary disclosedness—the disclosedness of the there, a disclosedness which the reflective gaze on the self covers over. If it is disclosed there before any reflective self-comprehension, how, then, does *Dasein* gain access to the being it has to be? How is *Dasein* brought back to the there where its own Being is disclosed to it in a primordial way if not by reflection on the constitution of its self?

Heidegger proposes that the answer lies in the description of *Befind-lichkeit,* which the English translators Macquarrie and Robinson render as "states-of-mind." Martineau's French translation renders this as *affection,* a translation which has the benefit of acknowledging the connection be-tween Heidegger's use of *Befindlichkeit* in *Being and Time* and his use of the same word to translate the Latin *affectio* when commenting on Saint Augus-tine during the religion courses of 1924.[7] Importantly, for Heidegger, *Befind-lichkeit* or affectedness is not a state of the soul or psyche: "the earliest sys-tematic interpretation of the affects that has come down to us is not treated in the framework of 'psychology'" (BT, 178).[8] Rather, for Heidegger, affect-edness has a fundamentally ontological-existential significance; it is the way in which *Dasein* is its there in such a way that its mineness, which is to say its ownmost Being, is disclosed. Affectedness is therefore at once a fun-damental characterization of *Dasein*'s being and (or, because of this) a meth-odologically significant aspect of Heidegger's existential analytic.

In bringing *Dasein* to the there where its own Being is revealed, affect-edness discloses a sense of being which is not available to consciousness and its perceptive acts. As Heidegger claims, "the possibilities of disclosure which belong to cognition reach far too short a way compared with the primordial disclosure belonging to moods, in which Dasein is brought be-fore its there" (BT, 173). Instead of theoretically grasping or beholding what *Dasein* is, affectedness discloses how it is—in the sense that when asked "how are you?" one responds with a word that designates a mood or an affect (scared, happy, angry, in love, hateful, etc.). This disclosure does not provide any information relevant to the constitution of *Dasein* as a what or an essential being but discloses being as existence. In affectedness, "the pure that-it-is shows itself, but the whence and the whither remain in darkness" so that moodwise disclosure is fundamentally deprived of the adequate evidence made in and through consciousness (BT, 173). The disclosure of affectedness does not arise through the immanent perception of an object in the passing stream of consciousness; for in a reflective act, the Ego's gaze is directed at essences or what a being is (intentionality: the *cogitationes* and their *cogitatum*), not that-it-is as disclosed in an affect.[9] Affects "are so far from being reflected on, that precisely what they do is to assail Dasein in its unreflecting devotion to the 'world'" (BT, 175). But, according to Heidegger, this does not mean that an affect is nothing at all or is consigned to the irrational. Rather, it means that the affects attune *Dasein* to a different sense of Being than that which is accessible in and through the conscious examination of consciousness.

Not only does the power of disclosure belonging to affectedness open a meaning of Being other than that within the scope of cognition, it also discloses in a fundamental way. Without the prior disclosure of Being in an affect, there could be no constitution of objects. According to Heidegger, "only because the there has already been disclosed in [affectedness] can immanent reflection come across 'Experiences' [*Erlebnisse*] at all" (BT, 175). Affectedness, the there of *Dasein,* therefore names something like the phenomenality of phenomena, their appearing in the sphere of *cogitatio* in such a way that they make up the material for subsequent reflection and the construction of objects. Heidegger will think this phenomenality in terms of a mattering, or Being-at-issue, which makes possible the relation with beings in concern (in opposition to the phenomenality of *cogitatio,* which becomes matter for the gaze that makes objects).

> For Dasein to be concerned with or to direct itself towards beings, it must be determined existentially beforehand in such a manner that what it encounters within-the-world can *matter* to it in this way. The fact that this sort of thing can matter to it is grounded in one's affectivity [*Befindlichkeit*]. . . . *Existentially, affectivity* [Befindlichkeit] *implies a disclosive submission or assignment to the world out of which we can encounter something that matters to us. Indeed from the ontological point of view* we must leave the primary discovery of the world to bare mood. (BT, 176–77, modified)

The mattering on which every concernful or theoretical relation depends is something to which *Dasein* must submit. This submission bespeaks a certain passivity in which *Dasein* is assigned or delivered over to the there where beings matter to it. It is only as first passively assigned to the there that *Dasein* has an interest in Being such that it can, on the basis of this assignment, direct itself toward beings. Unlike the acts of consciousness which proceed freely or voluntarily according to acts directed by the Ego, "a mood assails us," persecuting us in a certain way, without our being able to account for it in and through self-reflection (BT, 176). Assailed in its affectedness, *Dasein* is its affectedness in a way that must be distinguished from the way it might have certain habits which it itself constituted and which it might master. *Dasein is* in a mood; it finds its own being under the sway of moods. Finding its being there in an affect which assails it passively, *Dasein* is "always disclosed moodwise as that entity to which it has been delivered over in its Being; and in this way it has been delivered over to the Being which, in existing, it has to be" (BT, 173). This means that *Dasein* does not posit its own Being; it cannot justify its mineness by claiming that it made its own Being. Rather, mineness means, paradoxically, that the Being which is *Dasein*'s own is an existence to which it has been delivered over passively.

To designate this passivity of being delivered over to its that-it-is, Heidegger coins the term thrownness [*Geworfenheit*]: "the expression 'thrownness' is meant to suggest the *facticity of its being delivered over*" (BT, 174). Here, the expression 'facticity' (*Faktizität*) must be distinguished from 'factuality' (*Tatsächlichkeit*), the sort of being which Husserl's reduction suspended: whereas factuality designates objects present at hand which could, according to their essence, be otherwise, facticity is particular to *Dasein*. According to Giorgio Agamben, the origin of Heidegger's use of this term can be found in Saint Augustine

> who writes '*facticia est anima*,' the human soul is factic (*factice*), in the sense that it was 'made' (*faite*) by God. In Latin, *facticius* is opposed to *nativus* and means '*qui non sponte fit*,' what is not natural, what did not come to be by itself. . . . One must hear this term in all its crudeness, for it is the same adjective which Augustine used to designate pagan idols, in an acceptation of the term which seems to correspond perfectly to our term 'fetish': *genus faecticiorum deorum*, a genre of made (*factice*) gods.[10]

Through its connection with facticity, thrownness thus suggests a certain nonoriginarity (*non sponte fit*) in *Dasein*. As thrown into the there where the Being it has to be is disclosed, *Dasein* is not the maker of its own Being. It did not come to be by itself but is assigned to be the being it is in the passivity of its thrownness. As Heidegger writes, "Dasein is something that has been thrown; it has been brought into its there, but *not* of its own accord" (BT, 329).

Since *Dasein* has been thrown passively into its there where it is affected, rather than having brought itself there, *Dasein*'s that-it-is "stares it in the face with the inexorability of an enigma" (BT, 175). *Dasein*'s thrownness thus issues in a certain opacity or darkness, an unsolvable riddle, in the midst of the fundamental disclosure of its Being. It cannot know its own being from the ground up or come to full self-consciousness since "it never comes back behind its thrownness in such a way that it might first release this 'that-it-is-and-has-to-be' from *its* Being-its-Self and lead it into the 'there'" (BT, 330). Missing its own origin, *Dasein* can never appropriate fully the being to which it is nonetheless irremissibly delivered over; the Being which *Dasein* has to be, the only being which it is and can be, is a being it can never be fully.

As thrown into the there, *Dasein* not only does not make its own being but has no ground on which to stand or prior condition in which it could rest—*Dasein* is abandoned to itself, left on its own. Though *Dasein* is not the maker or originator of its own Being, it is in some sense fair to speak of it as first or ultimate, what Heidegger calls a thrown basis [*geworfene Grund*]: "as *this entity* to which it has been delivered over, it *is, in its existing,* the basis of its potentiality-for-Being. Although it has not laid that basis [*Grund*] itself, it reposes in the weight of it, which is made manifest to it as a burden by Dasein's mood" (BT, 330). *Dasein* is ultimate in that it alone bears the burden of (is responsible for?) Being,[11] and yet its facticity or its thrownness introduces a secondariness into this new subject of phenomenology: *Dasein* is the ultimate subject of phenomenological thought (it bears the burden of Being), yet it is not first in itself, not its own maker. *Dasein* is ultimate, though it is always preceded by an instance it can never name.

When Heidegger claims that *Dasein* "never comes back behind its thrownness in such a way that it might first release its 'that-it-is-and-has-to-be' from *its Being*-its-Self and lead it into the 'there'" (BT, 330), he suggests that if *Dasein* is a basis or ground, it is nonetheless a ground or basis that is irremediably haunted by an absence—the origin it can never be or the abyss it hangs over. Heidegger goes on to articulate the sense in which thrown *Dasein* is a basis or ground in terms of a certain belatedness: "In being a basis [*Grund-seiend*]—that is, in existing as thrown—*Dasein* constantly lags behind its possibilities. It is never existent *before* its basis, but only *from it* and *as this basis*. Thus 'Being-a-basis' means *never* to have power over one's ownmost Being from the base up" (BT, 330). Thrownness thus means that *Dasein* always comes after its own origin. Lagging behind itself, *Dasein* is too late to lay the basis which it is—it is a basis which cannot master its own base.

To summarize the description of *Dasein*'s disclosure in affectedness, it is useful to consider the particular form which Heidegger uses to illustrate it, namely, the affect known as fear. In his illustration, Heidegger outlines a sort of double intentionality belonging to *Dasein*'s affectivity: (1) it discloses a being, and (2) affectivity discloses being at issue for me or mattering to me. According to Heidegger, fear reveals both *"that in the face of which* we fear, the fearsome" and *"that about which* fear fears . . . Dasein" (BT, 179, 180). It is this latter form of intentionality which is particular to affectivity and distinguishes it from other intentional comportments. Like other forms of intentionality (the constituting intentionality of *Dasein* as Ego, the concerned intentionality of *Dasein* as being-in-the world), fearing discloses a being, the fearsome. However, this first intentional disclosure is possible only insofar as a second intentionality reveals *Dasein* to itself. "Only an entity for which in its Being this very Being is an issue can be afraid. . . . Fear always reveals Dasein in the being of its there" (BT, 180). Without being at issue (*um . . . geht*) for itself in fear, without having beings matter to it (*angegangen*) in fear, *Dasein* would not "know" to be afraid and so would not disclose the fearsome being.

Insofar as affections disclose the fact that beings matter [*angegangen*, from *angehen*] to *Dasein*, they bring us to see the ontical distinctiveness of *Dasein*: namely, that "Being is an issue [*um . . . geht*] for it." In its affectedness, then, the existential analytic has found a way in which the subject of phenomenology shows itself phenomenologically, that is, in and from itself in its very Being. It is not by the heroic activity of reflection or beholding oneself that *Dasein* reveals its ownmost Being but by abandoning itself to its affectedness which assails it in its passivity. But, again, a difficulty emerges: "Dasein constantly surrenders itself to the 'world' and lets the 'world' matter to it in such a way that somehow Dasein evades its very self" (BT, 178). Since its double intentionality means that affectivity reveals both mineness and beings, including others, affectivity is the possibility of *Dasein*'s authentic disclosure of its ownmost being at issue for itself *and at the same time* the possibility of its being alienated from mineness. That is to say, in affectivity, *Dasein* is thrown into the there which, at the same time as it discloses its ownmost Being, discloses the others or the publicness that tempts *Dasein* into falling into an alienation that hides its mineness or being at issue for itself.

Isolating *Dasein*

If even in affectedness, *Dasein*'s self-attestation is likely to lead the existential analytic astray, how can *Dasein* attest to itself? Since affectedness remains the disclosure of mineness, Heidegger does not abandon the description but finds "an understanding affectedness [*Befindlichkeit*] in which Dasein has been disclosed to itself in some distinctive way" (BT, 226). Such an affection must be one which discloses *Dasein*'s being at issue for itself (the second or passive intentionality of affectedness) while suppressing the accompanying directedness toward a being in the world (the first or active intentionality of affectedness). In suppressing the worldly being disclosed in affectedness, *Dasein* is brought before itself without being brought before that which tempts *Dasein* to fall into alienation from mineness. Heidegger claims that the affection which accomplishes this is anxiety.

In a certain sense, the choice of anxiety is dictated by the interpretation of falling: without the interpretation of falling as the everyday being of *Dasein*, Heidegger would not have been led to the description of anxiety as the distinctive way in which *Dasein* is brought before itself. As Heidegger himself says, "in working out this basic affectedness [*Grundbefindlichkeit*] and characterizing ontologically what is disclosed in it as such, we shall take the phenomenon of falling as our point of departure" (BT, 227). Starting with *Dasein*'s falling, a certain characterization of *Dasein*'s being and the mood in which it is understood is suggested to the existential analytic. "In falling, Dasein turns away from itself. That in the face of which it thus shrinks back must, in any case, be a being with the character of threatening; yet this entity has the same kind of Being as the one that shrinks back: it is Dasein itself" (BT, 230). Hence, as it discloses a threat, *Dasein*'s falling suggests that the fundamental affection resembles fear, and yet since falling flees not from an entity in the world but rather from mineness to an entity, this affection is not fear. It is instead anxiety. How then does Heidegger describe the phenomenon of anxiety; what does he see in it such that *"the turning away of falling is grounded in anxiety"* (BT, 230)?

As with any and all *Dasein*'s affectedness, Heidegger proposes a twofold interpretation of anxiety, dividing his analysis into a discussion of (1) that in the face of which one has anxiety, and (2) that about which one is anxious.

1. According to Heidegger, that in the face of which one is anxious is being-in-the-world as such or *Dasein* itself. In anxiety, unlike in fear,

> that in the face of which one has anxiety is not a being within-the-world. . . . [The indeterminacy and indefiniteness of the source of anxiety] tells us that beings within-the-world are not 'relevant' at all. Nothing which is ready-to-hand or present-at-hand within the world functions as that in the face of which anxiety is anxious. . . . The world has the character of completely lacking significance. In anxiety one does not encounter this thing or that thing which, as something threatening, must have an involvement. (BT, 231)

In reducing beings to irrelevance and insignificance, anxiety discloses to *Dasein* the nothingness, precisely, of the world. It thus stands apart from fear in that whereas fear fears this or that being, "anxiety is anxious in the face of the 'nothing' of the world" (BT, 393). By bringing *Dasein* up against no-thing at all, anxiety thus isolates *Dasein*—setting it apart from the beings, and others, to which it is exposed in other affects. When beings thus fall away into insignificance, we are left only with what is no-thing in the world: namely, Being-in-the-world itself, *Dasein*. The ontical nothingness disclosed in anxiety thus lets mineness appear as that in the face of which anxiety is anxious, thereby bringing *Dasein* back to its ownmost Being.

2. "That which anxiety is anxious about is Being-in-the-world itself" (BT, 232). As in all affection, anxiety thus discloses *Dasein*'s being at issue for itself in this being affected. Anxiety does so in a distinctive way, however, since, in it, beings and others sink away, leaving *Dasein* in the company of no-thing. This sinking away of beings and others thus removes the shelter, or cause, in which *Dasein* hides from its ownmost being at issue for itself.

> The world can offer nothing more and neither can the Dasein-with of others. Anxiety thus takes away from Dasein the possibility of understanding itself, as it falls, in terms of the 'world' and public interpretation. Anxiety throws Dasein back upon that which it is anxious about—its authentic potentiality-for-Being-in-the-world. Anxiety singularizes Dasein [*Die*

Angst vereinzelt das Dasein] for its ownmost Being-in-the-world. . . . Anxiety makes manifest in Dasein its Being towards its ownmost potentiality
for Being. (BT, 232)

Since beings and others fall away, anxiety throws *Dasein* back onto its mineness, without allowing it the possibility of understanding itself in such a
way that it might flee or hide from the dreadful nothingness of its own. It
thus isolates or singularizes *Dasein*, thereby serving the methodological function of a pure, uncontaminated disclosure of *Dasein*'s ownmost being and
making it possible for *Dasein* to attest to mineness purely from its ownmost
being. Since anxiety discloses *Dasein*'s ownmost being at issue for itself and
nothing else, Jean Greisch writes aptly of it, "I do not undergo or understand mineness truly except in and through anxiety. We could equally say
that anxiety is mineness undergone as affection."[12]

At this point, it again becomes possible to see how Heidegger's method
radicalizes, at the same time as it criticizes, the phenomenological practice
of Husserl. For anxiety, in a sense, has effected the reduction. It leads *Dasein*
back to itself in such a way that *Dasein* can now show itself as itself from
itself, and it does so precisely by suspending beings. Like Husserl's reduction, this annulment of beings makes manifest that which is not a being
among them (here, *Dasein*; for Husserl, the sphere of consciousness) but
which is the very possibility of Being: "Being 'is' only in the understanding
of those entities to whose Being something like an understanding of Being
belongs; namely, Dasein" (BT, 228). Anxiety isolates the 'being' in which
the Being of beings is to be found. But, this isolation of *Dasein* does not
mean that *Dasein* is a windowless monad or even a separate thing which
only reaches out to a world after being closed in itself. Instead, anxiety
isolates *Dasein* as openness or exposure since it isolates the mattering by
which any being is at issue for and has an affect on *Dasein*.

Insofar as anxiety reveals mineness or *Dasein*'s being at issue, it is not just
one affection among others but is in fact the fundamental or primordial
affectedness accompanying all others—Heidegger even calls it the "basic
state of mind [*Grundbefindlichkeit*]." Since only a being for which being is at
issue can be affected and since anxiety is the disclosure of mineness in
which being is at issue for itself, no affect is possible without a primordial
anxiety accompanying it. "Only because anxiety is always latent in Being-
in-the-world [*Dasein*] can such Being-in-the-world [*Dasein*] . . . ever be
afraid" (BT, 234). This is so not only because anxiety is affection by the
mineness that accompanies all affection but also because it is precisely anxiety which *Dasein* flees in its falling toward beings. *Dasein* is affected, in fearing, for instance, only because it flees its primordial anxiety toward beings
which can then threaten it.

Even if "from an ontological-existential point of view the not-at-home
[of anxiety] must be conceived as the more primordial phenomenon," it
remains second in the order of discoveries made by the existential ana-

lytic—coming after the analysis of *Dasein*'s falling into the world of concern and publicness. One can only wonder, at this point, if the privilege accorded to anxiety does not devolve from the interpretation of concern and publicness as falling: would Heidegger's path have crossed anxiety and would this anxiety have taken on the distinct and fundamental methodological function of isolating *Dasein* and its mineness if publicness and concern were not interpreted as *Dasein*'s falling or inauthenticity? These questions will be developed more fully below in light of Levinas's consideration of the extraordinary everydayness of fear for the death of the other.

Anxiety isolates *Dasein*, bringing it back to its ownmost Being and annulling the beings within-the-world which tempt it to interpret itself in terms of others or the world of its concern. Anxiety thus assails *Dasein* without there being any other assailant but *Dasein* itself—*Dasein* is anxious about the nothing it itself is. There is, in other words, a coincidence or "selfsameness of that in the face of which and that about which one has anxiety" (BT, 233). This coincidence suggests a certain reflexivity in *Dasein*'s primordial affect, a reflexivity which is not that of an immanent perception but which nonetheless suggests a certain self-relation. This reflexive structure of existence (it certainly is not consciousness's reflection on its self) would be expressed in the verb that Heidegger uses to designate *Dasein*'s primordial being affected: *sich ängstigen*, a reflexive verb. One might object that this verb should be taken passively, as is suggested by the fact that anxiety is an affect into which *Dasein* is thrown. However, when Heidegger writes that anxiety reveals "a threat which reaches Dasein itself and which comes from Dasein itself," he seems to acknowledge the existential-ontological significance of this grammatical reflexive (BT, 234). In a sense, then, *Dasein* gives its anxiety to itself, even if it does this passively and without knowing the whence and whither. *Dasein*'s passivity is rooted in an existential and reflexive auto-affection.

My Death

Holding *Dasein* open or exposed to a threat that comes from nothing and nowhere, anxiety is closely connected to the phenomenon of death since "death, as possibility, gives Dasein nothing" (BT, 307). In other words, the nothing that is revealed in anxiety is given to *Dasein* by its own death: "in [anxiety], Dasein finds itself *before* the 'nothing' of the possible impossibility of its existence [i.e., death]" (BT, 310). Since it emerges in anxiety where *Dasein* is isolated or brought back to its ownmost being, death, too, will constitute and reveal the mineness of *Dasein*. For this reason, no account of the meaning of *Dasein*'s ownmost Being is complete without a consideration of that possibility, death, which necessarily always accompanies anxiety. If anxiety is the affection in which mineness is revealed, then death is the very meaning of *Dasein*'s ownmost Being.

Heidegger's account of death begins by noting a curious fact, one that seems to contradict the claim that death is the meaning of *Dasein*'s being: when *Dasein* reaches its death, "it simultaneously loses the Being of its 'there.' By its transition to no-longer Dasein [*Nichtmehrdasein*], it gets lifted right out of the possibility of experiencing this transition and of understanding it as something experienced" (BT, 281). This observation of the obvious seems to imply that death marks the loss of the very being whose meaning it is supposed to reveal. At the very moment when the meaning of its ownmost being will have been disclosed, *Dasein* is cast out of the there where such a disclosure would happen, so *Dasein* always misses its own Being.

According to Heidegger, the impossibility of experiencing death leads an everyday understanding to take the death of others as a substitute theme where death is observed or experienced. Such an understanding overlooks the phenomenon of death in at least two ways. First, in funeral rites and mourning rituals, it overlooks the loss which death is by dealing with the loss experienced by those who remain. "In suffering this loss, however, we have no way of access to the loss-of-Being as such which the dying man 'suffers'" (BT, 282). Second, and more importantly, "this is what one presupposes when one is of the opinion that any Dasein can be substituted for another at random, so that what cannot be experienced in one's own Dasein is accessible in that of a stranger" (BT, 283). Such an access to death is therefore thoroughly determined by *Dasein*'s falling into publicness where everyone is the other, a they-self, and no one is his own. To experience death by observing it in another is already to overlook the mineness of *Dasein*'s Being, the mineness which is revealed in the radical isolation and individualization of anxiety. As such, it results from *Dasein*'s flight from the very thing which is being sought.

In my death, by contrast, it is a matter of what no one can do in my place. In denying the possibility that another might represent or substitute himself for me, my death singularizes me radically, leaving me alone with my own. In *Dasein*'s dying, Heidegger writes, "there is by its very essence no representing. These are the facts of the case existentially; one fails to recognize this when one interposes the expedient of making the dying of Others a substitute theme" (BT, 284). It would seem, then, that the facts of the case make it impossible for the existential analytic to arrive at an adequate interpretation of the very meaning of *Dasein*'s ownmost being: at the very moment my own is revealed, in death, I am unable to be there to disclose it. Having disclosed *Dasein*'s ownmost Being in anxiety, is the existential analytic now doomed to halt the moment it attempts to interpret the meaning of this being as death?

This would be the case if *Dasein* were a being like others, but as existing, *Dasein*'s end belongs to its being in a unique way: "Dasein always exists in such a manner that its 'not yet' *belongs* to it. . . . As long as any Dasein is, it *is already its 'not yet'*" (BT, 287, 288). Always "not-yet" as long as *Dasein* exists, death is not encountered in some future present moment (like the completed ripening of a fruit ready to be plucked), nor has it come when all that is outstanding for *Dasein* has come together in a whole (like a mortgage repaid). Rather, as long as *Dasein* exists, death is always impending or yet to come, like an infinite debt or an obligation that cannot be met. Death is a not yet which *Dasein* has to be as long as it is there since if death were to reach it *Dasein* would no longer be there. This means that in its ownmost being *Dasein* is always somehow lacking or not sufficient to itself; an inexpugnable not-yet belongs to mineness.

Since death as "not-yet" belongs to the constitution of *Dasein*'s own Being, the existential analytic interprets this Being as "Being-toward-the-end." *Dasein is* toward an end, an end at which *Dasein* never arrives as long as it *is* but which it is only by being toward. "The 'ending' which we have in view when we speak of death does not signify Dasein's Being-at-an-end, but a *Being-towards-the end* of this entity. Death is a way to be, which Dasein takes over as soon as it is" (BT, 289). Since the existential analytic discloses death as Being-toward-the-end, the possibility of death is revealed before the "end" of Dasein. If death is not a point at which *Dasein* arrives or which arrives to *Dasein* but a way for *Dasein* to be, then *Dasein* is, in a certain sense, its death; or, *Dasein* is by dying.

Disclosed in *Dasein*'s being toward, but never at, an end which is always impending, death is nevertheless certain: it cannot be doubted that one dies. But, according to Heidegger, this certainty is misunderstood when theoretical understanding relegates it to a merely empirical certainty. For theoretical understanding, death is certain in the sense that it happens to everyone; yet, since we are never able to make it present to us and so can know nothing of it, this certainty "necessarily falls short of the highest certainty, the apodictic" (BT, 301). Heidegger wrote these lines before Husserl's *Cartesian Meditations* and so at a time when apodicticity and adequacy of intuition went hand-in-hand. The certainty of death therefore falls short of the highest certainty in that it is never presented with adequate intuition. I should note that in *Cartesian Meditations*, however, Husserl suggests that there might be an apodictic certainty which is not given in an adequate evidence. In these terms, Being-toward-death might have the highest or apodictic certainty. In the terms used by *Being and Time*, however, death is never presented in the adequacy of evidence that would render it apodictically certain, and for a thought of such an apodicticity, it becomes a nonphilosophical or empirical problem, one that befalls beings present-at-hand in the world: death happens to others or to everyone (the they-self: "one dies," but that won't happen to me). When death is merely certain, as it is here, it becomes possible for *Dasein* to evade its being-certain of this death by saying, "'death certainly comes, but not right away.' With this 'but . . . ,' the 'they' denies that death is certain" (BT, 302).

But in this denial, the death which is denied is not the death that is integral to the doing and undoing of *Dasein*'s ownmost Being. Taking the certainty of death in this way "covers up what is peculiar in death's certainty—*that it is possible at any moment.* Along with the certainty of death, goes the indefiniteness of its 'when'" (BT, 302). Thus, for the existential analytic, since it inquires into *Dasein*'s being, another certainty appears. This certainty sees death as a possibility that is *Dasein*'s ownmost precisely because it is a possibility belonging to any and every moment. It is in a sense the one event that could befall *Dasein* at any time. Even if the arrival of death cannot be expected, awaited, or in any way calculated such that it appears in the present, it is nonetheless certain—but with a certainty that is not that of an evidence, neither of merely empirical evidence nor of adequate theoretical evidence. This certainty falls short of apodicticity only when apodicticity is equated with adequate evidence, an evidence reached only in theory. Following the distinctions, Husserl adopts in *Cartesian Meditations,* however, death can be said to be apodictically certain, though it cannot be known adequately.

Death is not only one way to be among others but is in fact a distinctive way for *Dasein* to be. According to Heidegger, as that which nobody can do in my place or take away from me, death brings *Dasein* to stand before its ownmost being by tearing it away from the they in which the Being of the I has been interpreted in such a way that it can be exchanged with any and every other. In death, *Dasein*'s very Being is precisely the issue since death threatens to take away just that, existence. "Death is Dasein's *ownmost* possibility. Being toward this possibility discloses to Dasein its *ownmost* potentiality-for-Being, in which its very Being is the issue. Here it can become manifest to Dasein that in this distinctive possibility of its own self, it has been wrenched away from the 'they'" (BT, 307). As in anxiety, death isolates *Dasein,* leaving itself to itself and detaching it from the seductiveness by which they have interpreted the being of *Dasein.*

> Death is a possibility which Dasein has to take over in every case. With death, Dasein stands before itself in its ownmost potentiality for Being. This is a possibility in which the issue is nothing less than Dasein's Being-in-the-world. Its death is the possibility of no-longer-being-able-to-be-there. If Dasein stands before itself as this possibility, it has been fully assigned to its ownmost potentiality for Being. When it stands before itself in this way, all its relations to any other Dasein have been undone. (BT, 294)

Bringing *Dasein* to stand before itself, death assigns *Dasein* to its ownmost possibility of being with an assignation that takes place in what Courtine calls "the mortal reflection."[13]

This "mortal reflection," while bringing *Dasein* before itself, also brings it before its own undoing; it is a reflection with mortal consequences. In this way, the reflection would signal not *Dasein*'s return to itself but its separation from itself.[14] *Dasein* would be brought before itself, in death, as if by a mirror whose glass bars it from laying hold of itself. This is contained in Heidegger's formulation: "death is the possibility of the absolute impossibility of Dasein" (BT, 294; see also 307). It brings *Dasein* before its ownmost possibility as before one that is impossible for it to be. As the possibility of impossibility, death gives *Dasein*'s ownmost possibility at the same time that it takes away all being-possible: *Dasein*'s "uttermost possibility lies in giving itself up," emptying itself of its Being (BT, 308).

Not only is the possibility of death distinctive in that it brings *Dasein* before its ownmost Being, it is also the possibility that opens all possibility, or "the possibility that possibilizes all others."[15] This is so for at least two reasons: (1) In bringing *Dasein* before its own Being-in-the-world, death brings *Dasein* back to its thrownness into the there where it has its possibilities to be or not to be. In bringing *Dasein* back from the inauthenticity of publicness to the possibility of authenticity, death opens an alternative which makes possibility possible. (2) More importantly, as always imminent, impending, or not-yet, death makes it possible for *Dasein* to be ever ahead of itself and thus to have its being as ever more possibilities to be or not. The possibility of death "discloses to existence that its uttermost possibility lies in giving itself up, and thus it shatters all one's tenaciousness to whatever existence one has reached" (BT, 308). Since as long as *Dasein* exists, the possibility of death remains, *Dasein*'s existence is never fully actual but always still remains possible. In this way, the possibility of death opens the possibility of the possible by disclosing to *Dasein* that at least one more possibility remains possible for existence as long as it is not yet dead.

Since death is not an end at which *Dasein* arrives like a ripened fruit nor a possibility which it actualizes by making use of its availability, being toward death opens immeasurable possibility, measureless because even the possibility of the impossible is included. In anticipating death,

> one does not tend towards concernfully making available something actual; but as one comes closer understandingly, the possibility of the possible just becomes "greater." . . . The more unveiledly this possibility gets understood, the more purely does the understanding penetrate into it *as the possibility of the impossibility of any existence at all*. . . . In the anticipation of this possibility it becomes "greater and greater." (BT, 306)

In Being-toward-death, *Dasein* by no means narrows down its possibilities but opens them more and more, ever more, to the point that even the impossible appears possible. So long as *Dasein* exists, its possibilities are not exhausted since the possibility of impossibility, as impossible, remains ever ahead of it, opening immeasurable possibilities before it.

Ethical Phenomenology and Prephilosophical Experience

My reading has suggested that the drive to push philosophy to more closely realize the phenomenological insight leads Heidegger and Levinas to discover a subjectivity that is structured in quite similar ways. To summarize these similarities: (1) Both *Dasein*'s mineness and the responsible self subvert the phenomenological I, pure or absolute consciousness, by an analysis of what precedes and undoes it. (2) Both thereby accomplish an immanent critique or a correction of phenomenology that was called for by phenomenological analysis itself. (3) Both undo the self-grounding a priori of consciousness and do so in terms of a de-posited subject—one that is first deposited before positing itself and so one that is de-posited or displaced in its very position of subject. (4) This deposited subject is expressed in terms of a singularity or uniqueness of the self which precedes and undoes consciousness. (5) Both deposit the subject and find its uniqueness in the description of a certain affectedness, which for both entails an irreducible passivity. (6) This irreducible passivity is articulated in terms of a belatedness of the deposited subject and an inescapable exposure to the burden that it supports. (7) Therefore, both *Dasein* and the responsible self name an ultimate which, as ultimate, is first or the condition of all but which is not its own origin and so, even as first, is always preceded by . . . , always open or exposed to the burden it supports. Commenting on a similar set of observations relating to Heidegger and Levinas, Jean-Luc Marion has written, "Inasmuch as its facticity, its thrownness, and its anticipatory resoluteness oppose it radically to the Husserlian *I*, Dasein could also be translated by *me voici* (here I am [Levinas's formulation of the subject]): *da-sein* (being-there), Being exposed here (*être exposé ici*), Being insofar as exposed here. Dasein does not receive any other privilege except to be exposed to, to put itself in play and to decide for the sake of the Being of beings; it can do so only by virtue of its exposedness. . . . Exposure thus characterizes Dasein as much as 'here I am.'"[16]

I suspect that the claim to have brought together the structure of the responsible self and the mineness of *Dasein* will not be admitted by many of Levinas's more zealous adherents. This is to be expected, since Levinas himself would reject my interpretation of Heidegger—most notably on two points: (1) The passivity of thrownness, according to Levinas, is recovered or assumed in a project whereby *Dasein* throws itself forward into the possibilities it was thrown into; in this way, the passivity of thrownness is converted into an act or is accepted and assumed in resolute decision. The task of existence is, roughly, to want all that happens to it, even if I am not the origin of it. (2) *Dasein*'s exposure is fundamentally an exposure to itself, an exposure which rests on a reflective structure. I have tried to show how the ambiguity of passivity and reflexivity does indeed remain in certain passages of *Being and Time* but also how the remnants of a reflective subject might be undone by the analysis of death. Granting these significant distinctions, let me point out three evidences in favor of my proposed rapprochement.

1. Levinas himself seems to offer evidence in support of my view when he writes, "*My* substitution. It is as *my own [mienne]* that substitution for the neighbor is produced" (OBBE, 126). Thus, the mineness which Heidegger uncovers in anxious being toward death echoes in the substitution of the responsible self. Just as anxious being toward death reduces the ego to its

ownmost and unique *Dasein* by bringing it before a possibility (death) which it alone has, so too does substitution reduce the self to its own and unique self: "no one can substitute himself for me who substitutes himself for all" (OBBE, 126).

2. Since the mineness of *Dasein*'s being does not mean an affirmation of its self that is produced by returning from its negation to itself but the undeclinability of its death, *Dasein*'s mineness (death) deprives it of its being. Depriving *Dasein* of its being in the very move by which it gives its being to it, death resembles substitution. In substitution I am myself in that only I substitute myself for every other and thereby dispossess myself of myself: "in substitution my being that belongs to myself . . . is undone, and it is through this substitution that I am not 'another' but me" (OBBE, 127).

3. Finally, just as the responsible self is unique in that only it is exposed radically in the passivity of affectivity, so too is *Dasein* alone the being who in its very being is exposed radically. To be sure, anxiety isolates *Dasein* but it isolates *Dasein* as the very place of exposure, as the exposure that precedes all exposure to this or that. For *Dasein,* what is at issue in its own being is not only its own being but much more than that: *Dasein*'s exposure is so radical that in its own being it is open not only to its own being but to the Being of beings, to such a point that *Dasein* is the scene where the question of Being is worked out. Even Levinas himself seems to admit that Heidegger's existential correction to phenomenology might have already uncovered what his own ethical correction does when he asks, "Did not Heidegger, despite all that he wants to teach about the priority of the 'thought of being'—here run up against the original significance of ethics?" (EN, 168).[17]

If one is convinced by these philosophical similarities between *Dasein* and the responsible self, what then accounts for the gap, sometimes a battlefront, separating the two? How are these subjects different if philosophy articulates a similar structure for each? In a sense the answer is obvious: In responsibility, the subject is exposed to the Other; I am responsible for others. In existing, *Dasein* is exposed to Being; *Dasein* supports the burden of Being. The philosophical issue between Heidegger and Levinas concerns less the structure of subjectivity than it does the question whether or not this subject signifies in existential or ethical terms: Does the uniqueness or subjectivity of the subject consist simply in giving itself up (Heidegger) or in giving itself to another (Levinas)? Between Heidegger and Levinas, philosophy does not choose different structures of subjectivity but different orders in which it might signify.

Now, how is phenomenological philosophy to decide between the two? Or, on what basis does Levinas, coming after Heidegger, decide that the subject of phenomenology is responsibility and not existence? I'd like to suggest that such a decision depends less on the necessities of phenomenological philosophy than it does on an interpretive decision taken by Levinas. This would be the point where nonphilosophical "experiences" exercise a determining influence over philosophy: If Levinas decides ultimately that the subject is responsibility, despite the seeming philosophical undecidability between the responsible self and *Dasein,* this decision is made in response to appeals or claims coming not from philosophy but from—where? From the Other. Would Levinas's decision to treat the subject of phenomenology as responsible thus indicate the point at which ethics is no longer philosophy, the point at which philosophy yields to a prephilosophical experience of ethics? The ethical, before philosophy, would be found in Levinas's decision to interpret the appeal as having come from an other. This is why Levinas can draw the introduction of *Otherwise than Being, or, Beyond Essence* to a close with the rather frank admission, "No doubt [the progress of this work] is not completely disengaged from pre-philosophical experiences" (OBBE, 20).

In addition to this, one can also look to the characterization of the Other as "the widow, the orphan, the poor" and the response of the responsible self as "Here I am!" At least once this response appears in quotation marks with a reference to the Hebrew Scriptures, Isaiah 6:8 (see OBBE, 199, n. 11), and the characterization of the Other is clearly also biblical. It could be said that these references, precisely as quotations, indicate an appeal to what is no longer given simply in phenomenological description but in religious tradition. They would once again mark the place at which nonphilosophical or prephilosophical experience intervenes to decide, or at least determine, the interpretation of the scene in which the subject is affected primally as responsibility. I will return to this point in part 3 of this book.

Love Strong as Death

If the issue between Heidegger and Levinas comes down to a question of interpreting the subject, this battle is fought over the interpretation of one phenomenon in particular: namely, death. In defense of his claim to a primarily ethical significance of the subject, Levinas offers an interpretation of death that challenges Heidegger's. He claims that the first sense of death is found not in anxious anticipation of it as my own but in the ethical concern of fearing for the death of the other. By challenging Heidegger's interpretation of death, Levinas seeks to undo the single most crucial phenomenon in the existential analytic, the one through which Heidegger is able to lay bare *Dasein*'s ownmost being.

My fear for the death of the other, according to Levinas, does not fall within the existential analysis of affectedness (*Befindlichkeit*), and it certainly does not fall within the existential analysis of fear in particular. "Fear for the death of the neighbor is my fear, but it is in no wise a fear *for* me" (GCM, 176). As in no way a fear for myself, the death of the other affects me in a fear which, according to Levinas, is not structured by the double intentionality of *Dasein.* As such, this fear strikes me without my being at issue for myself and therefore is not reducible to an anxiety in which this being at issue would be revealed. Unlike the affection of *Dasein*, "fear for the other man does not turn back into anxiety for *my* death. It overflows the ontology of Heideggerian Dasein. An ethical troubling of being, beyond its good conscience of being 'in view of this being itself' for which being-toward-death marks the end and the scandal" (GCM, 176). On this reading, fear for the death of the other is finally free of any reflexive foundation of the phenomenological subject. Whereas the Heideggerian analysis based all affectedness on the auto-affection of anxiety and thus let the passivity of *Dasein*'s affectedness hover in the ambiguity of passivity and reflexivity, Levinas's analysis of fear for the death of the other finally purges affectedness of any and all reflexive foundation: "the fear for the death of the other man is my fear, but is not in any way a being afraid of my own" (EN, 131 [modified]).

Since it suspends my own being at issue for myself, according to Levinas, fear for the death of the other casts me out of the *Da* of *Da-sein* where this being at issue is exposed. In fearing for the death of the other, I am no longer there where being is at issue for me. Far from being thrown into Being, the responsible self is thrown out or exiled from its place in Being (*Da-sein*), an utter re-ject, totally dis-inter-ested with regard to being. It is thus not there (*Da*) in the place where the question of being is asked but in a nonplace or utopia from which being is put into question. In fearing for the death of the other, responsibility is "the fear of occupying in the *Da* of my *Dasein* the place of someone; the incapacity of having a place, a profound utopia. Fear which comes to me from the face of the other" (EN, 130 [modified]). In fearing for the other's death, the responsible self fears being born into the world, being thrown into the place others might already occupy. It thus fears for the other before it is thrown into the place where it is at issue for itself, and even before it is.

By finding the signification of the phenomenological subject in fear for the other's death, not in anxiety about my own, Levinas claims that I am already myself in the everydayness of public life which Heidegger saw as the deepest alienation. Levinas uncovers "the signification of subjectivity in the extraordinary everydayness of my responsibility for other men, the extraordinary forgetting of death" or in "an ignorance of being and death which would not be an evasion, a cowardice, or a fall into the everyday or the courage for suicide" (OBBE, 141, 177). That is to say, when the everydayness of being with others is seen in an extraordinary way as responsibility above and beyond mere publicness, I am called as unique and irreplaceable in such a way that phenomenology has no need of a further reduction—like that effected in anxiety—to isolate the subject. Fear for the death of the other would thus introduce an "authenticity that, precisely, is not measured by what is proper to me, by *Eigentlichkeit*, or by what has already touched me, but rather by pure gratuity toward alterity" (GCM, 165). Interpreted as responsibility, the extraordinariness of the everyday or fearing would attest to the subject before its disclosure in anxiety. The subject would be disclosed in the everydayness of fear, and thus its disclosure would dispense with valorizing the lonely bout with anxiety.

According to Levinas, then, death already regards me in and through the face of the Other before it concerns me as the death I encounter as my own in anxious anticipation. The first sense of death is delivered to me not in my anxious anticipation of my own but in the ethical appearance of the face—"as though the invisible death that the face of the other is facing . . . were my affair. As if, ignored by the other, whom it concerns already in the nudity of his face, death 'regarded me' before its confrontation with me, before being the death which stares at me myself" (GCM, 162). In the face, death concerns me without being my own death and without my own being at issue in this death which affects me. The issue here is not so much whether I can die in the place of the Other. I obviously cannot; for he will surely die someday whether or not I stand on the gallows in his place ("'Tis a far better thing I do than I have ever done before"). The issue is whether I can be affected by his death before or without concern for my own.

For Levinas, then, the responsible self is the birth of a "'being able to die' subject to sacrifice" (OBBE, 128). Responsibility means the possibility of a sacrifice of self in which the self sacrifices even its own death in order to offer itself, gratuitously, to the neighbor—"the capacity for the ultimate gift of dying for the other" (GCM, 163, modified).[18] Against reducing the subject, ultimately, to the anxious anticipation of its own death, this ultimate gift or sacrifice witnesses a "love as irrefragable as death," and so a love which would rival the place of death in determining the subjectivity of the subject (EN, 169 [modified]). In responsibility, Levinas claims to have found "the future of death in the present of love" (EN, 217).[19] This love is not the reciprocity of an amorous couple. If Levinas adopts the term "love," it is only because he comes to see it as a sacrifice of self, a gratuitous devotion of all oneself to the other. In such a love, I am no longer at issue for myself but obsessed by the death of the other; it is not my death but the other's which individualizes me. When I love, I sacrifice all my possibilities, even the possibility most my own (that of my own death), in dying for the other.

PART 3
Levinas and
the Philosophy of Religion

7

The Death of God and Emergence of the Philosophy of Religion

After having practiced the reduction to the point at which it laid bare the transcendental ego, Husserl asked himself, "As one who is meditating in the Cartesian manner, what can I do with the transcendental ego philosophically?" (CM, 27). This question should be heard as an exclamation that one utters upon discovering a rich field of untapped treasure. For Husserl, the answer is found in the phenomenological exploration of consciousness as "an infinite realm of being of a new kind, as the sphere of a new kind of experience: transcendental experience" (CM, 27), and what can be done in and through this exploration is nothing less than the constitution of the entire objective world in its possibility.

Now, the same question might very well be asked of Levinas's ethical philosophy: "What can I do with [the responsible subject] philosophically?" Of what is philosophy capable if it adopts the figure of ethical phenomenology? What phenomena appear to a philosopher venturing into this strange land? In the third and final part of this book, I want to follow Levinas in exploring this land and show that one of the things of which such a philosophy is capable is a philosophy of religion—but not just any philosophy of religion. In Levinas's phenomenology, religious and theological thought find relief in the philosophy of religion: this philosophy of religion is capable of salvaging the intelligibility of religious notions (chapter 8) and of guaranteeing the significance of a transcendent God (chapter 9) in a postmodern or postmetaphysical age, an age which has been deemed the most irreligious or atheistic.

Metaphysics and the Necessity for the Death of God

If Levinas's phenomenological philosophy does indeed open the significance of religious phenomena, including God, then it is something of an
aberration in contemporary times. In the twentieth century, or in the so-
called postmodern age, those thinkers who stand at the end of metaphysics
have, for the most part, also stood for, or at least borne witness to, the death
of God. I need name only a few of these postmetaphysical or postmodern
thinkers for one to see the common destiny of metaphysics and God at the
end of metaphysics: Friedrich Nietzsche and Jean-Paul Sartre, Karl Marx
and Sigmund Freud, etc. This fact has been formulated well by Jean-Luc
Marion:

> Since metaphysics was coming to an end, being completed and disappear-
> ing, the question of God was coming to a close. Throughout the century
> that is now ending, everything happened as if the question of God could
> do nothing other than make common cause, positively or negatively, with
> the destiny of metaphysics.[1]

But why should the question of God stand or fall with the fate of metaphysics? According to Marion, this observed fact can be explained by reference
to the conceptual definition of metaphysics worked out by Martin Heidegger in his essay "The Onto-theological Constitution of Metaphysics." In
brief, Heidegger argued that metaphysics is constituted by forgetfulness of
the difference between Being as such and beings—the ontological difference. Even when it claims to think Being, metaphysics never thinks Being
as such but rather as a being since it thinks Being without distinguishing
it (that is, without discerning its difference) from beings. Being, then, is
determined as the indispensable and inseparable ground of beings. When
metaphysics thinks beings, it accounts for them in terms of their ground in
what is most general, or universally valid, in them: namely, Being as the
highest universal. Heidegger calls this the metaphysical reduction of Being
as such to beingness or the beingness of beings and claims that it has been
thought traditionally in onto-logy. But, Heidegger claims, metaphysics is
also theo-logy because, having forgotten the ontological difference, metaphysics thinks this highest universal only by thinking it in terms of a highest being or being par excellence—that is, by thinking Being as grounded in
God. In this way, metaphysics is, integrally and inescapably, linked to the
question of God.

    If, in God, metaphysics represents the ultimate ground or foundation of
universal being, then this God must be conceived in such a way that it is
adequate to this role, which means that it must be a cause or ground beyond which there are no others. Consequently, metaphysics conceives
God as *causa sui*, the self-caused cause which as self-causing needs no more
ground. According to Heidegger, "Being as the ground is thought out fully
only when the ground is represented as the first ground. . . . The Being of

beings is represented fundamentally, in the sense of the ground, only as *causa sui*. This is the metaphysical concept of God."[2] Thus, the metaphysical God is, as Marion says, always a concept of "the being par excellence that operates as and through efficiency such that, in special metaphysics, it can thereby ensure a ground for every common being."[3] In other words, God enters metaphysics as the being who is conceived under the concept of causality in order to account for Being in general by serving as its foundation or ground. Such a concept of God is indispensable to the metaphysical truth of beings. Inversely, the metaphysical understanding of the truth of beings is indispensable for such a concept of God.

In Marion's view, the Heideggerian conception of metaphysics "also allows us to understand how it was possible to speak of an 'end of metaphysics.'"[4] How so? As the search for a cause, reason, or ground of beings, metaphysics arises in response to the question "why is there something rather than nothing?" Now, on Nietzsche's analysis, the end of metaphysics, nihilism, means that "the aim is lacking; 'why?' finds no answer."[5] With the advent of nihilism, according to Nietzsche, the metaphysical question "why?" or "on what grounds?" is turned against metaphysics itself, rendering questionable all grounding institutions by endlessly asking every supposed ground "why?" or "on what grounds?" it is instituted. The nihilistic question is thus the same question as that to which the metaphysical institution of the ground responds—only now the question finds no stopping point. As Nietzsche has written, "the nihilistic question 'for what?' is rooted in the old [metaphysical] habit of supposing that the goal must be put up, given, demanded, *from outside*—by some *superhuman authority*."[6] Nietzsche's understanding of the end of metaphysics is, thus, only the extreme consequence of metaphysics—nihilism is metaphysics pushed to its extreme, logical conclusion.

Insofar as one can speak of the end of metaphysics, one will also speak of the death of God since the end of metaphysics renders inoperative that which produced or justified the concept of God—the institution of the ground. Conceived as part of the metaphysical operation of grounding Being in general, God loses his place and function when the ground collapses on itself. Hence, God dies. But, the metaphysical God does not die in an optional or arbitrary way—that is, by the will or choice of particular thinkers. If the end of metaphysics is implied in its concept, then as soon as God appears in metaphysics, his death has already begun.

Another reading of Nietzsche confirms that God's death is inevitable from the moment he appears in metaphysics. This can be seen in the fact that the forces who (1) create God are the same as those who (2) kill God.

1. According to a well-known Nietzschean thesis, God is the name for the highest ideals and for the ideal world in general, so whenever Nietzsche speaks of God (at least the old God, the Christian God, the dead God), he means also metaphysics. This is what is meant by the famous pronouncement of Christianity as "Platonism for the people."

Now, according to Nietzsche, metaphysics, and its God, are rooted in a shape of the moral consciousness. These moral roots of metaphysics are identified in one of the five great "No's!" that Nietzsche states in a fragment from *The Will to Power:* "Insight into the *moralization* of all previous philosophies and valuations."[7] Importantly, it is not just any morality which has determined the tradition of metaphysical philosophy, but a particular brand of morality: namely, the morality belonging to the forces of *ressentiment.* In Nietzsche's philosophy, the history of metaphysics and its God is reduced to its ground in a will to power driven by the reactive forces of *ressentiment.* That is to say, it is *ressentiment,* or the spirit of revenge, which drives the will to create a metaphysical world beyond the immanent or finite world of becoming. "This, indeed this alone is what revenge is: the will's ill will against time and its 'it was.'"[8] Suffering the passage of time and becoming, angry at the becoming past of all things, and unable to discharge itself ("powerless against what has been done . . . an angry spectator of all that is past"), the will of *ressentiment* seeks revenge by inventing an ideal world of essences or true Being—in a word, in God—beyond time wherein the really real resides. *Ressentiment* thereby achieves its revenge against time and becoming by evaluating it from the perspective of the divine world beyond, in view of which the value of this world is negated.

Along with this metaphysical world, even as the name for this metaphysical world, God is produced when the reactive forces of morality become creative. In a perhaps more familiar version of this story, God is born in the "dark workshop" of reactive forces. In "this workshop where *ideals are manufactured,*" "subjection to those one hates [is being lied] into 'obedience' (that is, to one of whom they say he commands this subjection—they call him God)."[9] Unable to discharge their will against those who persecute them, the forces of *ressentiment* invent an ideal world which deems their suffering a virtue commanded by God and rewarded in heaven. The forces of *ressentiment* invent a God in order not only to justify the suffering inflicted upon them by their persecutors (my suffering means that I am Good and will be rewarded in Heaven), but also to assure that their suffering will be avenged by the eventual punishment of their oppressors (those who cause pain are evil because they break the Law of God; they will be punished in Hell). Whether as revenge against time or the strong, both God and the metaphysical world are made and sustained by the forces of *ressentiment* seeking an imaginary revenge against a cause of their suffering.

2. Now, according to a perhaps less well-known Nietzschean thesis, it is these same forces of *ressentiment* that are responsible for the death of God. One of the accounts of the death of God given by Zarathustra helps us see this. According to Zarathustra, God dies at the hands of the ugliest man. When the ugliest man asks, "What is the revenge against the witness? . . . Who am I?" Zarathustra responds, "I recognize you well. . . . You are the murderer of God. . . . You could not bear him who always saw you—who always saw you through and through, you ugliest man! You took revenge

on the witness."[10] So not only does Zarathustra identify the murderer of God, he also provides a motive—revenge. It thus seems that God dies for the very same reason he was born: originally created as man's revenge for the suffering caused by life (its becoming past and the pain inflicted by the strong), God is now killed as revenge for man's having suffered through his vision into man's ugliness. With the death of God, *ressentiment* totalizes its revenge, taking revenge on the last thing that withstands its rage: namely, the instrument of its own vengeance. Not only does the end of metaphysics follow from its concept, but so too does the death of God follow as the necessary and logical conclusion of his birth in metaphysics, that is, *ressentiment*.[11]

If this literary account is not enough, consider the following historical observation from Nietzsche:

> During the moral epoch of mankind, one sacrificed to one's god one's own strongest instinct, one's 'nature': this festive joy lights up the cruel eyes of the ascetic. . . . Finally—what remained to be sacrificed? . . . didn't one have to sacrifice God himself and, from cruelty against oneself [i.e., asceticism], worship the stone, stupidity, gravity, fate, the nothing? To sacrifice God for the nothing.[12]

Nietzsche here sees the death of God, the sacrifice of God for the nothing, as the climax of the same forces of cruelty operative in the essentially religious ideal of asceticism or cruelty against oneself: namely, the forces of *ressentiment*. "An ascetic life is a self-contradiction: here rules a *ressentiment* without equal. . . . 'Triumph in the ultimate agony': the ascetic ideal has always fought under this hyperbolic sign."[13] Triumphing only in ultimate agony, the ascetic, driven by forces of revenge, achieves this ultimate triumph by murdering the God who saved his life—a victorious murder that is, by the very same blow, a suicide in which ascetic self-abnegation and cruelty consummates itself. For *ressentiment*, then, God's death is the rigorous statement of his birth.

Now, on this reading both the birth and the death of God belong to a particular form of morality such that the genealogy of morals appears to go hand-in-hand with a genealogy of religion.[14] What, then, if there were another form of morality? Might there be a morality for which the murder of God would *not* be the necessary and inevitable consequence? Levinas's responsible self offers one such possibility since this self, according to Levinas, is free of *ressentiment*. Having swallowed its own intentionality, this self does not seek to discharge itself when struck by its persecutors but takes upon itself responsibility for its persecution. Its extreme passivity means that it is a pure supporting, bearing the blows of others without reciprocating or discharging itself of the passion it undergoes in a reaction triumphantly acted out (imaginarily or not) against the cause of its persecution. Always too late, the responsible self neither finds nor knows a cause against which it could seek revenge; for the persecuting other is always leaving, precisely, traces. Taking responsibility even for the pain it suffers, the responsible self short-circuits the logic of revenge which leads inevitably from the birth to the death of God.[15] In marking an important transformation in the history or genealogy of responsibility, would Levinas's ethical phenomenology open a new moment in the genealogy of religion? I will explore this possibility in chapter 8.

Hegel and the Enlightenment "Death of God"

About the same time as metaphysics was coming to an end and God was dying, something else was emerging: the philosophy of religion. This is evident in Nietzsche's account of religion through a reduction to the philosophy of will to power. In Nietzsche, the genealogical account of religion in terms of the will to power both accomplishes and presupposes the death of God. It accomplishes the death of God in that the philosophy of will to power (the genealogy of religion) shows morality that it is rooted in the will to power which it despises; this philosophy of religion thus completes the death of God by bringing about the self-destruction of the forces which sustained God. Nietzsche's philosophical account of religion also presupposes the death of God in that its genealogical form is impossible if the highest values exist as metaphysical realities or things in themselves; that is to say, there can be no philosophy of religion as will to power when it is supposed that religious beliefs, values, and actions achieve their significance through a God outside them. Nietzsche is thus an exemplary figure of the connection between the death of God and the emergence of the philosophy of religion.

This connection is first apparent, however, in the philosophical thought of G. W. F. Hegel and his interpretation of modern philosophy, especially Kant, and so it is to a consideration of the death of God and the philosophy of religion in Hegel to which I now turn.

"God is dead" appears in Hegel's writings for the first time when in the work *Faith and Knowledge* (1802), he writes, "Formerly, the infinite grief existed historically in the formative process of culture. It existed in the feeling that 'God Himself is dead.'"[16] Even if Hegel's first statement of the death of God thus claims that this is "the feeling upon which the *religion* of more recent times rests," this statement is part and parcel of a critique of *philosophy* as figured in the leading philosophies of his time, the reflective philosophies of subjectivity found in Immanuel Kant, Friedrich Heinrich Jacobi, and Johann Gottlieb Fichte. The Enlightenment God is a dead God, according to Hegel, insofar as it is a totally abstract God who does not manifest himself in knowledge and since "spirit that does not manifest itself or reveal itself is something dead."[17]

On Hegel's reading, the death of God in modern philosophy began when Luther and his Reformation followers instituted an unbridgeable separation between finite human existence and transcendent or infinite divine

existence. Fearing that mediating structures such as icons and the sacra-
ments would pose a crisis for the faithful asked to believe, for instance, that
the (finite) bread and wine experienced at the Eucharist are in fact (divine,
infinite) body and blood, Protestantism banished the infinite from the intu-
itable, perceivable finite. Protestantism located religion in finite and limited
subjective feeling but in a subject still separated from God by the infinite
abyss of sin such that, across this distance, divinity remained an object of
longing and desire. For the Protestant, on Hegel's reading,

> beauty and truth present themselves in feelings and persuasions, in love
> and intellect [understanding]. Religion builds its temples and altars in the
> heart of the individual. In sighs and prayers, he seeks for the God whom
> he denies to himself in intuition, because of the risk that the intellect will
> cognize what is intuited as a mere thing, reducing the sacred grove to
> mere timber.[18]

According to Hegel, then, the unbridgeable gap between sighing, yearning
subjectivity and the God for whom it longs was established in order to ward
off the risk that knowledge, in the act of comprehending its object, will
reduce God to the level of man—or worse, that of a mere thing.

What Luther instituted as a prophylaxis of sorts—a prophylaxis against
denying the divinity of God in and through the act of reducing him to
finitude and immanence—backfires, or succeeds all too well, in its functioning and leaves an abstract, unknowable God whose transcendence is
preserved at the same time that his relevance is denied.[19] Frustrated by the
impossibility of satisfying its yearning for the infinite, sighing subjectivity
reconciles itself with the finitude to which it is confined and admits no
reality beyond empirical existence and the ordinary, everyday world. Hegel
writes,

> The infinite longing that yearns beyond body and world, reconciled itself
> with existence. But the reality with which it became reconciled, the objec-
> tive sphere acknowledged by subjectivity, was in fact merely empirical
> existence, the ordinary world and ordinary matters of fact [*Wirklichkeit*].
> Hence this reconciliation did not itself lose the character of absolute oppo-
> sition implicit in beautiful longing. Rather it flung itself upon the other
> pole of the antithesis, the empirical world.[20]

Subjectivity puts its longing to rest by absolutizing the position of finitude
and empirical reality—one might say, simply by forgetting what it could not
know and then forgetting this forgetting. This forsaking of transcendence
in the distance that was meant to protect it results in and belongs to the
good conscience of a subject "allowed to confide in ordinary life and surrender to it without sin" tarnishing its clean conscience and recording the
absence of the transcendence it has forsaken.[21] Such a God is not alive for
such a subject. This is at least one of the things Hegel means when he writes
that "the religion of more recent times rests" on "the feeling that God Himself is dead."

Thoroughly entrenched in the culture of the age, modern or Enlightenment philosophy, as represented by Kant, Fichte, and Jacobi, conceptual-
ized what existed historically as this "feeling that 'God Himself is dead.'"
Whereas Enlightenment philosophy by the time of Kant no longer absolutized empirical reality, it nevertheless, according to Hegel, had absolutized
the subjective experience wherein the possibility of this reality was constituted. Knowledge was confined to the phenomenal realm where the activity of the finite, human mind contributed to the experience made.

> The fixed standpoint which the all-powerful culture of our time has estab-
> lished for philosophy is [one where] philosophy cannot aim at the cogni-
> tion of God, but only at what is called the cognition of man. This so-called
> man and his humanity conceived as a rigidly, insuperable finite sort of
> Reason form philosophy's absolute standpoint. Man is not a glowing spark
> of eternal beauty, or a spiritual focus of the universe, but an absolute sen-
> sibility.[22]

Like the Protestant culture in which it was rooted, Enlightened philosophy
absolutized the distinction between the finite and infinite, man and God,
and took man as its absolute standpoint—a man, moreover, determined
by finitude and sensibility and so a man incapable of elevating himself,
through knowledge, to God.

Confined to the finite and the limits of sensible, human intuition, the
Kantian philosophy employed reason in the critical project of reflecting on
itself and thereby removed God from the sphere of its applicability. For
Kant, as is well known, man's reason turns in on itself in order to analyze
itself and discover its own limits. This critical turn was meant to secure the
possibility of knowledge by specifying the a priori structures of the mind
which make knowledge and experience possible. Knowledge was possible
so long as it was confined to the phenomenal realm of experience where
the mind is active; but when the mind attempts to extend knowledge beyond the realm of experience and make a claim to know things-in-them-
selves, it falls into illusion, what Kant called the transcendental illusion.
Prey to the transcendental illusion, finite man mistakes the structures of
thought for structures of reality. In the case of God, reason is particularly
prone to this "transcendental illusion." The so-called proofs for the existence of God, for instance, rest on the illusion of supposing that the principle
of causality applies outside the field of our understanding, that is, of supposing that causality is not a category of the understanding but a category
of being. To infer from our experience of the world that the world must
have a cause outside it (named God) is "a judgment of purely speculative
reason, since the object which we are inferring is not an object of possible
experience," and therefore this cause is not a possible object of knowledge.[23]
The result of Kant's critique of pure reason was that knowledge was secured from its skeptical attackers, but only at the price of removing God
from this well-defended fortress.

Having removed God from a knowledge confined to the limits of sensible experience, Kant believed that he had actually made room for faith, as he wrote famously in the "Preface to the Second Edition" of *The Critique of Pure Reason:* "I have therefore found it necessary to deny *knowledge,* in order to make room for *faith.*"[24] What knowledge gave up was found again in faith, though in a faith which could not know what it nevertheless held as its own. Knowledge renounced God with the express purpose of surrendering God to a faith where God might be preserved from the threat posed by knowledge. When Kant claims that his philosophy aims to abolish knowledge in order to make room for faith, he illustrates almost to perfection what Hegel means by the death of God. Kant's God is a dead one, for Hegel, to the degree that it is apprehended in a faith which cannot know what it nevertheless talks about, believes in, and longs for. Transcendent—that is, separated from knowledge by the absolute opposition between the finite and the infinite, the God of faith must always remain abstract and dead, apart from the living world of knowledge and experience.

The Death of God and Enlightenment Philosophy of Religion

It is precisely in this Kantian context that the modern philosophy of religion emerged. As Walter Jaeschke, one of the chief editors of Hegel's *Lectures on the Philosophy of Religion,* notes, "The first works to bear the name of philosophy of religion are written by committed Kantians. Karl Heinrich Pölitz in particular expressly took his stand in 1795 wholly on the practically grounded doctrine of God and religion."[25] While it might seem surprising that the philosophy of religion should emerge at the moment when God was being cast from knowledge to faith, it was precisely this act of banishment that opened the possibility for the philosophy of religion, determined its task, and guided its future. As Jaeschke writes, "as long as it seemed as though the idea of God was not only conceivable but indispensable to theoretical philosophy, indeed, properly speaking, its central point, the philosophy of religion had only marginal importance. What first released it from this shadow existence was Kant's demonstration of the failure of traditional philosophical theology."[26] How? How did removing the idea of God from philosophical knowledge of God make an opening for the philosophy of religion? And what tasks belonged to this emergent philosophy of religion?

What theoretical reason gave up with Kant (namely, God) practical reason recovered. That is to say, though theoretical reason cannot have any knowledge of God, God nevertheless appears as a necessary postulate of practical reason. In his *Critique of Practical Reason,* Kant starts from the idea of the moral good and the presupposition of moral experience. On this basis, he goes on to show how morality necessarily presupposes the a priori operation of the categorical imperative. Just as theoretical reason acts in knowledge in and through the forms of the intuition and the categories of the understanding, practical reason contributes the category of the ethical imperative to our moral life.

Now, according to Kant, along with the categorical imperative, practical reason postulates the idea of God—and it is just that, a postulate. It is a postulate, and therefore it is not known, and in fact can never be known, if there is a reality corresponding to this idea. Kant's argument is well known. According to Kant, the chief end of the moral life is virtue rewarded by happiness. To be morally virtuous we must never do the good in expectation of reward, for then we act out of a motive other than love of duty and hence are not virtuous. However, Kant says, we anticipate and even believe that this virtue will be crowned with reward. In order that this end might be upheld, the practical form of reason operative in morality necessarily postulates three ideas: (1) freedom, since only if we can do what we ought to do will this end be realized; (2) immortality, since the infinite distance between our sinful nature and the good we desire cannot be overcome in this life; and (3) God, who assures that virtue receives its just reward by apportioning happiness according to merit. The idea of God thus belongs to the practical faith that moral behavior will receive reward, and this idea is perfectly rational insofar as it is a postulate of reason in practical form.

The place where God is found has thus been shifted from theoretical knowledge to the practical reason active in morality; and with this shift, Kant has "made room for faith." The man of the Enlightenment, according to Kant, "needs no speculative proofs for God's existence. He is convinced of it with certainty, because otherwise he would have to reject the necessary laws of morality which are grounded in the nature of his being. Thus he derives theology from morality, yet not from speculative but from practical evidence; not through knowledge but through faith."[27] The idea of God remains and is fully rational because it is rooted in the a priori structure of reason in its moral operation.[28]

Having banished the possibility of knowing God in order to save God for faith, the critical philosophy faced the task of deciding what to do with the traditions and dogma of the historical religions. Within the philosophical disciplines, reflection on actual religions thus replaced speculation on God. The philosophy of religion in Kant and especially his followers made no claim to uncover knowledge of God; rather, it aimed to save what of religion was in accord with the activity of practical reason or in the service of its demands. Submitted to the definition of religion as the practical knowledge of our moral duties as divine commands,[29] religion would comprise nothing more than morality and practical reason could tolerate. With this identification, it became possible for a philosophical reflection on actual, historical religions to assess the extent to which particular doctrine or dogma did and did not conform to the religion of reason. This was the task with which the philosophy of religion was initially charged: not knowledge of God but critique of the representations, positive forms, and doctrine found in historical religions.

The classic expression of Kant's philosophy of religion is *Religion within the Limits of Reason Alone* (1793), where the historical institutions and beliefs of Christianity are evaluated and reinterpreted in light of the ethical religion of reason. To such a project, the revealed elements of religion obviously posed the largest obstacle insofar as the claims of revelation introduced a transcendence and authority beyond reason, even in its practical form. For the will to submit to determination by a revelation or revealed content would be for it to abandon the autonomy and self-determination it discovers in submission to practical reason. The dismissal or reduction of the possibility of revelation is evident in the Kantian reinterpretation of the Christological problem. Whereas traditional Christology sought to explain the relation between the human and divine, the finite and the infinite, the worldly and the transcendent, the Kantian Christology concerned the relation between the historical and the ideal in the person of Christ. For the Kantian philosophy of religion, the Christ of history is no longer a revelation of a transcendent God but a material example of the ethical ideal, something like a role model that is needed because the sluggish and sensuous nature of finite man prohibits him from attaining the ideal moral behavior he should be able to reach in and through reason alone. "Thus [Hegel writes] Christ is dragged down to the level of human affairs, not to the level of the commonplace but still to that of the human."[30]

Responding to the Kantian victory of Enlightened reason over religion, Hegel is quick to observe that what philosophy had vanquished was only the positive and therefore inessential forms of religion and that the reason which was victorious was in fact only a very impoverished and limited reason. "Seen in a clear light the victory comes to no more than this: the positive element with which Reason busied itself to do battle is no longer religion, and victorious Reason is no longer Reason."[31] Hegel, therefore, doubts that this victory really defeated the foe it intended. The philosophy of religion may have emptied the religious form of its positive content, and it may have preserved whatever of this content still stood after it had passed through the tribunal of reason; but, precisely in this way, the philosophy of religion failed to capture the essential content of real religious faith: namely, God. The religion over which it won out was not a real faith but only a weak caricature of faith, and therefore the victory is no victory at all.

The fact that faith still reached outside and above what so-called Reason could comprehend was the best sign that Reason's victory was still incomplete even in the post-Kantian philosophy of religion. Enlightened reason "acknowledges its own nothingness by placing that which is better than it in a *faith outside and above* itself, as a *beyond*."[32] Lacking its better part, Enlightenment philosophy, on Hegel's reading, was unsatisfied—and unsatisfactory—because it had won a victory over religion only by leaving what was essential to the content of religion, God, over and above Reason. Once again, Hegel is asserting that Kantian philosophy is both embedded in and the actualization of what exists in the surrounding culture as the feeling "God Himself is dead."

Understood as the denial of knowledge of God and the supposition of a faith reaching beyond it, the death of God becomes a problem for philosophy itself. The death of God means that philosophy has failed to reconcile within itself the distinction between faith, with its transcendent God, and knowledge. Faith still reaches beyond knowledge toward a God who cannot be known, a God who is in this sense dead and whose death leaves knowledge incomplete precisely in what concerns its highest object.

The Hegelian Death of God

The truth of the Enlightenment—"that heaven be transplanted to the earth below"[33]—was in need of assistance, according to Hegel, in that philosophy needed to recover knowledge of God. This is why Martin De Nys and Walter Jaeschke speak of Hegel as undertaking a "project which one legitimately names philosophical theology."[34] Through the resources of philosophy, they argue, Hegel hopes to develop the knowledge of God omitted from modern philosophy and thereby bring philosophy to completion. This project is only imperfectly grasped, however, when one—like Jaeschke, for example—does not add that this philosophical theology, this transplantation of heaven to the earth below, is propelled by the introduction of an idea that first appeared historically in a particular religious tradition: namely, the idea of the death of God that appeared in Christianity.[35] It is this second (Christian) sense of the death of God which allowed Hegel to revoke or overcome the death of God in Enlightenment philosophy; and it is this same death of God which allows the emergence of philosophy of religion in Hegelian philosophy.

To understand how Hegel's appropriation of this second sense of the death of God can revoke the death of God in Enlightenment philosophy, I want to return to the important passage from the conclusion of *Faith and Knowledge* where Hegel first uses the phrase "God is dead."

> But the pure concept or infinity as the abyss of nothingness in which all being is engulfed, must signify the infinite grief [of the finite] purely as a moment of the supreme idea. Formerly, the infinite grief existed historically in the formative process of culture. It existed in the feeling that "God Himself is dead," upon which the religion of more recent times rests; the same feeling that Pascal expressed in so to speak sheerly empirical form: "la nature est telle qu'elle *marque* partout un Dieu *perdu* et dans l'homme et hors de l'homme" [Nature is such that it *signifies* everywhere a *lost* God both within and outside man]. By *marking this feeling as a moment of the supreme Idea*, the pure concept must give philosophical existence to what used to be either the moral precept that we must sacrifice the empirical being (*Wesen*), or the concept of formal abstraction [e.g., the categorical imperative]. Thereby it must re-establish for philosophy the Idea of absolute freedom and along with it the absolute Passion, *the speculative Good Friday in place of the historic Good Friday. Good Friday must be speculatively reestablished in the whole truth and harshness of its God-forsakenness. . . .* The highest totality can and must achieve its resurrection solely from this harsh

consciousness of loss, encompassing everything, and ascending in all its earnestness and out of its deepest ground to the most serene freedom of its shape [emphasis mine].[36]

There are two important points to notice here.

1. The first sense of the death of God is now superseded, not annihilated, by a second, according to which the first is only a moment in the unfolding of its idea. The proposition "God is dead" is no longer absolute in its first sense but is now read as a truth which belongs to God Himself. As Eberhard Jüngel writes,

> By designating the feeling that "God Himself is dead" as a moment of the supreme idea, talk about the death of God gains a twofold meaning. First of all, in talk about the death of God, the situation of absolutized finitude expresses itself, which corresponds to abstract infinitude as empty negativity. Once that feeling is grasped as a moment of the supreme Idea, then the death of God is understood as an event of the *self-negation* of God, who does not desire to be "in and for himself" and does not desire to forsake the world in its finitude.[37]

Jüngel's point is twofold: first, on Hegel's reading, talk about the death of God gives expression to the Kantian standpoint insofar as it had absolutized finitude and correlatively posited only an abstract and empty infinite; second, Hegel has made that death of God a moment in the procession and return of God Himself. Thus understood, the atheistic feeling of the modern age, given philosophical articulation in Kant and the Enlightenment *philosophes*, stands within the unfolding of the Absolute, not as having truth on its own but as the moment of God's self-negation, the moment when God passes over into his opposite, leaving behind the remoteness of his transcendence and infinity in order to enter finitude, where he can be known.

2. By philosophically interpreting an idea (the death of God) given in revealed religion (in particular, the Christian religion), Hegel finds relief for and from the atheistic feeling of modern times. Hegel's task, as Jüngel says, was to reconcile faith and knowledge, heaven and earth, "against the apparently satisfied Enlightenment, by recapturing philosophically the content of faith. Philosophy had to grasp that in revealed religion heaven itself *has come* to earth. Philosophy had to reconcile Christianity with the Enlightenment. To do that, it needed and used the dark statement, the Death of God."[38] In Christianity, as interpreted by Hegel the philosopher, the death of God means that the abstract and unknowable God has descended into finitude, even to the point of submitting to death, where he reveals himself in order to be known by man. The process of revelation begun by the Incarnation is thus on the Cross. The feeling upon which modern religion rests, "God is dead," is therefore true in what it feels; but this feeling must be reinterpreted in light of the Christian tradition if it is to realize its truth and complete its project of reconciling heaven and earth. Only in and through its acceptance of the Christian sense of the death of God will philosophy achieve its final satisfaction.

The Hegelian Philosophy of Religion

If the death of God is a truth belonging to God, or if the wisdom of the heavens has indeed died and descended to earth, overcoming the separation of God and man, then the so-called Hegelian philosophical theology does not find its object in the remote or abstract heavens but here on earth. Where? In religion, where the knowledge of God is actual. As Hegel himself says, "the doctrine of God is to be grasped and taught only as the doctrine of religion."[39] Hegel's philosophy of religion will therefore differ significantly from that which issued from Kant. Whereas the Kantian philosophy of religion arises precisely out of the unknowability of God, the Hegelian belongs to and serves the knowledge of God. Jaeschke will speak of Hegel's philosophical theology "passing over into philosophy of religion, or vice-versa: the philosophy of religion is for Hegel only one part of philosophical theology, that part in which philosophical theology reaches its conclusion."[40] In recovering knowledge of God, not just reflecting on the positive forms of religion, Hegel's philosophy of religion revokes the death of God which had been instituted in Kant's philosophy. In so doing, it reconciles the last distinction within itself, overcomes the last transcendence resisting it, and realizes the death of God taught in Christianity. The Hegelian philosophy of religion at once presupposes the death of God and completes it.

This interpretation of the death of God as a fundamentally Christian truth about God is closely related to Hegel's description of Christianity as "the revealed religion." For a religion to be revelatory, according to Hegel, means precisely that its God can be known or cognized by the finite, human subject.

> Those who say that Christianity is not revelatory do not speak from the standpoint of the Christian religion at any rate, for the Christian religion is called the revealed religion. Its content is that God is revealed to human beings, that they know what God is. Previously they did not know this; but in the Christian religion there is no longer any secret—a mystery certainly, but not in the sense that it is not known. For consciousness at the level of understanding or for sensible cognition it is a secret, whereas for reason it is something manifest.[41]

The Christian religion is revelatory in its demand that no secrets be kept, that every mystery submit to manifestation. No secret being made of the divine mystery, the Christian consciousness can know God completely and unreservedly, thereby realizing the conquest or descent of the heavens.

The revelatory character of Christianity stems from its determination of God not as substance but as spirit. The acceptance of this determination of God as the starting point of Hegelian philosophy, as with its appropriation of "the death of God," marks another instance in which a historical religion (Christianity) has given concepts that are essential to the operation of this philosophy of religion, a philosophy which ultimately will dispense with the need for historical religions and proceed conceptually and speculatively. Whereas substance consists entirely in remaining in itself and needing no other for its existence, spirit is itself by manifesting itself in and for an other. "Spirit is an absolute manifesting. Its manifesting is a positing of determination and a being for an other. 'Manifesting' means 'creating an other,' and indeed the creating of subjective spirit for which the absolute is."[42] The determination of God as spirit means that God is not God if he does not manifest himself, does not leave his abstract and empty infinitude to manifest himself in and as the finite. If God as Infinite spirit has emptied himself into finite spirit, the finite knowledge of God is not simply a relation of the finite to the infinite but the infinite's self-relatedness back to itself. The religious consciousness is not simply knowledge of God—or it is knowledge *of* God where the genitive is read as both objective and subjective. In the knowledge *of* God actual in the religious consciousness, God knows himself and thus returns to himself from his self-othering in finitude.

Religion, however, does not yet know its own consciousness as such. A philosophy of religion is therefore needed to comprehend the truth which religion already is. This is why, as Hegel says in the passage from the conclusion of *Faith and Knowledge*, "Good Friday must be speculatively reestablished" and why the "pure concept must give philosophical existence" to what previously was a historical or moral doctrine. Noting the difference between the subjective perspective of religion and the speculative perspective of religion, Hegel writes, "In its concept, religion is the relation of the subject, of the subjective consciousness to God who is spirit. In its concept regarded speculatively, it is therefore spirit conscious of its own essence, conscious of its own self."[43] The difference here noted stems from the standpoint adopted. For the understanding that starts with man, religion is a relation of two independent and external beings, a subject and object transcending one another. For speculative philosophy, by contrast, where the starting point is God as spirit, religion is the closure of the circle whereby infinite spirit realizes itself in and through the subjective consciousness of it itself.

In this way, the philosophy of religion is not simply a description of man. Likewise, the philosophy of religion is not simply an interpretation of religion in light of philosophical knowledge, salvaging what accords with it and discarding what does not; nor is it an attempt to demonstrate the necessity of religious views. Rather, religion is of interest to Hegelian philosophy because religion is a self-relation of spirit to itself; considered in the speculative philosophy of religion, the religious consciousness of God is the return of spirit to itself. This is why the philosophy of religion completes the philosophical theology undertaken by Hegel. And, if philosophy itself remained incomplete to the degree that it failed to reconcile itself with what faith holds of God, then the philosophy of religion brings about the end of metaphysics.

But, the philosophy of religion achieves this task only on condition that it accept the determination of God by the harsh word "God himself is dead" or else by the determination of God as spirit whose essence is the full manifestation of all mystery. Though Hegel negates the Enlightenment death of

God and thereby brings metaphysics to its end, he does so only by a second, Christian death of God where the first is revoked in and through the full manifestation of God as spirit. There is thus no escape from the death of God, only its being enshrined as the very essence of God grasped in a finally completed and fully revelatory immanence.

The Nietzschean Conclusion

If Hegel enshrines the death of God in a philosophy of religion that recovers God in a positive sense, then Nietzsche does the same in a negative sense. As in Hegel's critique of Enlightenment philosophy, for Nietzsche, too, the death of God is a word directed against those who posit an unknowable, unintelligible God. When Zarathustra desires "that your conjectures should be limited by what is thinkable . . . that everything be changed into what is thinkable for man, visible for man, feelable by man," he joins Hegel in criticizing any philosophy or thinking that "recognizes something higher above itself from which it is self-excluded." Like Hegel, Zarathustra announces the death of God in order that philosophy might free itself from this willed servitude to an authority above or outside it. "If there were gods, how could I endure not to be a god! Hence there are no gods."[44] Zarathustra teaches the death of God in order that man might escape belief in or subservience to a transcendent power standing over against him.

However, whereas Hegel saw this infinite gap being overcome by a death of God which belongs to the very essence of God, Nietzsche saw it being overcome in a death of God that puts an end to the essence of God. "Hence, there are no gods." Having entered philosophy in Hegel's thought, the death of God, by the time it reaches Nietzsche, no longer belongs to the essence of God; it no longer maintains its Christian roots, and so when Nietzsche, the madman, and Zarathustra all claim "God is dead," this death is expressed in an unsurpassable way. Divorced from the Christian context where it was a truth about God, the death of God does not mediate or reconcile the atheistic feeling of modern times and the Christian faith.

In Nietzsche, the death of God no longer means the self-othering of spirit but the emptiness of all talk about God that is divorced from the will to power which employs God. Thus, for Nietzsche, the death of God issues in a philosophy of religion that is not charged with the task of completing the knowledge of God but one that reduces God to the will to power. Thought in a philosophy that reduces all religious meanings to the form of will to power which they express and enhance, God is no longer over against thought as in the Enlightenment, and he is no longer living in thought itself as Hegel taught. In Nietzsche, then, the happy alliance of the philosophy of religion and philosophical theology is rent asunder by the thought of the death of God, the very thought which Hegel had introduced in order to join the two tasks. In accepting Hegel's introduction of the death of God into philosophy but rejecting his reading of it, Nietzsche bequeathed to the twentieth century a philosophy of religion no longer attached to the project of some sort of a philosophical theology that seeks to know, or even over-come, an already revoked transcendence.

Levinas as Philosopher of Religion

The history of metaphysics thus ends with the death of God and the emergence of the modern philosophy of religion, positively in Hegel and negatively in Nietzsche. In a postmetaphyscial age, the death of God would be the sign under which philosophy lives. As such, the philosophy of religion would be incapable of any thought which does not recognize this as its highest and inaugural truth. In both sources of the postmetaphysical age, it is denied that any account of religion could ever recover something like the meaning of God's transcendence or his infinite distance.

In identifying the death of God with the end of metaphysics (positive and negative), however, the scope of this death is restricted: it is limited to the metaphysical understanding of God—thus leaving open the possibility of another significance of God. But, where might one find such a significance of God? It should be evident at this point that for such a significance to appear, the first question is where and how can thought find a meaning or an order of signification that evades metaphysical determination.

At this point, it is appropriate to recall the restatement of Husserl's exclamation with which I opened this chapter: "What can I do with [the responsible subject] philosophically?" For, in part 2 of this book, I argued that the phenomenology of responsibility opens a new field or order of meaning. In the next, and final, two chapters, I want to use the responsible subject philosophically, first in a philosophy of religion (chapter 8) and then in a philosophy of religion that might save the significance of divine transcendence (chapter 9).

I call this use of the responsible subject a philosophy of religion because, like the philosophy of religion begun in Hegel's time, it guarantees the significance of religious meanings through the resources of philosophy. It does not rely on the authority of dogma or tradition—though, again as in Hegel's use of the death of God, it might be the case that Levinas's philosophy would be inconceivable without drawing key ideas from historical religious traditions. Like Hegel's philosophy of religion, the phenomenology of responsibility does not let God and other religious phenomena fall into the irrationality of assent to dogma or tradition and it does not leave religious "experience" in a silent faith; it articulates their significance. Philosophy thus comes as a relief to theological thought.

Unlike the philosophy of religion in Hegel and Nietzsche, however, Levinas's phenomenology surpasses the origins of the philosophy of religion in the death of God. The phenomenology of responsibility thus relieves theological and religious thought from the necessity of having to surrender religious phenomena to a philosophy where they are reduced to the sphere of immanence (constituted under the sign "God is dead") in order not to be consigned to the silence of faith.

8

Ethical Phenomenology and the Religiosity of the Subject

To this point, my discussion has given no cause to believe that Levinas's phenomenology of ethics has anything to do with religion. In fact, one might at first suspect that any intrusion of religious themes or language would only annul the responsibility of the responsible self—for at least three related reasons: (1) Religion, as it is often understood, consoles and promises man that ethics will be rewarded in the hereafter, if not tomorrow. This reward would introduce a return to and for the self, thereby erasing the goodness, generosity, or selflessness of the responsible self. If there is a religiosity or a religion of the responsible self, it would have to be a religion without reward and without a consoling theodicy. (2) A religious determination of ethics might mean that responsibility was in fact dependent upon a highest being, called God, who issues the command to which I respond. This dependency would infuse responsibility with the certitude of a consciousness knowing it did what was required by the order, the orderer, of the universe. It would perhaps transform responsibility into the application of a technique (a God-given or prescribed way of acting) to a given situation (what should I do here and now?) and would thus entail the reinstatement of deliberation, judgment, and knowledge—in short, all that Levinas disqualifies when he locates responsibility outside the order of the universal, the logos, and consciousness. (3) Finally, as I showed in chapter 2, it was precisely the operation of a theological conceptuality which compromised the claims of *Totality and Infinity*. There, the presence of religious themes implied an unthought theological determination of ethics. This unthought determination meant that ethics was not absolute or unconditioned and therefore was not the first philosophy that Levinas claimed.

Why would the same not be true if there were again a religion, a religious language or a religious conceptuality operative in the determination of responsibility?

Despite these suspicions, Levinas's thought of the responsible self does indeed entail a religious dimension, which he himself admits when he claims, "the deposition by the I of its sovereignty as an I . . . signifies the ethical, but probably also the very spirituality of the soul" (GCM, 177), and when he writes, "In the prehistory of the ego posited for itself speaks a responsibility. . . . Beyond egoism and altruism, [what is at stake in responsibility] is the religiosity of the self" (OBBE, 117). In this chapter, I want to investigate this religiosity of the self. Since this religiosity of the self or this essence of religion is here discovered after the reduction has led to a subject outside the amphibology of being and beings, it is ordered neither in terms of onto-theology nor consciousness. And yet, since it is discovered at the end of a reduction and therefore in immanence, this religiosity remains nonetheless perfectly intelligible to philosophy—if by philosophy we understand a phenomenology that takes responsibility as its subject. In this way, Levinas's phenomenology opens the possibility of a religiosity that lives on in a postmodern or postmetaphysical age. Not only is this religiosity intelligible to a phenomenology of responsibility, according to Levinas, it is discovered by it. That is, a possible religiosity opens after the end of metaphysics insofar as the phenomenology of subjectivity describes its genesis in responsibility. There is no religion without responsibility (here Levinas agrees with Nietzsche), and Levinas's phenomenology, by uncovering the responsibility that undoes modern metaphysical thought, thereby saves religiosity for the postmetaphysical or postmodern age.

The Religiosity of the Responsible Self

Several components of this religiosity can be identified.

1. *Creation.* Since this self has been called into being before it exists, it is a creature:

> In creation what is called to Being answers to a call that could not have reached it since, brought out of nothingness, it obeyed before hearing the order. Thus, in the concept of creation *ex nihilo*, if it is not pure nonsense, there is the concept of a passivity that does not revert into an assumption. The self as a creature is conceived in a passivity more passive than the passivity of matter, that is, prior to the virtual coinciding of a term with itself. The oneself has to be conceived outside all substantial coinciding of self with self. (OBBE, 113)

Creation thus signifies in terms that are not comprehensible for knowing consciousness but that are to be found in the ethical subject. As not present when called into being, the creature is created in an extreme passivity that cannot be converted into an act; the creature cannot assume or become master of its own origin. Rather than answering the metaphysical question,

Why is there something rather than nothing? the notion of creation founded in ethics "defies myth in which tales about the origin of the world are
fixed" (OBBE, 177). To a phenomenology of consciousness, such creation is
pure nonsense, an excessive or insane thought: it is an impossible thought
since consciousness is its own origin as well as the origin of all that is and
since in consciousness, all the passivity of affectivity is assumable, convert-
ible into an act that constitutes beings. To a phenomenology that takes responsibility as its subject, however, the meaning of creation is a possibility
insofar as it belongs to the subject laid bare by a reduction.

It is important to notice this nonmetaphysical significance of creation
seeing as in modern thought the doctrine of creation has had a special relation to the metaphysical operation of the concept "God." Understood meta-
physically, creation, like God, is subject to the primacy of causality, becoming thereby the divine act by which God, the self-causing cause of all, causes
the creature to be. When creation is subject to the primacy of causality, it
becomes the coordination or synchronization of a cause, God, and that
which it grounds or effects, the world. At the end of metaphysics, however,
when the radicalization of nihilism casts doubt on the legitimacy and necessity of ground, the meaning of creation as causal operation is rendered
obsolete. In contrast, Levinas's notion of creation lives on after the Heideggerian and Nietzschean critique of metaphysics because it construes this
doctrine in terms of the responsible self which precedes and undoes the
metaphysical subject. For Levinas, when creation is thought in terms of the
more ancient significance opened up by the description of responsibility, its
meaning no longer depends on the synchronizing effects of causality but on
the diachrony (temporal delay or belatedness) of a subject called to be out
of nothingness before it was present to receive or condition that call.

If the analysis of responsibility thus broaches the religious notion of creation, it does so only by adopting something of a heterodox or heretical
stance.[1] That is to say, Levinas's phenomenology "saves" the religious notion of creation only by interpreting it outside of its orthodox, dogmatic or
traditional context. Levinas's phenomenology is the heir of religious tradition; it claims its language and employs it but deviates from a dogmatic
or theological interpretation of these religious notions. This is best seen in
that Levinas contends, "It is perhaps in this reference to a depth of anarchi-
cal passivity that the thought that names creation differs from ontological
thought. It is not here a question of justifying the theological context of the
former [the thought that names the creature]; for the word creature designates a signification older than the context woven about this name. In this
context, this said, is already effaced the diachrony of creation" (OBBE, 113).[2]
Theological traditions of interpreting the doctrine of creation overlook or
even repress a more ancient meaning of creation, a meaning which exceeds
the metaphysical intelligibility that, according to Levinas, orders theological thought. For this ancient meaning to be broached, then, only the phenomenology of responsibility will suffice. Somewhat like a heresy, Levinas's

phenomenology of responsibility articulates the secret meaning of creation or creatureness, a secret which has been borne by the theological traditions to which this notion has belonged but which has not yet received a thematic development. The phenomenology of responsibility takes a certain heretical distance in opposition to the dogmatic interpretations of tradition, in order to penetrate this secret. In thus broaching the secret of creation, phenomenological philosophy (not theology) saves religion from the demise it shared with metaphysics in the so-called postmodern age.

A heretical or heterodox stance does not contest the authority of the texts belonging to a tradition but simply their interpretation or the shape of the religion which has been constructed on their basis. A heretic is, importantly, a member of the community from which his stance diverges, but he is a member who has chosen or opted to construe the meaning of religion in terms other than those authorized by the authorities in power. An example of Levinas's heterodox reading of the Judeo-Christian tradition with which he identifies can be found in his reading of the scriptural story of Job. We are accustomed to treating this text in the context of theodical concerns: the text is made to harmonize the problem of an innocent man's suffering with the belief in a good and almighty God; asking why an innocent man, Job, should suffer, it teaches religious man to have faith in a God whose reasons are unknown but nevertheless just. On Levinas's reading, however, this text becomes a reproach against metaphysical or idealistic philosophers who have forgotten the sense of creation: "We have been accustomed to reason in the name of the freedom of the ego—as though I had witnessed the creation of the world, and as though I could have under my charge only a world that would have issued from out of my free will. These are presumptions of philosophers, presumptions of idealists! Or evasions of irresponsible ones. That is what Scripture reproached Job for" (OBBE, 122). The reproach to which Levinas here alludes is found in Job 38:4: "Where were you when I laid the foundations of the earth?" Referencing this verse in one of his Talmudic commentaries, Levinas writes, "Condition of the creature. Responsibility that Job, searching in his own impeccable past, could not find. 'Where were you when I created the World?' the Holy One asks him. . . . Even if you are free, you are not the absolute beginning. You come after many things and many people. . . . You are responsible for all. Your liberty is also your fraternity" (NTR, 85). That is to say, Job was reproached for having forgotten the ethical significance of creation, namely, that creation means my lateness in a world for which I am nonetheless responsible. This reproach is precisely the one that Levinas will make against metaphysical or idealist philosophies which fix their gaze on a consciousness that produces itself and then the world on the basis of itself: they have forgotten the belatedness that comes with the self's creation.[3]

More, in the common interpretation of this text, Job is an innocent man; he suffers without having done anything to merit his suffering. This unjust suffering is the peculiar scandal of the text, requiring faith in the justice of a God who speaks from the mysterious whirlwind. Job's apparently unjust sufferings test or try our faith in a God whose reasons and justice are beyond what appears to us. But in Levinas's phenomenological recovery, the fate of Job (to have suffered for what he never did, to have suffered without knowing why), a fate that hitherto seemed unintelligible or meaningless or intelligible only in terms of some inarticulate faith in a God whose reasons are unknown or unapparent—this fate is now understandable in and through an immanent analysis of responsibility, the very subjectivity of the subject.

> He would have known how to explain his miseries if they could have devolved from his faults! But he never wished evil! His false friends think like he does: in a meaningful world one cannot be held to answer when one has not done anything. Job then must have forgotten his faults! But, the subjectivity of a subject come late into the world which has not issued from his projects does not consist in projecting, or in treating this world as one's project. The lateness is not insignificant. The limits it imposes on the freedom of subjectivity are not reducible to pure privation. To be responsible over and beyond one's freedom is certainly not to remain a pure result of the world. (OBBE, 122)

That Job should suffer for crimes which were not his own makes philosophical sense when the subject of philosophy is structured as responsibility—responsibility for what it did not intend, what it did not commit. Job was not simply innocent; for, as a creature, he has come late into the world for which he is responsible and so is at fault, guilty of what he could not possibly have committed himself to.

Levinas's description of the responsible self also leads to the significance of

2. *Election.* Since the responsible self has been assigned, before choosing, an identity that is radically singular, the self can be termed elect or the chosen one. According to Levinas,

> The identity aroused behind identification is an identity by pure election. Election traverses the concept of the ego to summon me as me through the inordinateness of the other. It extracts me from the concept where I continually take refuge, for I find in it the measure of an obligation which is not defined by this election. Obligation calls for a unique response not inscribed in universal thought, the unforeseeable response of the chosen one. (OBBE, 145)

The notion of election does not explain my salvation, the fate of my being after my death, nor does it justify a nation's claim to a particular piece of the terrestrial world. Rather, election signifies through the ethical notion of a self that is radically singular in its assignation to responsibility. The self is elect insofar as in responsibility it is chosen for or assigned to itself before being free to choose or commit itself to responsibility. Elect in responsibility, the self is assigned to itself without regard for its having merited such election or for its capacity to meet this responsibility.

According to Levinas, then, "a philosopher can give to this election only the significance circumscribed by responsibility for the other" (OBBE, 122). Importantly, Levinas is here speaking of the significance of election for a philosopher, not for a theologian or believer committed to a religious tradition. The religious notion of election is philosophically comprehensible when philosophy adopts the figure of a phenomenology of ethics—but only then. A phenomenology of consciousness cannot reach the notion of election without distorting it, without losing the religiosity of that notion: such a phenomenology reduces every notion to the intentional acts whereby a subject constitutes phenomena in a present to which it is equal because it makes it; it thereby loses the sense of an election which happens before me, without my having intended anything that would merit it or not. In contrast, when the subject of phenomenology is responsibility, such foolish, mad, or excessive notions can be articulated in philosophy.

The description of responsibility conducts Levinas to the signification of the religious response par excellence,

3. *"Here I Am!"* Since the self is created by the call, being nothing before its call, the call to responsibility calls before there is an I to answer. The call calls me. To the call that summons me, the only answer is the one uttered by the prophets, "Here I am!" In French, this is rendered as *"me voici"* which, like the Hebrew *"hinneni,"* eschews the nominative "I" and employs the accusative "me." Levinas writes, "There is an assignation to an identity for the response of responsibility, where one cannot have oneself replaced without fault. To this command continually put forth only a 'here I am' [*me voici*] can answer, where the pronoun 'I' is in the accusative, declined before any declension, possessed by the other"; "[t]he word *I* means *here I am*, answering for everything and everyone" (OBBE, 142, 114). As such, the "here I am" clearly belongs to the subject that is discovered after the reduction to responsibility.

"Here I am" is found by a phenomenology that practices a reduction to the saying, a saying which it interprets as responsibility. Levinas writes,

> Saying [responsibility] is without noematic correlation in the pure obedience to the glory it orders. It is without dialogue, in the passivity from the first subordinate to the 'here I am'. . . . Already a sign made to the other, a sign of the giving of signs, that is, of this non-indifference, a sign of this impossibility of slipping away and being replaced, of this identity, this uniqueness: here I am. (OBBE, 145)

In other words, "here I am" is the saying that says nothing, the saying that delivers every said but is itself nothing said. In the "here I am," the self is exposed in an exposure that makes it possible for signs to be exposed as signs, for meaning to be meaningful. As such, the "here I am" does not belong to the dialogue where information is stated and circulated between an I and a Thou (divine or human, it does not matter) co-present to one another. Rather, "here I am" is the saying that precedes and opens all dialogue in that it exposes me to the other.

As the answer to my creation in responsibility, the saying of *me voici* does not posit or claim the place where I stand ("here") as my own, as "my place in the sun."[4] It marks the first experience of myself as reception of a me that was not first constituted in and by consciousness itself. As a response to my summons, "here I am" means that the summons affects me first before I am there to affect myself with the possibility of this affection. I say "here I am!" before all else, even before I am there to be conscious of what affects me or who is calling me. Moreover, in saying *me voici*, I do not recognize myself outside myself as a conscious I sees itself in the mirror of the world and others; rather, I testify to a me that I did not see in reflection but which was created by the accusation with which the other claims me.[5]

Levinas's analysis of responsibility also develops the significations of

4. *Expiation* and *Martyrdom*. The self is an expiation, a martyr, and even a *Sacrifice*, insofar as it sacrifices all concern for itself in responsibility for every other, to the point of expiating for the faults of others.

> The self, a hostage, is already substituted for the others. . . . Impassively undergoing the weight of the other, thereby called to uniqueness, subjectivity no longer belongs to the place where the alternative of activity and passivity retains its meaning. We have to speak here of expiation as uniting identity and alterity. The ego is not an entity capable of expiating for the others: it is this original expiation. This expiation is involuntary for it is prior to the will's initiative. (OBBE, 118)

Expiation here appears during the practice of phenomenological philosophy; the notion of expiation appears and appears perfectly intelligible when phenomenology takes the subject to be responsibility. Expiation is not an act that an I, after conscious deliberation, chooses to do, nor is it something that happens to a self on the basis of the self affecting itself with the possibility of expiating. Rather, expiation befalls me from the other; and in its befalling me, I am myself—as if I, the I, were a hostage. I am myself in my being an expiation for others without my willing it. I am myself in my being sacrificed for others without this happening on my own initiative. "The subjectivity of the subject is persecution and martyrdom" (OBBE, 146). The self itself, in the anarchic depths of its genesis, is the very expiation by which others are removed from responsibility for the crimes they commit, even the crimes against the self. In the reduction to responsibility, the self passes "from the outrage undergone to the responsibility for the persecutor and in this sense from suffering to expiation for the other" (OBBE, 111).[6] In and through the sacrifice of the self, being is redeemed from the violence of being. "In this sense the self is goodness. . . . [The self] consists in my being faced with everything that is only because I am by regard for all that is. It is an expiating for being" (OBBE, 118).

I should add that phenomenology also uncovers a trace of *God* in the responsible subject. Responsibility is the place where notions such as infinity, glory, and, of course, transcendence all take on a meaning; but this "phenomenon" seems so important and so controversial that I will defer consideration of it until the next chapter, where I can treat it more fully.

A Religious Philosophy . . . for Better or Worse?

At this point, I need to emphasize that this phenomenology describes neither a positive, determined religion nor actual, historic religious experience. This philosophical thought of religiosity does not intend to start from the events of revelation as these have been experienced or handed down in texts belonging to any religious tradition. Against the alternative of appealing to either a religious experience that must "justify itself before philosophy [metaphysics]" or a silent faith for which "what the Bible raises above all comprehension has here not yet reached the threshold of intelligibility" (GCM, 55, 57), Levinas's recovery of religion appeals strictly to a phenomenology of responsibility whose resources suffice to recover the possibility of religion.

If it is not based in religious experience or in the authority of religious tradition, however, does this phenomenological account of religiosity submit religion, nonphilosophical by definition, to forms and orders of meaning that are foreign to it? I believe it is possible to answer this question with a "No!" and to claim that when the subject of phenomenology is taken to be responsibility, phenomenology articulates—philosophically, that is outside the silence of faith or the authority of dogma—the significance of religious phenomena without losing sight of what is religious in them. This is so because in responsibility, phenomenology reaches a subject that is open to the appearance of the unconditional, of what is not given in the plain evidence of a present made by consciousness, and of what is impossible to account for by reflection on the self—that is to say, the appearance of what, at least in the West, would characterize the religious claim to the event of revelation.[7] For the appearance of religious phenomena to be intelligible as such, for them not to fall into either the less than zero or the intentional acts to which Husserlian phenomenology would consign them, a subject ordered as the responsible self is demanded.[8]

According to Levinas, when religious thought starts from religious experiences, it is unable to detach itself from metaphysics or onto-theology and consequently links its fate to theirs.

> A religious thought that appeals to religious experiences allegedly independent of philosophy insofar as it is founded on experience, already refers to the "I think," and is entirely connected to [metaphysics or onto-theology]. . . .[9] It is possible that the word "God" may have came to [metaphysics or onto-theology] from a religious discourse. But [they]—even if [they] refuse it—understand this discourse as that of propositions bearing on a theme, that is to say, as having a sense referring to an unveiling, to a manifestation of presence. The messengers of the religious "experience" do not conceive of another signification of meaning. . . . From the outset, then, the religious being interprets what he lived through as experience. He already interprets God, of whom he claims to have an experience, in terms of being, presence and immanence. (GCM, 62)

A thought of religiosity that is based on religious experience cannot avoid referring to the conscious subject, or the transcendental I, who stands behind every experience as that which constitutes it. As Husserl taught, experience is possible only if it finds its meaning and possibility in the immanent life of consciousness which identifies beings and makes the present in which they appear. Experiences do not so much befall me from the outside as they are made by consciousness in accord with the limits of its capacities.

According to Levinas, then, the reference to experience, even interior experience, does not only doom the thought of religiosity to the fate of metaphysics; it also, more importantly, suggests that a religious thought based in religious experience is unable to accede to the significance of religious phenomena. Since it finds all meaning in the sphere of immanence constituted by and constitutive of the I, such a thought loses phenomena which make a claim to transcendence or to a move beyond this world or to a dissatisfaction with terrestrial goods.[10] On this reading, as soon as religious phenomena are brought into consciousness, as soon as they are experienced, they are thought in terms of the objectivity of the world. Their religious character is the price they must pay if they want to earn their intelligibility in an experience of consciousness.

In contrast, Levinas's thought of religiosity starts from what he has called "the latent birth, in the other, of religion; prior to emotions and voices, prior to 'religious experience' that speaks of revelation in terms of the disclosure of being" (GCM, 72). Born in the other, religiosity belongs not to experience and consciousness but to ethics or responsibility. As a subject wherein the I is affected before it is there to condition or measure the appearance which affects it, responsibility is the order of meaning where unconditional or absolute phenomena belonging to the religious are articulated.

A latent possibility of responsibility, Levinas's phenomenological account of religiosity also stands outside the authority of religious tradition and established faiths. His having discovered a religiosity in the depths of the subject (responsibility) does not qualify Levinas's thought as belonging to a religious tradition, and the responsible subject is not committed to a particular, historic faith. This can be seen in the division of his work into a philosophical side that presents itself as some form of phenomenology and a Jewish side that takes up political, theological, and even philosophical problems in the history of Judaism by commenting on the authoritative texts of this tradition. Such a division of his work is meant to indicate that the religiosity uncovered in the ethical subject belongs to the subject as such, not to a Jewish or Judeo-Christian subject.

In many places Levinas has explicitly disavowed the authority of Jewish tradition over his philosophical work. First, in response to Jean-François Lyotard's description of Levinas's philosophy as a thought of the Old Testament God, Levinas responds, "I am not for all that an especially Jewish thinker; I am a thinker, *tout court*" (AQS, 83). And, as Lyotard himself recalls, Levinas has objected to him, "It is not under the authority of the Bible that my thought is placed, but under the authority of phenomenology. . . . You make of me a Jewish thinker" (AQS, 78–79). Next, when asked if it is possible to have a phenomenology of the other without first recognizing revelation, Levinas responds, "is all this phenomenology inspired by the Bible? I believe it free of it" (AQS, 81). If we take him at his word, then, it belongs to another part of his work, the Talmudic commentaries, to start from the revelations, the textual records, and authorities given in a historical tradition.

For this reason, I must wonder if those commentators who attempt to claim Levinas as a "Jewish philosopher" or to uncover the "biblical archetype" of his thought are not betraying their master. In commenting on the significance of God uncovered in the phenomenology of the subject (responsibility), Richard Cohen writes, "the knowledge that Levinas's thought is committed to the Jewish tradition, to a properly Jewish conception of God, already provides a preliminary indication of the direction the task at hand will take."[11] What is meant here by commitment? Is this a commitment in the sense that one assents or lends credence to certain truths or doctrines held by a religious tradition? Even if it is not, to claim that a commitment to a historic religious tradition—be it dogmatic or otherwise—guides in advance or provides preliminary direction for the phenomenological discovery of the subject's religiosity suggests that the religiosity of the subject is not religiosity as such but the religiosity of an actual and particular religion. By implying that an actual, historical religion has determined the religiosity of the subject, it compromises the phenomenological status of Levinas's phenomenology. Wouldn't the reduction have to bracket or suspend such determinations and all commitments as precisely contrary to the principle of the absence of presuppositions? Read in this way, Cohen's remark fails to appreciate the sense in which the discovery of the subject's religiosity happens in Levinas through a phenomenology, a description of the subject as such, a subject that we all are (even if each says I alone am responsible) regardless of historical or cultural context—as unfashionable as such considerations might currently be. Moreover, what is meant by "properly Jewish"? Would the "properly Jewish" be uttered in this phenomenological French? Wouldn't the religiosity of the subject have been discovered from the improper or somewhat heterodox or heretical stance of choosing to articulate meanings of religious notions that had not yet been thematized by the traditions that keep or transmit them?

Similarly, when Robert Gibbs adopts Levinas because his philosophy is formed by an encounter with the "Jewish other" and claims that through Levinas "Judaism can again reorient philosophy," it again seems that Levinas is being read contrary to his intentions.[12] On Gibbs's reading, and Cohen's too, the responsibility of the subject is very nearly equated with a Jewishness of the subject, an equation that is figured by the apposition in a phrase such as "this Jewish other of philosophy, this radical ethics."[13] With such an apposition, Gibbs suggests that the responsibility and hence the religiosity of the subject is identifiable with the religion of an historical people, the Jews. Would such a subject still merit the adjective "unconditioned" or "unconditional"? Or would it instead be a subject conditioned by its belonging to a particular religious tradition? As Gibbs himself says, "Religion here [in the essay entitled 'Ethics and Spirit,' an essay appearing in one of Levinas's 'Hebrew' writings, *Difficult Freedom*] appears by its proper name: Judaism. (Not that this is a religion only for Jews, but that it is the determining perspective of Judaism)."[14] How would such a religiosity belong to the very subjectivity of the subject if it is the religiosity of a particular religion? How is it that every subject is Jewish? Likewise, if religion's proper name is "Judaism," the name of an actual, historic religion, in what sense has the phenomenology that uncovers this religion really succeeded in its practice of the reduction?

Both Gibbs and Cohen address these questions through reference to a notion of Judaism's universalizing tendency. Citing Levinas, Cohen writes, "the extent to which Levinas's ethics is 'Jewish' then, is that wherein the Jewish message is a message for all mankind. 'Whenever one sees Israel in the sacred texts,' Levinas writes, 'one can substitute humanity.'"[15] But, this seems equally to imply that one cannot speak anymore, as Cohen does, of the "properly Jewish" and that one need not be what Gibbs calls a "Jewish philosopher" to discover responsibility and religion. It also risks repeating (in an inverted form) the crime that has been attributed to most of nineteenth-century Christian theology: namely, the identification of one religion as the consummate or archetypal religion, the religion which achieves the essence of religion.

As I have already suggested, the position taken by Gibbs and Cohen (names which figure a tendency operative in other authors as well) goes against the expressed intentions of Levinas insofar as he disavows the authority or priority of Judaism in his phenomenological account of the self, its responsibility and its religiosity.[16] Levinas presents his philosophy as a description of the self as such, undetermined by history, traditions, or civilizations: "This saying [responsibility] is prior to all civilization" (OBBE, 198, n. 6). Saying or responsibility is "not any sort of cultural gesture" (OBBE, 144). In claiming that responsibility precedes civilization and culture or is found only by a "reversion to the hither side of civilization" (OBBE, 198, n. 7), Levinas implies that responsibility stands outside actual, determinate religions such as Judaism; for what is Judaism if not a culture, a civilization having a body of literature, an authorized interpretation, and a tradition transmitting it?

Gibbs, and also Cohen, is aware that he reads Levinas somewhat contrary to his expressed intentions, acknowledging that "Levinas resists the title Jewish thinker."[17] I do not dispute the legitimacy of such a creative appropriation or use of a text, but I do want to point out the dangers that such a reading invites and the consequences that it holds. It seems that more than simply disavowing a master, an overcoming that every teacher wishes from his students, such readings risk delivering him over to his accusers. They confirm a reading which forms the basis of what others count as an objection.

According to the objectors, most notably Dominique Janicaud, contemporary French phenomenology (represented by Levinas, Marion, Jean-Louis Chrétien, and Michel Henry, even to some extent Ricoeur) masks an a priori determination by commitments to religious traditions. This determination compromises its claim to the status of phenomenological philosophy. In Levinas's thought, according to Janicaud, "phenomenology was taken hostage by a theology which does not want to say its name."[18] On this reading, Levinas and the others abandon the methods which permit phenomenology to be rigorous science. The methodological presuppositions which permit their phenomenology to be open to transcendence, revelation, exteriority, etc., are not imposed rigorously but dogmatically, that is, in accord with commitments to proper religious dogma—to what Cohen calls a "properly Jewish conception of God." According to Janicaud, "all is established and imposed from the beginning; this 'all' is considerable: it is nothing less than the God of the biblical tradition. Exact betrayal of the reduction. . . ."[19] Far from uncovering responsibility and religiosity through rigorous phenomenological practice, Janicaud claims, Levinas has merely imposed them on phenomenology by recourse to an unstated, undescribed, and unshared commitment—worse yet, a commitment which is unstat*able,* undescrib*able,* and unshar*able.* "By virtue of which experience," Janicaud asks, "does this phenomenology speak?"[20] Isn't one letting oneself be seduced by authority and ideology, religious dogma, if one accepts the results of a phenomenology that claims access to unutterable secrets of subjective life? How could this phenomenology of the ineffable speak if not in formulae given by dogma?

Thus, the readings of the first camp (e.g., Cohen and Gibbs) prove to the second (e.g., Janicaud) that Levinas's thought is nonphenomenological since they imply determination by a received tradition that precedes phenomenology. Could it be that the disciples' attempt to read Levinas as a Jewish philosopher plays into the hands of his critics by giving them more on which to base the accusation of a theological hijacking of phenomenology? Any confrontation between the two camps will come to an impasse since each side agrees with the other's claim to a religious determination of Levinas's phenomenology—only for one this counts as highest praise, while for the other it is a serious crime.

Before offering a suggestion as to how one might work through the resistance offered by such an impasse, I need to make it clear that I do not agree with Janicaud. While Janicaud's objections lead me to be wary of appropriating Levinas's philosophy for a particular religious tradition, it should be evident that I do not agree with Janicaud precisely because I think that, just as the other camp misrepresents the significance of the religious language in Levinas's phenomenology, so too does Janicaud base his objection on a weak reading of Levinas's phenomenology. In the first place, it seems that Janicaud's demand to know the experience speaking in Levinas's phenomenology begs the question; for, in Levinas, it is precisely a question of what is not given in an experience directed by an I and constituting objects of knowledge. Janicaud will never see the rigor of Levinas's phenomenology unless he accepts an order of meaning that exceeds that which is measured by consciousness and its experience. Janicaud also overlooks the ways in which Levinas's thought of responsibility is in fact imposed not through a lack of rigor but through an exceedingly rigorous thought of key notions in Husserl's phenomenology. It does not abandon the reduction but pushes it beyond itself to the point where it even describes the genesis of the pure ego in an assignation to responsibility that constitutes a transcendence in immanence which Husserl himself claimed was a major phenomenological difficulty.

Levinas addresses an objection like Janicaud's when it is made to him by Lyotard. Lyotard asks,

> Is it not that Revelation is necessarily inscribed in your thought, in contradistinction to that of Husserl—who is a true phenomenologist, if I might dare say so, that is to say someone for whom Revelation is not proposed to recognition? . . . I would say that, in a certain way, all your thought departs from the failure of the Fifth Cartesian Meditation, and it can relieve it only by the production of this absolutely primordial relation which is Revelation, that is to say the encounter of the other and the dispossession of the self by such an encounter. (AQS, 79)

Lyotard, like Janicaud purged of a polemical tone, thus suggests that Levinas corrects Husserl's phenomenology of the other by recourse to Revelation. Levinas responds that the inverse is the case:

> [Husserl] would not consider the way to the other as original, and because of that he did not have Revelation. This relation to the other [responsibility] is so extraordinary . . . that it can bring us to the problem of Revelation in the religious sense of the term. I do not identify the two, but I say that this brings me close to the possibility of giving a meaning to Revelation instead of attributing it to moments of pure madness and abuse. (AQS, 80)

In other words, it is not that a religious revelation makes possible the phenomenology of responsibility. Rather, the reduction to responsibility makes it possible for phenomenology to articulate a meaningful concept of revelation insofar as this notion is found to belong to the order of meaning structured as responsibility. Contrary to Janicaud's reading, Levinas's thought is, or points toward, a philosophy of religion and not a theology or religious philosophy of any sort.

A Philosophy of Religion

If Levinas is neither a philosopher committed to a particular religious tradition (a Jewish philosopher) nor a phenomenologist who betrays phenomenology to theology (a representative of the theological hijacking of phenomenology), what is going on in his thought? Interpretation reaches a point of indecision. Derrida has written of a similar impasse in reading the Czech philosopher Jan Patočka. Concerning the identification of Patočka's text, Derrida writes,

> The fact that Christian themes are identifiable does not mean that the text is, down to its last word and in its final signature, an essentially Christian one, even if Patočka himself could be said to be. . . . The alternative between these two hypotheses (Christian text or not, Patočka as a Christian thinker or not) is of limited pertinence. If it does involve Christianity, it is at the same time a heretical and hyperbolic form thereof. Patočka speaks and thinks in the places where Christianity has not yet thought or spoken of what it should have been and is not yet. (GD, 49)

The same might be said about Levinas: Jewish themes can indeed be spotted: Gibbs, Cohen, and Janicaud have all pointed to them. But the religion, the Judaism, operative in Levinas's phenomenology is certainly not articulated in a dogmatic or orthodox form, and the fact of Levinas's own Judaism does not decide the phenomenological status of his text—neither for better nor for worse. If Judaism does appear in this phenomenology, it is a Judaism that thinks or speaks—heretically, hyperbolically, or perhaps heterodoxically—what Judaism has not yet said about what it has always secretly harbored.

What, then, is happening in this phenomenology that, admittedly and to all eyes, discovers a religiosity in the heart of responsibility? If "the alternative between these two hypotheses ([Jewish] text or not, [Levinas] as a Jewish thinker or not) is of limited pertinence," what is happening in this phenomenology that proceeds in indisputably religious language? In parallel to one strand in Derrida's reading of Patočka, I want to suggest that the analysis of responsibility produces the pure possibility, the nonnoematic meaning or even "essence," of religion—the possibility of religion before any recourse to religious experience and before any recourse to the revelations kept by historical traditions.

Following the phenomenological tradition of Husserl, Levinas's philosophy is an analysis of possibility and significance—though the order of possibility and significance found in the responsible subject is far broader than that measured by the phenomenology of consciousness. For phenomenology and the phenomenology of religion, the actuality of religions does not prove difficult to accept or scandalous to describe. Rather, it is the possibility of religious phenomena that causes embarrassment—embarrassment for a phenomenology as well as for a religious believer who wants to explain or render intelligible the fact of religious phenomena. How can mad and excessive phenomena such as creation, election, expiation, and inspiration (the facts of religion) even be possible? Indeed, most often when they are denied as nonsense, it is with a claim such as "but that's impossible." Conversely, if one can discover how such phenomena might be possible, one has no difficulty accepting them. In its concern for establishing possibility, this problematic stands apart from that confronting a certain theology seeking to justify or ground the truth claims of its dogmatic content.

> Let us now come to the main problem. It is certainly not a problem of an apologetic nature requiring the authentication of the various revealed contents, confessed by the religions described as revealed. The problem lies in the possibility of a rupture or breach in the closed order of totality, of the world, or of the self-sufficiency of its correlative, reason. . . . If the possibility of such a fissure in the hard core of reason could be thought, the most important part of the problem would be resolved. But does not the difficulty come from our habit of understanding reason as the correlative of the possibility of the world: a thought which is equal to it? Can it be otherwise? Can a model of intelligibility be sought in some traumatic experience in which intelligence is broken, affected by something that overflows its capacity? . . . Is not the model of revelation an ethical one? (BTV, 145–46)

Phenomenology describes the possibility of revelation, not a possibility that is then actual and not the conditions for the possibility of it becoming actual, but a possible revelation in broaching the rupture of the self-sufficient subject in responsibility. "Admittedly, it is not a matter of deducing from this responsibility the actual content of the Bible: Moses and the prophets. We are concerned rather with formulating the possibility of a heteronomy" (BTV, 147). Against readings that identify Levinas as a Jewish philosopher or one committed to a Jewish conception of God, the religiosity met in the phenomenology of responsibility is, admittedly, not an actual religion and the analysis of responsibility is not intended to deduce the actual content of the Bible. That is to say, Levinas's phenomenology does not move from the possibility of religion (the analysis of responsibility) to an actual religion (the religion of Moses) that would be the exemplary historical embodiment of the essence of religion.

Derrida describes a similar sort of religious discourse in Patočka. With regard to the Christian themes, Derrida writes,

> What engenders all these meanings and links them, internally and necessarily, is a logic that at bottom (that is why it can still, up to a certain point, be called a "logic") has no need of *the event of a revelation or the revelation of an event*. It needs to think the possibility of such an event but not the event itself. This is a major point of difference, permitting such a discourse to be developed without reference to religion as institutional dogma and proposing a genealogy of thinking concerning the possibility and essence of the religious that doesn't amount to an article of faith. (GD, 49)

I have been trying to make the same point with regard to Levinas. Phenomenology has no need of the event of revelation or the revelation of the event in order to articulate a discourse on religion. If phenomenology need only think the possibility of such an event, it finds this possibility in the analysis of the responsible subject to which the possibility of religious phenomena belongs. The analysis of responsibility thus articulates a religious discourse outside the authority of institution, dogma, and assent to creedal formulations. Levinas, like Patočka, belongs to a philosophical "tradition that consists of proposing a nondogmatic doublet of dogma, a philosophical and metaphysical doublet, in any case a *thinking* that 'repeats' the possibility of religion without religion" (GD, 49).[21] Phenomenology thinks and speaks, articulating the meaning of religion; it is not like a faith that cannot speak but only believes in what it does not know.

To summarize, by putting forth a religious discourse that has no need of dogma or authority, what Derrida calls "a nondogmatic doublet of dogma," Levinas joins a tradition of philosophers that includes, at least, Kant, Hegel, and perhaps Kierkegaard. Kant's deduction of the religion of reason from the principles of practical reason and Hegel's deduction of Christian truths from the speculative concept of God in the *Lectures on the Philosophy of Religion* or from the experience of consciousness in the *Phenomenology* would offer possible forefathers or at least parallels to Levinas's recovery of a certain religion in and through the resources of philosophy. Of course the differences are legion: Kant's practical reason is not Levinas's responsibility; Hegel's claim to deduce the necessity of actual, historical faiths finds no parallel in Levinas or Kant; the speculative concept from which Hegel starts is precisely what Levinas argues is the suppression of responsibility. But nevertheless, the formal similarities or the similarities in the schematization of philosophy and religion seem persuasive enough to hazard the claim that Levinas can be placed in the ranks of a tradition of thought that would be called philosophy of religion. I will return to this point.

The Contribution of Judaism

Without basing itself in the authority of tradition and faith, Levinas's thought of responsibility nonetheless outlines the possibility of religiosity—but only the possibility since this philosophy is a stranger to actual experience and historic faiths. An obvious question then arises, one that Derrida suggests when he writes of Patočka,

> Everything *comes to pass* as though only the analysis of the concept of responsibility were ultimately capable of producing Christianity, or more precisely the possibility of Christianity. One might as well conclude, conversely, that this concept of responsibility is Christian through and through and is produced by the event of Christianity. . . . There is no choice to be made here between a logical deduction, or one that is not related to the event, and the reference to the revelatory event. One implies the other. (GD, 50)

Does the analysis of responsibility lead phenomenology to the possibility of religion? Or, conversely, is the notion of responsibility itself already religious, already produced by actual, historic religions? Does the phenomenology of responsibility produce, in a circular fashion, a possible religion that repeats an actual, particular religion precisely because responsibility was originally produced by it? We might suspect that (1) the responsibility described by Levinas first appears in the historical event that has come to be known as Judaism (and perhaps also Christianity, though that would take me too far afield) and that, therefore, (2) it is not simply the case that the analysis of responsibility leads to the essence or possibility of religiosity; rather, the historical event of determinate religions, Judaism and Christianity, endowed our historicity with the notion of responsibility whose philosophical analysis produces a religiosity that dispenses with the necessity of historical reference.

In this sense, the work of Cohen, Gibbs, and others adopting a similar position returns in an interesting way. Their descriptions of parallels between Levinas's ethical phenomenology and Judaism do not so much make Levinas a Jewish philosopher as they show how Judaism, the fact or event of it, has contributed to our history notions without which there would have been no responsibility for phenomenology to analyze. As Catherine Chalier has written, "a mind not educated by the Book [the Bible], with eyes not opened thanks to its teaching, would remain unskilled in the perception of the face transmitted by philosophy. This perception does not impose itself evidently or spontaneously; it is undeniably guided by the reading of the Torah, preceded by the idea of man fashioned in the image of his Creator."[22] This claim makes sense to me if it is taken as pointing out a certain historicity to the notion of responsibility—that is to say, if it does not claim that Levinas is a "Jewish philosopher" or a philosopher "committed to a properly Jewish conception of God" or that responsibility and Judaism coincide. Rather, it makes sense to me if it says that Judaism has made it possible for phenomenology to articulate such a religiosity because Judaism has produced, in the history of (Western) man, the responsibility whose analysis articulates this religion without religion. There would be a certain historicity to the notion of responsibility, and the event of Judaism would mark an important moment in this history; for it inaugurates the epoch which Levinas's phenomenology inhabits and bequeaths to it the notion of responsibility it analyzes.

This point can be made through reference to Levinas's own confrontation with the texts and sources of Judaism. "The man announced to humanity in Israel [Levinas writes] might also signify the possibility of interrupting its *conatus essendi*, the possibility of answering for the other, who is 'none of my business,' who is nothing to me" (ITN, 133). That is to say, Israel has announced the responsible self in the history of humanity at large, marking a new moment in the paired history of responsibility and religion. Though one can always read such a remark as a patent example of excessive Jewish pride, claiming that the particular religion, Judaism, contains what is universally human about man in general;[23] if it is read more generously, it says that the subjectivity of the subject, its responsibility, has been endowed by or historically conditioned through the event of Judaism—not that this historical condition marks a reference to personal history, but that such a historicity frames the subjectivity of the subject in an almost Heideggerian fashion of enframing and epochal withdrawals. This does not mean Levinas's phenomenology belongs to or is committed to Judaism proper. It does, however, suggest that the responsibility discovered at the heart of the subject (a phenomenological discovery) entered or was announced to historical subjects through Judaism and that without the event of Judaism, phenomenology would be denied access to the themes and logic necessary to articulate such a responsibility.

Judaism's contribution to the phenomenology of responsibility can be seen in Levinas's own confrontation with the fact of Judaism and its texts —as, for example, when he considers a text by the Rabbi Haim of Volozhin, a rabbi living in the late eighteenth and early nineteenth century. For Levinas, this text, *Nefesh haHayyim,* exemplifies the purest form of Judaism, a Jewish sensibility and piety "that were cut off from external influences and tapping their own roots . . . nourished—already or still—by purely traditional elements. [Rabbi Haim's] was a time when that tradition seemed to renew itself from within" (ITN, 119). As Levinas emphasizes, Rabbi Haim wrote his work only a few hundred kilometers from Königsberg and Jena where, during his lifetime, Kant and Hegel, respectively, had taught and written; and yet, "there is nothing, absolutely nothing, of the philosophy or the science of the new times" (BTV, 154). This text thus takes on, in Levinas's thought, the role of exemplifying Judaism as such. What it contains, for Levinas, is a purely Jewish expression of God, man, and the world. It is therefore most useful to my understanding of how the Jewish figure of man might have contributed the notion of responsibility to phenomenology.

This text contains the notion of an "interiority" or life of the subject which is not included in the consciousness to which it belongs most intimately. In the hierarchical cosmology of Rabbi Haim,

> Every force, from the lowest to the highest, is but the extension of the existence and life of *Elohim,* an extension which reaches the force below it through the intermediary of the force above it, which is the soul poured forth in its interiority. And as we know from Ari's Kabbalah, the light and interiority of every world and force is the external being of the force and the world which are above it.[24]

In other words, as Levinas comments, "that which is higher is always internal in relation to that which is lower: height and interiority coincide" (BTV, 157). Just as the soul is animated by the higher forces of *Elohim* found in its inmost depths, so too does consciousness bear in itself an other in the midst of its sameness, and this other is the possibility of the very life or living of the consciousness which it haunts. Such a notion clearly belongs to much Neoplatonic thought and so does not necessarily lead to the conclusion that Judaism per se has endowed phenomenology with the figure of the subject which it probes.[25] In other instances, however, this text figures the subjectivity of the subject in terms of responsibility and thereby stands out from other Neoplatonic forms of thought in which the interiority of the subject transcends itself in a relation not specified in terms of responsibility. As Levinas points out, for Rabbi Haim, "man is interiority through his responsibility for the universe" (BTV, 162). Man's psyche or soul is the fact of his supporting a world of which he is not the origin. Man is figured as "ground" of the universe without his being an *arché* which precedes the world or generates it from his self.

This is seen in the following interpretation of Genesis 2:7, where the phrase *nefesh hayyah*, from which the rabbi's work takes its name, appears. The text comments:

> But the verse literally does not say that the breath became a living soul *in* man; it says that man became a living soul [*nefesh hayyah*] for the countless worlds. . . . Just as the body's behavior and movements are due to the soul that is inside man, man as a whole is the power and living soul of the upper and lower countless worlds.[26]

On this interpretation, a hyperliteral reading that produces a profoundly spiritual content, when God breathed the breath of life into man, he did not make man a living being but a living soul, and as a soul, man animates the world. Haim's rendering of the verse rests on a reading of the Hebrew that is not reflected in the translation of the Revised Standard Version, which renders the verse as follows: "Then the lord God formed man of dust from the ground and breathed into his nostrils a breath of life; and man became a living being [*lenefesh hayyah*]." In this rendering, the Hebrew word *nefesh* (soul or breath) is interpreted in decidedly ontological language, a being; such a rendering is far from obvious in Hebrew. More importantly, however, the phrase *nefesh hayyah* is being read as a noun modified by an adjective which follows it. Again this reading is not obvious, since the word *hayyah* is also attested as a noun ("life" or "the living")—in which case the phrase is a construct where a noun modifies another noun (similar to the Latin genitive) and could be rendered not "living soul" but "soul of the living." It is this latter reading which Rabbi Haim emphasizes in his reading of the phrase, a reading which is made easier by rendering the phrase, as does Rabbi Haim, *nefesh haHayyim*. On this reading, man himself is the soul of the living, or what Haim calls a "soul for the countless worlds." Man's very life, his soul, animates the universe or is where the fate of the universe is decided. Man, in the depths of his interiority, as a soul for the universe, means to be responsible for a world which he did not create, which in fact was there before him—by about six days. What is this if not a figure of the responsible subject who supports a world which did not issue from him and into which he has come too late?

According to Haim, the biblical notion of man as the image or likeness of God needs to be thought in these terms. Man is the soul of the world just as is God, who in the passages expressing this likeness is named *Elohim,* that is master of the universe. Like God (*Elohim*), man has the power which decides the fate of worlds. As Rabbi Haim writes, "His will, blessed be He, confers upon man the power to free or to stop ('to open and close') thousands of myriads of forces and worlds, on account of all the detail and all the levels of his conduct and all his perpetual concerns, thanks to the superior root of his deeds, words and thoughts, as if man too were the master of the forces that command these worlds."[27] This mastery, *Elohim,* conferred upon man makes man God-like in that he too sustains the universe. Man's mastery, however, is operative not in and through the exercise of an absolute or arbitrary power but in terms of obedience to the commandments, *mitzvoth.* Man's deeds, his obedience to the commandments (*mitzvoth*) or his rejection of them, determine the fate of beings, whether or not the divine energy in being will be increased or diminished. In this way, "to practice the commandments is to endure the being of the world" (BTV, 161). In observing, or not, the commandments, man bears the burden of determining whether or not being is justified; he does not decide his own standing before God nor does he offend God in violating commandments—he destroys the world: "through the power of our sins, the force of the superior power is diminished."[28] There is in man more at issue than just himself. If bearing the world, deciding its fate, is what it means to be in the image of God, we would have found the historical figure or entry for what phenomenology means when it says that for the self "to support the universe is a crushing charge, but a divine discomfort" (OBBE, 122).[29]

The contribution historical religion has made to the articulation of Levinas's phenomenology is particularly evident in the role it has played in giving expression to one of responsibility's most important characteristics: passivity. "The rational subjectivity which we have inherited from Greek philosophy . . . does not entail the passivity which, in other philosophical essays, I have been able to identify with responsibility for the other" (BTV, 147). If this passivity does not come from our Greek inheritance, whence does it come? According to Levinas, it comes from the Bible and its reading in the Jewish tradition—most notably, from Exodus 24:7, a verse which appears in many of Levinas's Jewish writings and commentaries. This verse reads, "All that the Lord has spoken we will do and we will hear [understand]." According to this verse, as Levinas emphasizes, the Israelites respond to the revelation, the commandments, by doing before hearing and understanding. In such a shocking inversion of logic, and the logical order of moral action, it is not difficult to hear the strange structure of responsibility: the self is responsible before it commits itself to responsibility, before it knows or understands who and what it is responsible for. In doing before

hearing and understanding, the obedience of the Israelites precedes the calculation of a subject who would assess the situation, take stock of his own
capacities, and choose to accept or reject responsibility on the basis of a
rationality pertaining to what any I, the I in general, would do were it in his
place.

The absurdity or offensiveness of such a doing before hearing is regis-
tered by those textual variations, recorded in the notes to the *Biblia Hebraica
Stuttgartensia,* that have inverted the order and written, "we will hear and
we will do," almost as if they were posting an objection based on the Husserlian priority of consciousness. One of modern Judaism's great thinkers,
Martin Buber, in his translation of the Bible, also tries to mitigate the offensiveness of such a doing that precedes hearing and understanding when he
renders the verse, "We will do in order to understand," suggesting that
the doing is incomplete without the subsequent understanding to which it
leads.[30] According to Levinas's reading however, Talmudic Judaism teaches
that this apparent inversion or incompletion is in fact "a secret of angels";
as Rabbi Eleazar has said, "When the Israelites committed to doing before
hearing, a voice from heaven cried out: Who has revealed to my children
this secret the angels make use of, for it is written (Psalm 103:20): 'Bless the
Lord, oh, his angels, you mighty ones, who do His word, hearkening to the
voice of His word.'"[31] Thus, what Husserlian phenomenology would reject
as nonsense (a command by which I am affected before my consciousness
of it) Talmudic Judaism teaches as eminent uprightness, the ideal of man or
Temimut. The Talmud even goes so far as to record the objection of a Min
who also speaks as an early precursor of those objectors who base themselves on the primacy of a phenomenology of consciousness: "You should
have listened in order to know whether you were able to accept, and if you
were not able to accept, you should not have accepted."[32] But, as Levinas
emphasizes, for Talmudic Judaism—which he insists represents the Jewish
reading of Scripture—this offensive order is crucial to the notion of *Temimut;*
and the objections of the Min are dismissed.

Now simply pointing out or establishing a fact and interpreting it are different things. Not wanting to let these observed parallels between responsibility and the Jewish sources remain insignificant observations, I want to
recall the point of this comparison. It is as if the historical religions, or rather
the historical religion Judaism, has contributed notions without which phenomenology would not be able to access and articulate the responsibility
borne in the very subjectivity of the subject. One way to interpret this observed comparison would be to say that the contribution of religious traditions permits phenomenology to thematize the unthematizable saying and
to articulate the secret of subjectivity, a secret found in a responsibility that
arises before language and consciousness. In other words, without *quoting*
from religious traditions, without *citing* historical texts, phenomenology
could never have said the unutterable responsibility of the subject. As Derrida has observed, "It is not the presumed signatory of the work, E.L., who

says: 'Here I am,' me, presently. He *quotes* a 'Here I am,' he thematizes what is nonthematizable."[33] Often, though not always, appearing in quotation marks throughout Levinas's text, the "Here I am" (*me voici*) by which phenomenology articulates the responsibility of the subject is marked as a citation. Levinas once makes this citation explicit by footnoting one of the biblical texts from which it is drawn, Isaiah 6:8: "Here I am! send me" (OBBE, 199, n. 11). Without the texture of Jewish tradition, phenomenology finds itself unable to articulate the secret responsibility of the subject. Is this not because this secret was given to the subject by the event of Judaism? One could also add the frequent citation of "thou shalt not kill!" as the meaning of the face met in responsibility. The expression which precedes language, the face which says nothing, says Exodus 20:13 or Deuteronomy 5:17: "Thou shalt not kill!" If the meaning of the face is uttered by citing the interdiction against murder, one wonders if phenomenology is able to reach this meaning without recourse to the texture of religious traditions. Finally, I could add the biblical notion of the widow, the orphan, and the stranger, which identifies the face as a face of destitution and dereliction; and even Levinas himself will wonder if "perhaps, the reference to the face and the uniqueness without genre of the other man . . . is a recollection of the 'widow, orphan, and the stranger' in Biblical justice" (AQS, 81).

This is why I believe we must take Levinas seriously when he asks, "am I citing the Bible, or am I doing phenomenology" (AQS, 74). But, as he suggests later, the real question is "to know if this reference to the Bible falsifies phenomenology" (AQS, 80). That is to say, contrary to Janicaud, the mere reference or invocation of the Bible—the undeniable citation of its language and the appearance of biblical themes such as revelation, creation, election, inspiration—does not necessarily compromise the phenomenological status of phenomenology. As Levinas points out, even Husserl himself invokes the notion of animating someone (the inspiration I spoke of above) in the second volume of *Ideas* when he describes the constitution of the Other. And, I might add, *Cartesian Meditations* ends famously with an apparent collapsing of the distinction between philosophical and religious traditions when it cites together "the Delphic motto: 'Know thyself!'" and the *De vera religione* of Augustine: "*Noli foras ire,* says Augustine, *in te redi, in interiore homine habitat veritas*" (CM, §64).

Such a use of the Bible would suppose a theory of sacred scripture that is quite close to that held by certain thinkers of modern Judaism: Martin Buber and Franz Rosenzweig, for example. For them, the Bible is not considered to be of a supernatural origin which justifies its authority and the dogmatic use of its text. The citation of biblical and Talmudic texts does not serve as unquestionable proof or as the last word of any argument. As Buber and Rosenzweig before Levinas had said, the Bible is a text in which the testimony of man has been recorded—be it testimony to the I-Thou in Buber or to the epiphany of the face in Levinas. Biblical and Talmudic texts and formulae therefore appear in Levinas because these texts bear witness to the responsibility which Levinas also seeks to describe; they are not there because he intends his work to be Jewish or because he seeks to compel acknowledgment of his point. As he writes of his own work,

> My work, which is situated in the fullness of the documents beliefs and moral practices that characterize the positive fact of Judaism . . . , attempts to return to the structures or modalities of a *spiritual* that lends itself to, or consents to, or even tends toward, such treatment. These structures or modalities are hidden beneath consciousness, which is representative or conceptual, already invested in the world, hence absorbed in it. They are hidden but can be discerned by a phenomenology attentive to the horizons of consciousness, and in this sense (despite its use of biblical and Talmudic documents and formulations) it is a phenomenology prior to a theology that would use what it has borrowed as its premises. (ITN, 109)

Here, Levinas at once acknowledges that (1) his work is situated in the documents belonging to the "positive fact of Judaism—its historical and empirical content," and (2) the structure of the spirituality which he seeks is discernible by phenomenology. The two claims are not incompatible if one understands that while phenomenology alone can access the responsibility of the self as such, it can do so only insofar as it has received the notion of responsibility and the terms by which it will articulate it from the fact of Judaism, its documents and their reading.

Conclusion

If, in beginning this chapter, I suggested that there is no religion without responsibility, it now seems that I have been led to say that there is no responsibility without religion, that is, without the fact or event of historical religious traditions, in particular Judaism, which marks the opening of a new epoch in the history of responsibility and religion. The articulation of responsibility is possible insofar as religious traditions have endowed the history of the West with the themes and "logic" necessary for its phenomenological discovery in the heart of the self as such. It seems, then, that the phenomenology of responsibility and the historical fact of Judaism are co-implicated: through the investigation of responsibility, the former produces the latter as a possibility while the latter gives access to the notion of responsibility which the former articulates. This is why Levinas's phenomenology can appear to be at times more orthodox than the orthodox, at times heretical, and at times purely phenomenological. When he frequently wonders if his Talmudic commentaries have discovered the notion of responsibility in these texts or read it into them, he gives voice to this ambiguity.

The two hypotheses—phenomenology producing a certain religiosity; the event of Judaism producing or unveiling responsibility—need not be understood as exclusive or incompatible. There is indeed a precedent, or several precedents, in the history of philosophy and religious thought where they have been made to inhabit the same space of thought. I think, first and somewhat provocatively, of no one less than G. W. F. Hegel for whom the philosophy of religion moved precisely between a speculative deduction of religious truths and a hermeneutic recovery of Christian doctrine. As we saw in chapter 7, the Hegelian philosophy of religion aimed at a re-establishment of the Christian religion wherein the doctrines of the Christian faith, having been by and large abandoned by his theological contemporaries, were articulated in and through speculative philosophy, which therefore comes as something of a relief to a bankrupt theology. Consider this brief example of a project which permeates the work:

> Suppose that we take *God* as our point of departure. Then God or spirit is this judgment [or primal division: *Ur-teil*]; expressed concretely, this is the creation of the world and of the subjective spirit for which God is object. Spirit is an absolute manifesting. . . . 'Manifesting' means 'creating an other' and indeed the creating of subjective spirit for which the absolute is. . . . In a further and later definition we will have this manifestation in the higher form that what God creates God himself is, that in general it does not have the determinateness of an other, that God is manifestation of his own self, that God is for himself—the other . . . the Son of God or human being according to the divine image.[34]

Starting simply with the concept of spirit, thought thinking this concept is logically led to deduce the truths of the historical religions: creation, then man in the image of God, and ultimately the necessity for the second person of the Trinity. The remainder of the *Lectures on the Philosophy of Religion* are an extended working out of this project in which philosophical deduction, not faith, passes through each shape of determinate historical religion until it reaches the consummate religion, Christianity, where the concept of spirit is an object for itself. This ultimate end reveals the beginning. That is, the concept of Spirit, which speculative thought thinks in the course of deducing the religions, comes from the event of a particular religious tradition: namely, Christianity. Again, to cite Derrida, "Everything *comes to pass* as though only the analysis of the concept of [Spirit] were ultimately capable of producing Christianity. . . . One might as well conclude, conversely, that this concept of [Spirit] is Christian through and through and is produced by the event of Christianity" (GD, 50).

Thus, the relation between the historical event of Judaism and ethical phenomenology's recovery of religion could be compared to the relation between the Christian faith and the philosophy of religion in Hegel. Just as for Hegel philosophical thought of the concept of Spirit articulates a religious discourse without recourse to faith or the events of revelation transmitted by traditional authority, so too in Levinas does the analysis of responsibility produce a religious discourse without reference to faith and dogma. Just as for Hegel the concept of Spirit comes from a historical religion which is then deduced speculatively without reference to its event, so too for Levinas does the concept of responsibility come from a historical religion whose possibility is then repeated through the phenomenology of responsibility. Clearly delineating the many differences between the two projects in philosophy of religion is also certainly necessary, but it depends on first recognizing the points of convergence around which the debate could be conducted. Further study is surely needed.

9

The Ethical Possibility
of God

For the philosophy of religion, one phenomenon in particular poses a difficulty that has been almost insurmountable—that of God, more particularly, the transcendence of God. This difficulty is evident in the observed fact that the emergence of the modern philosophy of religion in the nineteenth century was simultaneous with what Hegel and Nietzsche both spoke of as "the death of God." When the modern philosophy of religion was born, nearly all religious phenomena were recovered or re-grounded with the exception of one—the transcendence or absoluteness of God and its corollary, a revelation that is not reduced to individual genius or a provisional necessity to be overcome by the freedom of reason. To be sure, each of the founding figures of this discipline claimed to have retrieved the sense of God in his very death—to God's benefit (Hegel) or not (Nietzsche); but none maintained the sense of God's transcendence or of a revelation that maintained this transcendence.

Even Kant, who claimed to have cleared a way for faith in the existence of a God transcending theoretical reason, did so at the price of excluding this transcendence from philosophy, leaving it only as a postulate of practical reason. While reason could say much about religion and so could reestablish religious notions on a new ground, it said little about God, except to postulate his existence, and nothing or nothing positive about a revelation of transcendence. Kant's philosophy was able to save religion at the price of rendering revelation (the breakthrough of a transcendence coming from beyond consciousness) at best a provisional aid to what reason can provide itself. This is evident in the fact that for Kant the Christ of history is but an example of the highest ideal held by reason, an example used to lead sluggish and sensuous man to an ideal which it should, in the best of all possible worlds, be able to attain without Him.

On this reading, Nietzsche's word, God is dead, spoken by the madman, consummates the vanishing of transcendence supposed and effected by the rational theology and philosophy of religion dominating the nineteenth century—and, if Heidegger is to be believed, by the entirety of theological and philosophical thought. Nietzsche, the last metaphysician, claimed to have revealed the hidden ground of the entire metaphysical tradition by a reduction of all phenomena, above all God, to an expression of the will to power, which thus grounds a vision of the totality of beings, without exception and hence without transcendence. This consummation issues directly in the phenomenology of Husserl; for it is this phenomenology that claims to be a method and movement to the sphere of immanence where there appears each and every possible being.[1] In Husserl, in contrast to Hegel, God is so dead that the sphere of immanence can be said without uttering his name; the transcendental subject, consciousness, is absolute immanence without in any way being identified with the mind or thought of God or Spirit. The name God appears only rarely in Husserl's text, and then only to be put immediately between quotation marks, scare quotes:

> What concerns us here . . . is that this being [a "divine" beyond the world] would obviously transcend not merely the world, but "absolute" Consciousness. It would thus be an *"absolute" in the sense totally different from that in which consciousness is* an absolute. . . . Naturally, we extend the phenomenological reduction to include this "absolute" and "transcendent" being. It shall remain excluded from the new field of research which is to be provided, since this shall be a pure field of consciousness. (Id, 134)[2]

But, what if "the field of research which is to be provided" is not consciousness? What if the aim of phenomenology is compromised by restricting its field to consciousness, as I tried to argue in part 2? Would God "appear" to such a subject?

Nineteenth-century philosophy of religion could be summed up in the following remark from Levinas: "The transcendent or the Absolute, or the One, cannot enter into relation with the soul [revelation] without beginning within it; but by doing so it ceases to justify its transcendence" (BTV, 126). This truth holds for the founding figures of the philosophy of religion—exemplified by Kant and Hegel—was uttered by their critic—Nietzsche—and was consummated in the phenomenology of Husserl. It thus appears that the test of any serious advance in the philosophy of religion will be its ability to maintain the transcendence of God and his revelation in a thought that is nonetheless submitted to philosophical criteria of intelligibility and rationality. In this chapter, I will argue that Levinas's phenomenology does indeed help make such an advance and that this advance goes hand-in-hand with his envisaging a field of research not restricted to pure consciousness.

The Idea of Infinity

According to Levinas, the idea of infinity permits a thought of God that does not immediately imply the death of this God or the reduction of transcendence to the immanence of an object thought by consciousness. "The idea of the infinite . . . conserves for reflection the paradoxical knot which is already tied in religious revelation. The latter . . . is knowledge of a God who, while offering himself within this openness, also remains absolutely other or transcendent" (EN, 245 [modified]). God, given to religion in the paradoxical revelation of that which transcends knowledge, is kept for philosophical thought by the idea of the infinite since this idea is precisely an idea of what cannot be included in any idea thought by a thought. It therefore repeats in philosophy the revelation of what reveals itself without being subjected to the conditions imposed on it by the concept. Thus, if the philosophical thought of God and God's revelation is not to imply, follow upon, or have as its consequence, the death of God, it must, according to Levinas, proceed through the idea of the infinite.

But, isn't the idea of the infinite pure madness, the pretense of a thought not yet fully rational, not yet fully satisfied with itself and unhappily pretending that the infinite remains, as such, outside it? Isn't it a willed servitude to claim to have an idea of a thing but not to accomplish fully the thought of it? And aren't madness and servitude the precise contraries of philosophy, which is reason and freedom? Hegel said as much in his discussion of the unhappy consciousness, Jewish religion, and the bad infinite. If he is right, wouldn't philosophy of religion be doomed to fail in its attempt to think transcendence and revelation without reducing them to a satisfied or happy consciousness?

In order that these questions not remain as unanswered objections, the following question must be asked: How can the possibility of the Infinite, transcendent to its idea, be established irreducibly? That is to say, in terms of what can the infinite, as such, appear as an originary and irreducible possibility? On what stage does the subject play when he receives the idea of infinity? Just as when discussing the significance of religious phenomena the real question was not to demonstrate that such phenomena or events actually occurred in the life of a subject but to show that such phenomena were possible, so too the problem posed to the thought of God is not to demonstrate an actual God who is infinite but to show that such an infinite is possible. For that, it falls to phenomenology to reconstruct the subjectivity in which such an idea might be significant. In two essays, "On the Idea of the Infinite in Us" and "God and Philosophy," Levinas undertakes precisely such a project, showing that the possibility of the infinite cannot be established by a phenomenological account that takes the subject to be exhausted in consciousness, the *cogito,* or I think.[3] Instead, it falls to a phenomenology that uncovers the subjectivity of the subject in responsibility to assure the significance of what is meant by the idea of the infinite, to make its possibility rational according to the broader rationality discovered by the phenomenology of ethics.

Somewhat surprisingly, the starting point for Levinas's discussion is Descartes's experience of the idea of infinity as that experience is recorded in the third of his *Meditationes*. It is no doubt significant that Levinas chooses a philosopher, and no less a philosopher than the founder of modern philosophy, as the source for his description of revelation and transcendence. This choice suggests that he means for his interpretation of the idea of infinite to be situated not in a religious reflection that starts from the authority of tradition or dogma but in philosophy, perhaps a philosophy of religion.

For Levinas, Descartes's "experience" is important not because it proves the existence of God nor because it establishes this existence on the basis of the certainty of the *cogito*, but because it figures the undoing of the consciousness that is conscious of it: "In his meditation on the idea of God, Descartes has sketched the extraordinary course of a thought, proceeding to the point of the breakup of the *I think*" (GCM, 62). Contrary to the traditional interpretation, which has it that Descartes is the thinker of an unimpeachable and unshakeable *cogito*, Levinas notes that Descartes's thought of the infinite interrupts the primacy of the *cogito*, suggesting that the *cogito* does not exhaust all there is of subjectivity but that it is preceded by another, anterior instance. Despite Descartes's confessed intentions, "it is not the proofs for the existence of God which interest [Levinas], but the rupture of consciousness" (GCM, 63). The rejection of these proofs entails the rejection of the principle of causality which was introduced in order to put them into operation. To prove the existence of God outside his idea of God, Descartes determines God in accordance with the principle of causality: first, God necessarily exists not because there must be an external reality similar to the idea which I have acquired through the senses but because my idea must have a cause, which can only be God; and, then, second, even God must have a cause, if only himself as *causa sui*.[4] In this, one can easily recognize the onto-theo-logical thought of God in terms of causality, a determination which proved fatal in the time of Nietzsche; and, in the second, one can also see the eventual, if not already actual, elimination of God's transcendence in that *causa sui* names a God whose existence is proven by the same principle as the existence of creatures is proven: the principle of causality, which thus stands over all. The Cartesian aim of proving the existence of God must therefore be rejected by a philosophy of religion that seeks to recover or establish the meaning of transcendence.

Though rejecting Descartes's intention to prove the existence of God based on his experience of the idea of infinity, Levinas nonetheless will employ his experience. For it "describes the meaning of what is designated by divine existence, rather than [the consciousness] of an object adequate or equal to the intention of a knowing intention" (EN, 220). How can the meaning of God that is described by Descartes's idea of the infinite be explicated so that it maintains transcendence and the possibility of a revelation to thought that does not annul this transcendence? For the sake of convenience, I have highlighted four points to help address this question.

1. As finite, *the idea of the infinite thinks what cannot be contained in the unity or immanence of the I think*. It is an idea of the noncontainable, what cannot be contained in any idea. As Descartes writes, "It does not matter that I do not grasp the infinite, or that there are countless additional attributes of God which I cannot in any way grasp, and perhaps cannot even reach in my thought; for it is in the nature of the infinite not to be grasped by a finite being like myself" (AT, 46). The idea of the infinite can never be thought adequately enough, can never achieve adequacy with its *ideatum* since this *ideatum* is infinite or in possession of innumerable attributes and therefore exceeds whatever can be thought about it. What is given in this thought or this "experience" of thought overflows what this idea could mean, contain, or intend. This is what Levinas is saying in the frequently repeated phrases "the *more* in the *less*," or a "thought destined to think more than it thinks," or when he writes of a "dazzling where the eye holds more than it can hold" (GCM, 67). Exceeding what can be equaled or comprehended by a thought which nonetheless "thinks" it, the idea of the infinite resists the noetic-noematic correlation or fulfillment which characterizes consciousness. "Non-encompassable" and "unable to be comprehended," the infinite resists the synoptic gaze that would grasp together each of its parts or moments of appearing in a present of consciousness. Failing thus to be phenomenalized in the present, it indicates the collapse of the a priori correlation of consciousness and its objects. As such, the possibility of the infinite will not be found by a phenomenology of consciousness, where all that comes to light does so in the present and as an object adequate to the intention that aims at knowledge of it.

But, though it eludes adequacy with the intentions of consciousness, the infinite is not unrelated to me and even is, in a certain way, thought by me—as Descartes claims. "The idea [of God as infinite] is utterly clear and distinct. . . . It does not matter that I do not grasp the infinite" (AT, 46); "by God I mean that whose idea is in me, that is, the possessor of all those perfections which I do not comprehend but which I can touch with my thought" (AT, 52); "to comprehend something is to embrace it in one's thought; to know something it suffices to touch it with one's thought" (Letter to Mersenne, May 26, 1630). In distinguishing a thought which comprehends from that which touches or nonetheless understands, Descartes envisions a thought or meaning of God that is not played out in the field of (Husserlian) consciousness, where every intentional act can be fulfilled by intuition that is at best adequate to it but most often lacking or deficient.

2. *The idea of the infinite does not originate in my own* cogito *but is put into me*. When Descartes considered all the ideas he could find in the *cogito* (ideas of God, things, angels, animals, and other men [AT, 43]), in every case but one he concluded that they could each have originated in the idea that he had of himself—the exception being the idea of God. He argues that the ideas of things, animals, angels, and even other men need not presuppose

the existence of the thing outside my *cogito* since these ideas could in fact have been formed from the idea I have of myself. This is so because each of the elements which make up these ideas—namely, extension, shape, movement, and position—is a mode of substance. "But since they are merely modes of substance, and I am a substance, it seems possible that they are contained in me eminently" (AT, 45). In the idea of God, however, the situation is different; for, "by the word God I understand a substance that is infinite, independent, supremely intelligent, supremely powerful, and which created both myself and everything else (if anything else there be) which exists. All these attributes are such that, the more carefully I consider them, the less possible it seems that they could have originated from me alone" (AT, 45). Of course, Levinas will not accept the substantialist language employed by Descartes, nor the interpretation of the relation between an idea and its *ideatum* in terms of causality; nor will he use the Cartesian evidence to establish a proof for the existence of God. What he will adopt is the "experience" of a subject who, reflecting on an idea in the *cogito*, finds in itself more than it can account for by itself from itself alone. If the meditating philosopher finds in himself an idea which could not have come from himself, Levinas following Descartes concludes, it is there only because it was put in him.

3. *This putting of an idea into me implies the passivity of an affected subject.* An idea put in me, the infinite affects me "despite myself" or without regard for what is possible for an I or consciousness. Before affecting myself with its possibility, I am subjected to the blow whereby this idea was put in me. As put in us, the idea of the infinite requires a certain fundamental passivity—what Levinas calls a "passivity unlike any other because it cannot be assumed," a passivity therefore "that one cannot assimilate to receptivity" (GCM, 63, 64). Lacking the capacity to receive, this passivity cannot hold or retain the infinite and therefore does not furnish material for the conscious work of generating a phenomenon in the present of consciousness present to itself. This means that the idea of the infinite or "the idea of God is, from top to bottom, affectivity," where affectivity does not mean welcoming in a form or an idea (EN, 221). The passivity of this affectivity would mark the idea of the infinite as, in a sense, an intuition that has given without respect for the limits of intentionality. Having been put in me, the idea of the infinite marks the appearance of what precedes the intentional a priori where all is "given beforehand" as a possibility for consciousness. Such an idea "perhaps reverses—*avant la lettre*—the universal validity of and originality of intentionality" (GCM, 63 [modified]). The origin of intentionality being reversed, I am no longer the agent of an intention but the recipient of an intention directed at me. Under this reversal of intentionality, the idea of the infinite reduces consciousness to its affectivity where it finds itself affected by what does not and cannot find an origin in the I who gives itself all its possibilities beforehand

Though Descartes finds the idea of infinity in reflection on his own *cogito*, it is found to have already been there before this *cogito* even was. After concluding that this idea must have been put in me without my intending to find it there, Descartes writes, "It only remains for me to examine how I received this idea from God. [It did not come from the senses, and I did not invent it.] The only remaining alternative is that it is innate in me, just as the idea of myself is innate in me" (AT, 51). The idea of the infinite thus precedes the beginning of the *cogito* in which it is discovered. The French translation is even more suggestive, reading: "Il ne reste plus autre chose à dire, sinon que, comme l'idée de moi-même, elle est née et produite avec moi dès lors que j'ai été créé [There remains nothing else to say but that, like the idea of myself, it (the idea of the infinite) was born and produced with me from when I was created]." Following this version, Levinas suggests therefore that the idea of the infinite suggests "the passivity of the created one" (GCM, 64), who, as such, lags behind his own origin and so has come too late to be able to account for or claim as his property all that is possible for him. This is why Descartes also declares, "the perception of the infinite is somehow prior in me to the perception of the finite, that is my perception of God is prior to my perception of myself" (AT, 45). Found there where a subject is not first related to itself but to what is other than it, the appearance of God is not restricted to the measure of the *cogito* or I think, thought thinking thought or present to its own thought.

In brief, then, the possibility of the idea of the infinite cannot be established phenomenologically by an interrogation of consciousness. To assure the significance of the meaning "intended" by the idea of the infinite, phenomenology must look to what precedes the conscious subject who gives itself all that affects it. As Levinas writes, the idea of the infinite marks "an exception to the commonly accepted phenomenology of thought which, in an essential sense, is atheistic precisely as thought equaling the thought that fills and *satis*-fies it" (EN, 220). This is why Descartes's meditation on this idea marks an interruption (the only one) in his reflection on the *cogito,* a pause in his attempt to reconstruct clear and certain knowledge of the world on the basis of the evidence of the *cogito:* "I should like to pause here and spend some time in the contemplation of God; to reflect on his attributes, and to consider, wonder, and adore the beauty of this immense light, so far as the eye of my darkened intellect can bear it" (AT, 52). The meditation on the infinite thus ends not with full or adequate knowledge of God but with admiration, adoration, and bedazzlement—the passivity of affectivity.

If the meaning of God can nonetheless be articulated, how are we to account for its significance? Is it just a play on words, a mere abstraction or a definition reached in and through pure speculation or imagination? Or, can phenomenology establish the infinite in its possibility such that its meaning no longer appears as the mere explication of a word but is assured of its significance? A further description of how the infinite comes to its idea—how it is thought—will help find its phenomenological possibility.

4. Up until now, the meaning of the infinite has appeared only with a negative sense; it exceeds the thought that cannot contain it and therefore

cannot be described positively. Nonetheless, Levinas argues, the subject has a "positive" relation to it. Returning to a key theme of *Totality and Infinity*, Levinas speaks of this affective relation with the Infinite as Desire: "a passivity, or passion, in which Desire is recognized, in which the *'more in the less'* awakens with its most ardent, most noble, and most ancient flame, a thought devoted to think more than it can think" (GCM, 67). *At the failing-point where the subject is summoned to think more than it can think, desire succeeds consciousness.*

But, this is a desire which is not interpretable in terms of my intentions. In the first place, this desire does not start with or find its origin in consciousness but in the infinite itself which awakens desire by the very fact of its idea having been put in me. Furthermore, as in-finite, the "term" of this desire exceeds all that could satisfy the needs or wants that consciousness could intend for itself. "The negativity of the *In-* of the Infinite—otherwise than Being, divine comedy—hollows out a desire that could not be filled, one nourished from its own increase, exalted as Desire—one that withdraws from its satisfaction as it draws near to the Desirable" (GCM, 67). As movement toward the infinite, this desire is not an intentional act of consciousness since this movement is not susceptible of fulfillment or adequation by any intuition belonging to a finite subject. Whereas the intentionality of consciousness finds a stopping point, at least an eventual one, in the object intended by an idea, the desire for the infinite grows deeper the more this idea is thought, seeing as this thought always contains more than thought can think. Hence, the desire for God does not mean possessing God but always wanting more. Levinas cites the following text from Kierkegaard: "In the case of worldly goods, to the degree to which man feels less need for them, he becomes more perfect. . . . But in the relationship between man and God, the principle is inverted: the more man feels the need for God, the more he is perfect" (GCM, 109). Theological desire does *not* rest secure with its object, perfectly adequate to it and correlative of it such that he needs no more of it; it is not perfected when it has attained its object, and if it could attain this object, it would be no longer. Theological desire grows more perfect the more it desires the infinite which is forever ab-solving itself from desire, ex-ceeding it, and so lacking from it.[5]

Here, a difficulty emerges: "Does not desire restore the contemporaneousness of the desiring and the Desirable? . . . Does not the desiring one derive from the Desirable a complacency [*complaisance*] in desiring, as if it had already grasped the Desirable by its intention" (GCM, 67)? That is to say, even if the intention is not intuitively fulfilled, isn't the desirable still correlative with desiring consciousness since, after all, objects are most often given in intentions lacking complete intuitive fulfillment? Wouldn't the pretended transcendence of the infinite therefore fall back into the immanence of a consciousness aiming at objects? I have already shown that for Levinas the infinite exceeds its idea and is therefore not given in a lack of intuition, but by exceeding its idea—absent by its excess. How then does he describe this desire such that it does not tend toward what it lacks? How does God maintain his distance from Desire?

5. *This desire for the infinite signifies in terms of goodness and responsibility for the Other.* According to Levinas, "the Desirable or God remains separate in Desire . . . only if the Desirable orders me to what is non-desirable, to the non-desirable, par excellence, *autrui*" (GCM, 68 [modified]). Ordered to the nondesirable by virtue of my desire, I am not able to rejoice in the end or term at which my desire would aim; for, in fact, this desire is completely disorienting and lacking in straightforwardness: it turns me from its end and directs me to what is most foreign to it—the nondesirable, *autrui*. This is what dictates that it be termed "Good." The infinite is good, above all, in that it does not accept what desire offers but directs this desire to an other, *Autrui*. The Good thus completely disorients desire, turning it away from the infinite which aroused it and which it wants, in order that the infinite might escape a present shared with desire. The infinite is "Good in this very precise, eminent sense: He does not fill me with goods, but compels me to goodness, which is better than to receive goods" (GCM, 69).

The idea of the infinite thus signifies goodness and a subjectivity ordered to responsibility for *Autrui*. As Levinas writes, "transcendence is ethical, and the subjectivity which in the final analysis is not the 'I think' or the unity of 'transcendental apperception' is, as responsibility for *Autrui*, subjection to *autrui*" (GCM, 68).

What Sort of an Argument Is This?

Having reached this conclusion, "God and Philosophy" proceeds with a description of subjectivity as responsibility. The descriptions are for the most part quite similar to those put forth in *Otherwise than Being, or, Beyond Essence* and therefore do not need to be repeated here as I have already described the structure of this subject in chapter 4. Nevertheless, I want to note that they do indeed follow; for they raise several questions regarding their relation to the preceding discussion of God.

On one such a reading, ethics or responsibility is preceded by a theological relation which either causes or implies in itself the ethical relation: the responsible subject would be the end term of a deduction or analytic unfolding of the idea of the infinite. On the other hand, the infinite or God might be seen as something like the condition for the possibility of ethics: ethical experience presupposes the idea of God as that without which it would not be possible to explain the fact of responsibility and subjection to others. Robert Gibbs, in his "Jewish Dimensions of Radical Ethics," seems to suggest such a theological starting point when he favorably compares Levinas and Franz Rosenzweig, writing: "The theological relations of [Rosenzweig's] *The Star of Redemption* lead directly to the ethics of relations with other persons. Hence as in Levinas we have an ethical reading of theological concerns. The responsibility we have to the infinite commits us to approach the nearest one." Does a relation to the infinite or God precede ethical relations into which it leads? Do I have a responsibility for the infinite in addition to and preceding, as it were, my responsibility for the neighbor? Though Gibbs's argument does not exactly claim that responsibility is unfolded from the infinite or that God is the condition for the possibility of ethics, he does seem to drift toward the latter claim, for instance when he writes, "without the radical transcendence that height provides for Levinas, nearness could not possibly serve as radically ethical."[6]

To be sure, Levinas's own manner of presentation in "God and Philosophy" would invite such interpretations insofar as he begins with the idea of the infinite and reaches responsibility only after an analysis of what the former implies. I believe, however, that, appearances to the contrary notwithstanding, such interpretations must be resisted. First of all, to interpret these arguments as an attempt to start with the infinite and then demonstrate ethics by inferences or unfold ethics by analysis of implied contents would be to place both God and the responsible subject in the order of causality—an order which pertains only to beings and thus directly contradicts Levinas's claim to Otherwise than Being. Second, and more importantly, to interpret the infinite as the starting point of a deduction or analytic unfolding or even as the condition for the possibility of ethics would be to ignore the primacy of the ethical in Levinas. How can the claim "ethics is first philosophy" be harmonized with an interpretation that makes the infinite or a theological relation the prior condition for the possibility of ethics? In replacing or avoiding the ethical starting point, this argument would seem to compromise one of Levinas's central claims. What is more, it would have done nothing to find or establish the possibility of the infinite or to guarantee that the analyses are anything more than a verbal abstraction, a play on words, void of significance. The idea is simply assumed, given as assumed—from where? From theology and religious tradition, one must suppose again, following Gibbs when he writes, "Does this mean that radical ethics needs Judaism? Yes. Not in an absolute sense, and certainly not in a dogmatic sense. Jews have no monopoly either on this God or the struggle for this ethics. . . . Ethics needs Jewish thought in the sense that it requires a true infinite, a radically transcendent God who can make the dimension of height turn into hyperbole."[7] On this reading, ethics inherits an idea of transcendence that is indispensable to the determination of the intersubjective space as radically ethical. This inheritance remains an assumption, something assumed from previous tradition, and this assumption serves as the basis for articulating the ethical relation. But such an assumption, any assumption in fact, is precisely what must be abandoned if the meaning of the infinite, or any phenomenon whatsoever, is to be assured a significance that is not instituted by authority (however nondogmatic) or by the mere explication of a word.

Seeking to respect the phenomenological starting point and to support the claim that Levinas's philosophy can be read within a philosophy of religion, what I would like to propose is this: In arriving at goodness and re-sponsibility, "God and Philosophy" has not completed an analysis of what is meant by the idea of the infinite. Though the presentation of the material starts with the idea of the infinite and arrives at responsibility, Levinas is not arguing that there is actual ethical experience because we have the idea of the infinite or God. Instead, as Levinas writes, "[If] it is the signification of the beyond, of transcendence, and not of ethics that our study seeks, it finds it in ethics" (GCM, 200, n. 23 [modified]). In other words, ethics de-scribes the horizon within which the meaning of the infinite acquires signi-ficance. As Levinas writes, "In order that the formula, 'transcendence to the point of absence' not signify the mere explication of an ex-ceptional word, it was necessary to restore this word to the signification of ethical intrigue" (GCM, 69). Such a task, to bring a word back to the situation in which it arose or to assure the significance of a word against a mere analysis of its meaning, clearly falls to phenomenology, which with Husserl's *Logical Investigations* originated with such a task in mind. With a few revisions, this citation from Levinas could easily have been written by Husserl himself; but, for reasons already discussed, when it is a matter of God and the idea of the infinite, the phenomenology of consciousness does not suffice. Instead, for the idea of God to be established in its possibility, phenomenology must revert to the significations found in responsibility. "Ethics . . . is the very possibility of the beyond" (GCM, 69). Though speculation on the idea of the infinite can give us the meaning of God's transcendence, such a God will seem abstract, a play on words, unless it can be shown to be possible; and for that, according to Levinas, the phenomenology of responsibility is needed. This is best expressed in the following intratextual gloss of a citation from Levinas: "This abstract idea [or empty meaning of the word 'infinite'] of something that precedes the originary [consciousness] which we seem to be constructing is provided for us in a concrete way [that is, a way in which its meaning is assured significance and possibility] by the responsibility pri-or to commitment" (BTV, 127).

On this reading, one might say that the often recurring, and sometimes confusing, path whereby Levinas's argument starts with the infinite and ends with responsibility is not a deduction but a reduction—a reconduction of the given back to the subject where it first appears. Levinas takes the in-finite as a point of departure (a given) and proceeds back to its anarchic be-ginning (to no longer taking this given for granted but to seeing it in its giv-enness) in the subject who passively receives it. As a reduction, the strange order in which the argument is presented can be explained: Levinas's argu-ment, like Husserl's, follows a way back to the beginning; it reconducts the given (the infinite) to the subject (responsibility) and the horizon (ethics) where it finds its possibility and its meaning is assured signification. Phe-nomenology, according to Levinas, can establish the possibility and signi-ficance of the infinite, that is to say God, insofar as it practices an ethical reduction.

This would explain, I think, why Levinas will often seem to repeat the analysis he has just undertaken—in other words, why in "God and Philosophy," after he seems to have articulated the meaning of the infinite as goodness and responsibility, Levinas will say, "The exposition of the ethical meaning of transcendence, and of the Infinite beyond being, can be carried out starting from the proximity of the neighbor and my responsibility for the other" (GCM, 70). What does it mean here to say the exposition can be conducted "starting from" responsibility? Hasn't Levinas already ended his exposition or explanation of the meaning of transcendence? Why now at the point where the essay seems to have reached its end does he say that the procedure can be started? What is this second beginning?

We encounter the same puzzling suggestion of a new or second beginning at the end of the essay "The Idea of the Infinite in Us." As in "God and Philosophy," this essay arrives at the point where the experience of the idea of the infinite suggests the affection of a subject that must be described as other than *I think*. This affection, Levinas concludes, is irreversible and so happens in a passivity that is not equal to the receptivity whereby consciousness assumes what affects it absolutely. Having reached this conclusion, Levinas asks "whether this affectivity of adoration and this passivity of bedazzlement can admit of further phenomenological interpretation, or whether they can be attained on the basis of an analysis situated at the level of the interpersonal order and the otherness of the other man, my fellow-man, my responsibility for the other" (EN, 221). Again, Levinas seems to suggest that the analysis of responsibility or intersubjectivity would mark a second starting point for an analysis concerned with establishing the possibility of the infinite.

In fact, however, this second starting point is the phenomenological beginning to which the ethical reduction would return us. Having practiced a reduction of the infinite to the subject wherein its meaning appears, it now becomes possible to pursue a phenomenological analysis of that subject and recover the significance of the infinite. In that analysis, the meaning of the infinite no longer appears as a play on words, a mere abstraction or definition, the analysis or unfolding of the meaning of a term, infinite. Levinas says, "to do phenomenology is not only to safeguard the significance of language, threatened, in its abstraction or in its isolation. . . . It is to research the human or interhuman plot as the fabric of the ultimate intelligibility. And that perhaps is also the path whereby the wisdom of heaven returns to earth" (EN, 221).

The "wisdom of heaven returning to earth" refers to a passage from no one less than Hegel. Commenting on the Enlightenment project of demystification and rational critique, Hegel claims that "heaven is transplanted to earth below"[8] only when his own speculative philosophy is able to reconcile the Enlightenment (Kantian) division between faith and knowledge by overcoming the transcendence of an unknowable God. That is to say, Hegelian philosophy presupposes and consummates the descent of God from his abstract and remote transcendence to the sphere of history and experience. Theological truths then can be recovered by a speculative philosophy, which therefore comes as something of a relief to an impoverished or dead theology. No doubt, it is strange that Levinas should refer favorably to Hegel, especially to a passage in which Hegel seems to promote the overcoming of transcendence and the realization of a total immanence. What is going on in such a reference?

I believe that this reference suggests that the relation between Levinas's phenomenology and his account of God should be read according to the Hegelian schema of philosophy of religion. That is to say, Levinas recovers theological notions through the resources of ethical phenomenology in such a way that philosophy, here in its figure of ethical phenomenology, can articulate theological notions in an intelligible or rational, that is philosophical, language—if we accept the broader sense of rationality and intelligibility opened by Levinas's ethical reduction. In the reduction to responsibility, Levinas's phenomenology achieves a philosophical thought of God (like Hegel) that articulates the significance of God without leaving divine transcendence in a silent faith or purely subjective opinion and at the same time without destroying transcendence or denying the possibility of a revelation. The difference from Hegel arises, obviously, in the continued claim to a divine transcendence; and this difference is explained by the different figure of philosophy adopted in each—ethical phenomenology, conceptual thought.

As "the wisdom of heaven returned to earth," ethical phenomenology in thinking God stands outside the traditional distinction between the God of Abraham, Isaac, and Jacob and the God of the philosophers.

> To ask oneself, as we are attempting to do here, whether God cannot be uttered in a reasonable discourse that would be neither ontology nor faith, is implicitly to doubt the formal opposition, established by Yehuda Halevi and taken up by Pascal, between, on the one hand, the God of Abraham, Isaac, and Jacob, invoked without philosophy in faith, and on the other the god of the philosophers. It is to doubt that this opposition constitutes an alternative. (GCM, 57)

The traditional distinction has posed the following alternative: either submit God to onto-theology and consciousness, reducing transcendence to objective immanence in order to know him fully; or remain unable to articulate the meaning of what faith holds—except by recourse to authority and dogma—in order that God might be absolute and unconditional, transcendent. Against this distinction, Levinas's phenomenology speaks of "the rationality, and the rationalism of transcendence," of "reasons that 'reason' does not know" since they did not begin in consciousness or immanence (GCM, 57, 77). In a phenomenology that practices the reduction to responsibility, the revelation of transcendence does not mean that rationality, where significance is given to meaning, is abandoned in a thought which, "in order not to be ontological, falls back on . . . views without necessity and words that play" (DQV, 125). Read this way, Levinas's phenomenological recovery of God does indeed bear a surprising—shocking perhaps—resemblance to the Hegelian project. This resemblance, I must stress, is formal or schematic and does not pertain to the content of each. Like Hegel, Levinas's phenomenology is concerned with articulating, in philosophy, a rational thought of God, if by "rational" we accept Levinas's extension of rationality beyond the strict sphere of knowledge, conceptual thought, and adequate evidence.

The Ethical Possibility of God

Having achieved the reduction to responsibility, how does phenomenology describe the possibility of the God appearing there? What significance does the phenomenology of ethics find for the word "God"?

In its articulation of the significance of God, Levinas's phenomenology displays something distinctive in contemporary thought of religion. When in the previous chapter I discussed a possible religiosity in postmodern or death-of-God culture, one might not have been especially surprised or impressed. For, after all, the psychologists, sociologists, and historians of religion have taught us to find the religious disseminated throughout social and private life in today's secular culture; they have taught us that, though God is dead, religion is everywhere. While reducing Levinas's thought of religiosity to another secular transformation of religion is overly simplistic and in fact eliminates many possibly interesting points of comparison with other such projects before even asking about them, such a reduction also overlooks, more importantly, Levinas's claim to give a meaning to the transcendence of God. It is here, above all, that his thought distinguishes itself not only from the Hegelian philosophy of religion, but from those secular transformations of religion. Levinas's thought opens both the possibility of religiosity *and* the possibility of the revelation of a transcendent God.

In finding a meaning of God's transcendence, however, Levinas does not return to the theism inherent to metaphysical thought before the death of God; this transcendence is not that of a God who inhabits a heavenly world behind the scenes. Like most postmodern thinkers for whom the overcoming of metaphysics is a task, Levinas insists that the self is an atheist. The responsible self "is a creature, but an orphan by birth or an atheist no doubt ignorant of its Creator, for if it knew it[,] it would again be taking up its commencement" (OBBE, 105). In responsibility, the creaturely self is an atheist insofar as it is forever delayed behind and therefore ignorant of its origin.[9] If the self were to assert knowledge of the God who created it or summoned it to be, it would make a claim to conceive its creator or its origin, a claim that it is barred from precisely because responsibility means suffering the irreversibility of a call that affects me before I am present to conceive it. The responsible self "is subject to being affected by the other, and this being affected, by reason of its very irreversibility, does not change into a universal thought" (OBBE, 84). The self cannot even affirm that God exists, insofar as every such affirmation affirms a concept of what is then called God, while it is precisely the order of such universals that is denied to the responsible self. For Levinas, then, it is the very description of responsibility which excludes this created self from ever holding to any theistic conception that knows with certainty of God, even if only that he exists.

In describing the responsible self as an atheist, Levinas seems to join those thinkers for whom, at the end of metaphysics, there might be a religiosity but only a religiosity without a transcendent God. Is this just another equation of postmetaphysical thought and the death of God? Not quite. To see why, consider the signifyingness of the face.

According to Levinas, the face assigns me to myself, in responsibility, without my being able to conceive the other for whom I am responsible. The face does not signify the other in the way that a sign does when it presents a meaning to a co-present auditor who can then grasp it and reduce it to a comprehensible significance. Rather, the face signifies an irreducible order or command that summons me to respond to the other but signifies it before I am present to respond. In the face "is heard a command come as though from an immemorial past, which was never present. . . . My reaction misses a present which is already a past of itself" (OBBE, 88). The other had already passed when I am there to respond and so is always absent from my meeting with the face. This is why Levinas will say that the face is in the trace of an absence: the face appears in the trace left by the passing of what never entered the present in which I have experiences but is always already past without this past being recuperable in a present.

Since the self is always late when responding to the other and since, then, the other is forever absent from the face to which I respond, this command of the face is one which is never fulfilled. It summons me to an approach whose term I cannot meet but which recedes—unto infinity—as I draw near to it. As for Descartes's idea of the infinite, it is important, here, to distinguish this infinity from an end which is infinite; as an end, the infinite would put to rest or satisfy my responsibility. In the infinity of responsibility, by contrast, the "term is not an end. The more I answer the more I am responsible. . . . This debit which increases is infinity" (OBBE, 93). For Levinas, infinity signifies in my unending and ever-increasing response to the face of the other. In this sense, according to Levinas, responsibility also harbors the possibility of another theological category, another divine name—glory: "[responsibility] increases in the measure—or in the excess of measure—that a response is made. It increases gloriously. . . . An infinite increase in one's exhaustion, wherein the subject does not simply come to consciousness of this expenditure, but is its site and its event and, if we may say this, its goodness. *The Glory of a long desire!*" (GCM, 72–73 [modified]).

Insofar as the face leads responsibility to the infinite and to glory, Levinas will speak of "the face as *à-dieu* [unto God]" (GCM, 168). Here it is important to emphasize the distinction between the face as *à-dieu* [unto God] and the manifestation of God. The face does not show me God. It does not present God, nor does it indicate God in the manner of a sign that synchronizes signifiers and signifieds. Rather, the face summons me to God, *à-dieu*, but to God who is forever departing, bidding *adieu*, from the face that presents itself to me. Always bidding *à-dieu* and *àdieu* in a face, "the Infinite could not signify for a thought that goes to a term and the *à-Dieu* is not a finality" (GCM, 176–77). In this sense, the face met in responsibility does not make God manifest in and for consciousness insofar as consciousness occurs precisely as the aim or intention directed at objects to which it could, eventually, arrive in the achievement of adequate knowledge. Transcending the ecstatic transcendence of consciousness in intentionality, such a God is, Levinas writes, "transcendent to the point of absence" (GCM, 69).

Levinas's analysis of the responsible self thus displays what he calls "the marvel of the *moi* claimed by God in the face of the neighbor" (GCM, 177). This means that the responsible self, the self that is unable to conceive its creator, is an atheist for precisely theological reasons, without these theological reasons "leading to any theological thesis" (OBBE, 196, n. 19). In saying that the responsible self is an atheist for theological reasons, I do not mean that its atheism rests on dogmatic assumptions or thematic propositions about God as an object that can be known and conceived. This is why Levinas adds that the theological reasons do not lead to any theological thesis. Rather, the term "theological" is used here because, for Levinas, my assignation opens or invokes a naming of God. Levinas uses the term "theology" in both senses, that of a set of dogmatic propositions about God and that of a discourse that utters the name "God," seeking to unsettle or disrupt the former while opening the possibility of the latter. Sometimes, he prefers the plural "theologies," claiming that "theologies, in the plural removes, I hope, any dogmatic pretension from the general idea which this word harbors in my collection. Theologies: the search for a theo-logic, for a rational way of speaking of God" (BTV, xiv).

It is precisely, and paradoxically, because God signifies in responsibility that theological theses are impossible; or, it is the very theological character of my assignation to responsibility that renders me unable to conceive of God or to include God in the present of consciousness. For Levinas, then, atheism is precisely the way in which the responsible subject is affected by God. This is so because the idea of God is an idea of the infinite which, by definition, cannot be comprehended or encompassed by the finite thought that thinks it. Since God is defined as incomprehensible, the ignorance of the responsible self turns into a relation to God, "as though the not-letting-itself-be-encompassed were also an exceptional relation with me" (GCM, 63). Paradoxically, then, the theistic thought that claims to know or to comprehend God is just as much a denial of God as is the atheistic thought that announces the death of this known God. On the other hand, the atheism of the responsible self is a witness to God without this witnessing becoming a new figure of theism.

For Levinas, the transcendence of God is not revealed by being put before the witness, since, after all, this transcendence is a "transcendence to the point of absence." Rather, it is revealed in the saying of "*me voici!*" to the face for whom I am responsible. In saying *"me voici!"* to the other, I reveal the infinite that the face signifies to me without stating it in language and thus without reducing it to a concept or theme. Levinas writes,

> In my "here I am," from the first present in the accusative, I bear witness to the Infinite. . . . "Here I am" just that! The word God is still absent from the phrase in which God is from the first time involved in words. It does not at all state "I believe in God." To bear witness to God is precisely not to state this extraordinary word. (OBBE, 149)

Responsibility itself, me, is thus the revelation of God: "the subject as hostage has been neither the experience nor the proof of the Infinite, but the witnessing of the Infinite, a modality of this glory, a witnessing that no disclosure has preceded" (GCM, 73). Revealed in the responsible subject itself, God is "revealed before appearing, before presentation before a subject" (OBBE, 147), and as a modality of the glory of God, the subject does not effect this revelation through the intentional acts or operations of a consciousness which makes beings present. As responsibility, the subject itself is this revelation: "I am the witnessing, or the trace, or the glory of the Infinite. . . . The infinite is not 'in front of' me; it is I who express it . . . : *me voici*. A marvelous accusative here: here I am under your gaze, obliged to you, your servant. In the name of God. Without thematization. The sentence in which God comes to be involved in words is not 'I believe in God!'" (GCM, 75). Witnessing is a revelation which precedes the conscious subject who looks and says, "I believe in this God whom I now experience or whom I now see before me. Listen to the experience I am sharing with you." The *me voici!* of responsibility is itself the revelation of God and not a result or after-effect of it. It reveals God without affirming a concept of God, without even stating the word "God," and without encountering this God in the present of an experience made by a subject.

Since the responsible self is not only the one to whom the revelation is made but is itself the revelation, transcendence is revealed without being subject to, conditioned by, or limited by what I can hear, by what I can find as a possibility in and for consciousness, or by what can be gathered into the unity of the I think. Levinas thus speaks of this self as prophetic or inspired.

> One must give the name *"inspiration"* to this intrigue of infinity in which I make myself the author of what I hear. Inspiration constitutes, on the hither side of the unity of apperception, the very psyche of the soul. It is inspiration or prophetism in which I am the medium channeling what I announce. "God has spoken, who will not prophesy?" says Amos, comparing the prophetic reaction to the passivity of the fear which seizes him who hears the roaring of the wild beasts. Prophetism as pure witness; pure, for prior to all disclosure. (GCM, 76 [modified])

Like a prophet, then, the responsible self does not report messages he has heard from God or speak about God so as to communicate the divine workings to an audience who listens. In the "Thus says the Lord" which prefaces the oracular speeches of the prophets, the prophet himself becomes "the medium channeling what I announce." The word by which God reveals himself to the patiently attentive and listening prophet is, in fact, the word which is spoken in the prophesying itself, and this word is not a statement about God, a statement in which the word "God" would appear, thematizing and communicating, what I have known or experienced of this God. Witnessing, as a prophecy "by which the Infinite passes, is not something added on as an information, expression, repercussion or symptom, to some experience of the Infinite or its glory, as though there could be an experience of the Infinite and something else than glorification" (OBBE, 148). Impressed on me from before the beginning of consciousness, this witnessing is pure or prophetic in that it happens without needing the activity of a subject or existence to bring it out of its hiddenness or disclose it. As the responsible self, the prophet who witnesses God has no business of its own, no project for its own sake, no involvement in the world, according to which it would disclose God.

Unlike Descartes, Levinas insists that the witnessing of God "must not be taken as a 'new proof of the existence of God'" (GCM, 168). Such a proof, according to Levinas, would indicate that its proponent has mistaken the à-dieu of the face for a "sign of a departure" and then has reduced the face to "the indicating of a signified" which, through its sign, could be grasped by an act of consciousness adequate to the being signified (OBBE, 93). Only through such a mistake is it possible for thought to synchronize an effect, my responsibility before the face, and its cause and thereby deduce from the existence of responsibility that God, too, exists and that he exists in such and such a way. But, "a face is not an appearance or sign of some reality, which would be personal like it is, but dissimulated by the physiognomy, and which would present itself as an invisible theme" (OBBE, 93). For Levinas, then, the argument that deduces the existence of God by starting from my responsibility is founded on irresponsibility to the face, a sort of response that forgets the infinite that leaves a trace in the face. Such an argument interprets witnessing not as responsibility but as knowledge, a way to know the existence of that which calls in the face.[10]

The question of the existence or nonexistence of God is the ultimate question only for those whose thought still "shows the prestige of the totality and of efficacity [that is, of causality]. . . . and holds to the unity of being and univocity of *esse*" (OBBE, 94). One must first decide whether God is or is not on condition that one submit God to the metaphysical definition of God as first cause or ground of beings. When God is conceived under the metaphysical primacy of causality, God must be first in order to achieve his function and title since only what is, first, can cause what is; for metaphysics, something cannot proceed from nothing, so God must first be (not nothing but something) in order to ground or cause beings. Likewise, one must first decide whether God is or is not on condition that one assume Being is a totality or is the highest universal admitting no meaningful beyond. When all phenomena must first be grounded in universal Being in order that they might affect me, the first decision with respect to God concerns existence or nonexistence. On Levinas's reading, this interpretation of witnessing "translates perhaps the logical necessity of fixing the object of religion in conformity with the immanence of a thinking that aims at the world" (GCM, 105). The assumption that God must be in order to be witnessed treats of God as if God were a being like other beings in the totality of the world. It assumes the primacy and ultimacy of the world as a totality admitting no beyond and also the univocity of *esse;* it thereby forgets the transcendence of God: in order to "ensure the efficacy of God in the world, [it] sacrifices transcendence" (OBBE, 95).

Against the injunction to decide of God first whether he is or is not, Levinas claims that God need not be to be witnessed if "one puts forth the Platonic word, Good beyond Being" (OBBE, 95). Far from witnessing the existence of God, then, my responsibility for the other witnesses God as the Good. "From the Good to me, there is assignation: a relation which survives the 'death of God'" (OBBE, 123). In other words, the *à-dieu* of the face incites me not to divine being but to the Good which does not die with metaphysics and its God.

According to Levinas, it is precisely as "Good beyond Being" that God departs and absolves himself from the present of my consciousness since it is the very goodness of the Good to "incline the movement it calls forth to turn it away from the Good and orient it toward the other, and only thus toward the Good" (GCM, 69). Here, the goodness of the Good does not consist in its being, in any way, an object intended or made to appear by consciousness. This goodness does not belong to the Good of Plato, which remains accessible to a theoretical or contemplative gaze aimed directly at it; it is, instead, much closer to the goodness of the Judeo-Christian (or Neoplatonic) Good, a Good which is self-diffusive and self-abandoning, overflowing itself. In declining the desire that it arouses so as to orient it to an other, the goodness of the Good issues in the responsibility of the subject; the responsible self is in this way the revelation of the Good: "the self is goodness. . . . Goodness invests me in my obedience to the hidden Good" (OBBE, 118); "the subject is . . . , if one can say so, goodness" (GCM, 73).

If God "is" Good without Being, in that he forever separates himself from or declines my offering by inclining it to the other, God is "neither object nor interlocutor"—neither a thing I possess nor a person to whom I answer (GCM, 69). Instead, according to Levinas, even as God affects me by turning me to responsibility for the neighbor, he remains absolutely remote or "transcendent to the point of absence" (GCM, 69).

For Levinas, then, God is inseparable from responsibility not as the other for whom I am responsible but as an other other, the other whose absence inclines me to responsibility for others. In responsibility, God "remains a third person: He at the root of the You [*Il au fond du Tu*]" for whom I am responsible (GCM, 69). In designating the always already absent God as *Il,*

Levinas names God with neither a proper nor a common noun but with a pronoun. This pronoun has no antecedent and is not reducible to a noun designating beings; for nothing, no noun, is before what is always already past. Levinas writes in the concluding sentence of *Otherwise than Being, or, Beyond Essence:*

> after the death of a certain God inhabiting the world behind the scenes, [responsibility] discovers the trace—the unpronounceable inscription—of what, always already past—always "he"—does not enter into any present and to which are no longer suited the nouns designating beings nor the verbs in which their *essence* resounds, but which, as Pro-noun, marks with its seal all that can bear a noun. (OBBE, 185 [modified])

With this agrammatical use of the pronoun *il,* Levinas seeks to reflect the way in which the responsible subject, after the death of God, is affected without being able to identify or fix the meaning of the absent source of its obligation. "This way for the order to come from I know not where . . . we have called *illéité,*" a neologism that Levinas formed from the French pronoun *il* or the Latin *ille* (OBBE, 150; see also OBBE, 12). Since God is already absent from the face before ever being present through it, Levinas claims that this God can be designated, if such a word is still meaningful, only by the paradoxical or agrammatical anteriority of the pronoun *il* to any nouns designating beings.

Of course, one could understand God to be the antecedent of the pronoun *il,* claiming that *il* is a pronoun that stands in for God. Levinas grants that it is possible to understand *il* in this way, but such an understanding of *il* makes of God a being: "I can indeed state the meaning borne witness to as a said. . . . The word God is an overwhelming semantic event that subdues the subversion worked by *illéité.* The glory of the Infinite shuts itself up in a word and becomes a being" (OBBE, 151). On this reading, the word "God" is situated in metaphysics: it designates a being who precedes the incomprehensible *il* and thereby subdues the subversiveness of *illéité* by identifying *il* as the being, God, who calls me to my obligation. But, it must be remembered that stating the name "God" designates the antecedent of *il* on condition that one reduce God to his metaphysical conception.

After the end of metaphysics, on the other hand, no nouns designating or identifying beings are antecedent to the anonymous *il.* How, then, can that which survives the death of God be identified with or determined as God? For Levinas, in a certain sense, it is not: after the end of metaphysics, that which survives the death of God can be called God only on condition that the word "God" no longer identifies or determines the God that it names. He writes,

> I can indeed state the meaning borne witness to as a said. It is an extraordinary word, the only one that does not extinguish or absorb its saying, but it cannot remain a simple word. The word God is an overwhelming semantic event that subdues the subversion worked by *illéité.* The glory of the infinite shuts itself up in a word and becomes a being. But it already

undoes its dwelling and unsays itself. . . . A said unique of its kind, it does not narrowly espouse grammatical categories like a noun (neither proper nor common noun). (OBBE, 151)

On this reading, the word "God" signifies like the third person pronoun *il* in that its meaning can never be determined finally but always escapes the word which states it. After the end of metaphysics, the word "God" is thus always at odds with, always contested by, or always undone by *illéité* such that God is never named finally or definitively with the word "God." Hence, after the death of God, the word "God," like a pronoun preceding its ante-cedent, no longer fixes a meaning; rather, it "designates" the anonymous which undoes and renders improper every name that is given to it, even "God."

Conclusion: "The Ambiguity of the Temple and the Theatre"

Insofar as God is inseparable from responsibility, "the He [*Il*] at the root of the You," we might say, an element of anonymity haunts responsibility. This would mean that ethics is not entirely an interpersonal affair. Such a thought becomes troubling because ethics was first conceived (in the work that culminated with Levinas's *Totality and Infinity*) as an interpersonal affair or face-to-face encounter which marked an interruption of obedience to the violence and horror of an anonymous existence—what Levinas calls the anonymity of the there is [*il y a*]. Thus, if responsibility bears within it an anonymous element, *il*, we might suspect that it would never realize the cause for which ethics was first introduced.

Levinas describes the *il y a* through the phenomenon of "the night" and our "horror of darkness." For Levinas, the *il y a* explains the way in which, even after the negation of all beings, there still remains the void or horrify-ing darkness which there is [*il y a*] in the absence of each and every being. The *il y a* thus designates the "irremissability" and anonymity of what Lev-inas calls "being in general."

> The *il y a*, inasmuch as it resists a personal form, is "being in general." The *il y a* in effect transcends interiority as well as exteriority, a distinction which it no longer even renders possible. . . . There is no longer [*il n'y a plus*] this or that. . . . *Il y a*, in general, without it mattering what there is, without our being able to fix a substantive to this term. *Il y a* is an imper-sonal form, like in it rains or it is warm. Its anonymity is essential. The mind does not find itself faced with an apprehended exterior. . . . What we call the I is itself submerged by the night, invaded, depersonalized, stifled by it. The disappearance of the I and of all things leaves what cannot disap-pear, the sheer fact of being in which one participates whether one wants to or not, without having taken initiative, anonymously. (EE, 94–95)

For the Levinas who wrote *Totality and Infinity*, this terrifying and violent anonymity is interrupted, on the one hand, by the interiority of subjective existence liberating itself from anonymous participation and, on the other hand, by the upsurge of the face. This interiority of the I and transcendence of the face meet in the asymmetrical distance of ethics, which annuls the bonds of participation in a common genus, project, or other horizon. According to this author, in ethics, instead of being "submerged by the night" which threatens one anonymously, I myself am commanded by a personal other whose face marks the emergence of exteriority and so an escape from the irremissability of Being in general or the anonymity of the *il y a*.

We might begin to suspect that responsibility troubles the cause of ethics when we see that violence, which Levinas intended to put to rest by ethics, returns, in a slightly different form, in responsibility. For Levinas, in the absence of any determinate or identifiable beings, the menace of the *il y a* horrifies one: "Before this obscure invasion it is impossible to take shelter in oneself, to withdraw into one's shell. One is exposed" (EE, 96). In other words, the *il y a* is horrifying, menacing, and threatening because one is entirely exposed to it, entirely vulnerable, without an interior into which one can retreat. "The *il y a* transcends interiority as well as exteriority, a distinction which it no longer even renders possible" (EE, 94). Such would be the violence of the *il y a,* an anonymity that penetrates interiority leaving one without a place of one's own to which one can flee. This violence returns in responsibility where the responsible self is so passive as to be unable to escape from God; "the impossibility of escaping God lies in the depths of myself as a self, as an absolute passivity. . . . [It is] the impossibility of slipping away, absolute susceptibility" (OBBE, 128). In fact, this impossibility of escape happens in terms that are very similar to those in which the *il y a* menaces one: the responsible self is "the breaking up of inwardness and the abandon of all shelter, exposure to traumas, vulnerability" (OBBE, 48). Thus, in both the phenomena of being delivered over to the *il y a* and the phenomena of the responsible self turning *à-dieu,* one is exposed without the possibility of withdrawing or taking shelter in an interiority that can be called mine. It would seem that the violence of the anonymous, a violence to be denounced and overcome by ethics, has nonetheless returned here as what Levinas from time to time calls the "good violence" or "trauma" that the responsible self suffers in the name of God.[11]

For Levinas, then, everything hinges on distinguishing two types of anonymity. Without distinguishing these two forms of anonymity, responsibility can hardly be distinguished from the menace of *il y a*. This raises a significant problem for Levinas's thought of God: how can forms of the anonymous be distinguished when anonymity means, by definition, our inability to discern or to identify it as this as opposed to that? It seems that Levinas's description of the responsible self implies that such a distinction cannot be made, at least not by this self. Since the responsible self always arrives too late to be conscious of or to identify the other, the self cannot tell whether it is exposed to God or to the *il y a;* it certainly cannot tell us since, as singular, the responsible self is outside and denied access to the order of the universal and the logos where it would be possible to know and to communicate such knowledge. The self may be a witness, but it is a witness who cannot say or identify, and so cannot testify to, that which it witnesses: is it God or the *il y a*?[12] Why not say, as John Caputo does, there is/*il y a* obligation—obligation happens? Everything undergone by the responsible self, and the very structure of this self, seem to indicate such a conclusion is just as warranted as is the conclusion that responsibility bears witness to God.[13]

If responsibility harbors an element of the radically absent or anonymous, we also must ask how this namelessness can be called God and not something, or everything, else—such as the unconscious and language (Jacques Lacan's discourse of the other), Being as such (the later Heidegger), or perhaps even the *il y a* and everything of Heidegger's *Es gibt* which it is meant to evoke. Here the problem confronting Levinas concerns the possibility of naming the absence I suffer in responsibility as an absence of God, that is as an absence to which God belongs and which belongs, definitively, to God. If the word "God" is absent from the phrase in which God is first witnessed (OBBE, 149), why, how, and with what consequences does Levinas repeatedly claim that, in responsibility, the self witnesses *only* God? Why does he say, "there is no pure witnessing except of the Infinite" (GCM, 75), identifying the Infinite with the capital letter marking a proper name, when that which is witnessed is *illéité* and therefore so anonymous as to be "designated" by a pronoun? In fact, at least once in his work, Levinas does seem to speak of an absence of God that does not, as an *à-dieu*, revert into the transcendence of God, a fact that suggests that God might not be the only name for the namelessness witnessed by the self after metaphysics. He writes, "rather than to God [*plutôt qu'à Dieu*], the notion of the *il y a* leads us to the absence of God" (EE, 99). Here, then, is an absence of God that is not the result of a transcendence named God and does not lead *à-dieu;* it is rather the result of the anonymous that Levinas calls *il y a*. What is to distinguish these two unidentifiable absences?

Such a possible meaning of the absence of God troubles the identification of the trace as a trace of God. To be sure, when Levinas says the trace is left by God, he does not mean to identify the being who, once present, left the trace when he became absent;[14] nonetheless, these observations suggest that in claiming that the trace is left by the unidentifiable or anonymous, Levinas can no longer say, to the exclusion of other namings, that this trace is a trace *of God* and not of another absence. If "God" does not identify a being but signifies the indeterminate or anonymous absence at the heart of responsibility, why is it the *only* word suited to naming this anonymity? Why is the trace a trace *of God* and not of another? In light of such questions, Levinas's attempt to find a possible significance of God is seen as an attempt to save, precisely, the name of God. After the end of metaphysics, for Levinas, nothing that is said, or has been said historically, of God can be maintained, save the name that says nothing of this God.[15]

After the death of God, Levinas's thought of God thus saves the name only, "God." But why save this name? From everything I have said, it appears we might just as well abandon the name; all the evidence for God could as easily be for "no-God" or some other name. Again, why not say only "obligation happens," "*il y a/es gibt* obligation"?

The problem of naming the anonymous appears again in Levinas's text when we notice that a description of the same phenomenon—insomnia or wakefulness—leads to different namings of the anonymous. The early Levinas "introduces into the impersonal event of the *il y a* not the notion of consciousness but that of wakefulness [*la veille*]" or insomnia (EE, 111). For this Levinas, insomnia is a form of attention—not yet a consciousness that thinks or intends—absolutely void of objects; it is a vigilance that is awakened not by something but by the *il y a* arising in the very absence of all beings. In the later work, however, insomnia is the wakefulness of a responsibility that opens *à-dieu:* there he identifies "relationship-to-God, the original insomnia of thinking" (GCM, 120). Here insomnia remains an objectless form of attention, but now this attention is awakened by God. In this way, the phenomenon of an anonymous insomnia gives access to both the responsible self awakened by God and the one who is menaced by the *il y a.*

I am thus led to conclude that in this philosophy of religion, God is given only in confusion or ambiguity. The singular self finds itself in a situation of indecision: perhaps it is God who incessantly awakens me by calling me in and through the face; perhaps there is [*il y a*] only incessant awakening. Levinas himself seems to recognize such an undecidable or indiscernible difference when he writes, "transcendent to the point of absence, to the point of his possible confusion with the agitation of the *il y a*" (GCM, 69). It is not a matter of deciding in the face of this confusion; rather, let the undecidability remain. I want to leave open, or once again open, the question—posing it in Levinas's own images: the religion of the God after the death of God, is it religion or is it an absurd comedy? After metaphysics, is the subjectivity of the subject, is responsibility, the "temple" or the "theater" of transcendence?

NOTES

Introduction

1. Friedrich Nietzsche, *The Gay Science* (New York: Vintage, 1974), p. 181.

2. Karl Marx, "Towards a Critique of Hegel's Philosophy of Right: Introduction," in *Karl Marx: Selected Writings*, ed. David McLellan (Oxford: Oxford University Press, 1988), p. 63.

3. Philip Rieff, *Freud: The Mind of the Moralist* (Chicago: University of Chicago Press, 1979), p. 257. It should be noted, however, that this is not necessarily the view that Rieff himself takes of psychoanalysis.

4. Clement Greenberg, *The Collected Essays and Criticism*, vol. 3, ed. John O'Brian (Chicago: University of Chicago Press, 1986), p. 178.

5. I must add a point of caution. It certainly is not the case that *all* discourses in the first half of the twentieth century were antithetical to religion or ignored its significance and that *all* recent cultural criticism is shaped by religious issues. There are, of course, important exceptions on both sides. Nevertheless, it seems fair to say that recent years have seen an opening to religion on the part of philosophers and of literary and cultural critics.

6. Mark C. Taylor has attempted to "establish the implicit and explicit spiritual preoccupations of leading twentieth-century painters and architects and to disclose the religious significance of their work" (*Disfiguring: Art, Architecture, and Religion* [Chicago: University of Chicago Press, 1992], p. 5). David Tracy, venturing into the history of psychoanalysis, has suggested that the relationship between Freud and Lacan can be read in light of the religious categories prophet and mystic. See Tracy's "Mystics, Prophets, Rhetorics: Religion and Psychoanalysis," in *The Trial(s) of Psychoanalysis*, ed. Françoise Meltzer (Chicago: University of Chicago Press, 1988). One can also consult *Lacan and Theological Discourse*, ed. Edith Wyschogrod, David Crownfield, and Carl A. Raschke (Albany: State University of New York Press, 1989).

7. "More audaciously than any recent developments in French criticism, Kabbalah is a theory of *writing*" (Harold Bloom, *Kabbalah and Criticism* [New York: Seabury Press, 1975], p. 52). For claims to a more far-reaching influence of rabbinic interpretation in contemporary discourse, see Susan Handelman, *The Slayers of Moses: The Emergence of Rabbinic Interpretation in Modern Literary Theory* (Albany: State University of New York Press, 1982).

8. See Julia Kristeva, *Powers of Horror: An Essay on Abjection* (New York: Columbia University Press, 1982), chapter 5 and, especially, chapter 6, where Kristeva reads sin and confession together with analytic speech and transference. See also Kristeva's *Tales of Love* (New York: Columbia University Press, 1987), especially part 4, which is devoted to readings of Paul, Bernard of Clairvaux, and Thomas Aquinas on love and desire.

9. Regina Schwartz, "Freud's God," in *Post-Secular Philosophy*, ed. Philip Blond (London: Routledge, 1988), p. 281. This claim is tempered by the conclusion of the essay, where Schwartz no longer considers Freud simply a religious thinker proposing a religious myth but the champion of "a condition that hovers, ambivalently, and I might add heroically, between theory and belief. And it may well be that

heroic ambivalence, rather than some clearer faith (illusion) or easier atheism (disillusion), that distinguishes a post-secular philosophy" (p. 302). The first position represents a mere reversal of previous readings of Freud, while the latter represents a more difficult attempt to walk the complicated and uncertain line between the two positions.

10. Kevin Hart, *The Trespass of the Sign: Deconstruction, Theology, and Philosophy* (Cambridge: Cambridge University Press, 1989), p. 45. For Hart's treatment of the early reception of Derrida and his objections to it, see *The Trespass of the Sign*, pp. 42–47, and "Jacques Derrida: The God Effect," in *Post-Secular Philosophy*, pp. 260–62.

11. *The Trespass of the Sign*, p. 43.

12. John D. Caputo, *The Prayers and Tears of Jacques Derrida: Religion without Religion* (Bloomington: Indiana University Press, 1997), pp. xviii and xix.

13. See Gilles Deleuze and Félix Guattari, *Anti-Oedipus: Capitalism and Schizophrenia*, trans. Robert Hurley, Mark Seem, and Helen R. Lane (New York: Viking Press, 1977).

14. To name but a few. See John D. Caputo's *Against Ethics: Contributions to a Poetics of Obligation with Constant Reference to Deconstruction* (Bloomington: Indiana University Press, 1993) and Edith Wyschogrod's *Saints and Postmodernism* (Chicago: University of Chicago Press, 1990). Mark C. Taylor, as early as *Altarity* (Chicago: University of Chicago Press, 1987), was re-imagining the category of otherness in ways that figure significantly in ethical discourse. Finally, Jacques Derrida, too, turned explicitly to ethics in his *The Gift of Death* (Chicago: University of Chicago Press, 1995). I will leave aside the question of whether or not his work ever repudiated or ignored ethics, something that is far from obvious.

15. See *Ethics as First Philosophy: The Significance of Emmanuel Levinas for Philosophy, Literature, and Religion*, ed. Adriaan T. Peperzak (New York: Routledge, 1995), and *Emmanuel Levinas: L'Ethique comme philosophie première*, ed. Jean Greisch and Jacques Rolland (Paris: Les Editions du Cerf, 1993).

16. The title "Jewish philosopher" is applied to Levinas by Robert Gibbs in his *Correlations: Rosenzweig and Levinas* (Princeton: Princeton University Press, 1992), p. 4. In this work, Gibbs adopts Levinas because his philosophy is formed by an encounter with the "Jewish other" and claims that through Levinas, "Judaism can again reorient philosophy" (p. 4). Similarly, without using the phrase as such, Richard Cohen in *Elevations: The Height of the Good in Rosenzweig and Levinas* (Chicago: University of Chicago Press, 1994) reads Levinas as a "Jewish philosopher"—as when he writes, "The knowledge that Levinas' thought is committed to the Jewish tradition, to a properly Jewish conception of God, already provides a preliminary indication of the direction the task at hand will take" (p. 173).

17. Rejecting Jean-François Lyotard's description of his philosophy as a thought of the Old Testament God, Levinas says, "I am not for all that an especially Jewish thinker; I am a thinker, *tout court*" (AQS, 83). Also, as Lyotard himself recalls, Levinas objects, "It is not under the authority of the Bible that my thought is placed, but under the authority of phenomenology. . . . You make of me a Jewish thinker" (AQS, 78–79). And, speaking of his own work, Levinas says, "is all this phenomenology inspired by the Bible? I believe it free of it" (AQS, 81).

18. "Phenomenology was taken hostage by a theology which does not want to say its name" (Dominique Janicaud, *Le tournant théologique de la phénoménologie française* [Paris: Editions de L'éclat, 1991], p. 31).

19. In regard to secularization, I am thinking of Mircea Eliade's work on the sacred and the profane, Emile Durkheim's description of society (especially of the

religious sentiment aroused before a nation's flag), and even of Sigmund Freud's description of obsessive actions as religious practices. For each of these thinkers, the transcendent God is quite decisively dead, but they nonetheless see religion or religiosity at work throughout contemporary culture.

20. G. W. F. Hegel, *Faith and Knowledge* (Albany: State University of New York Press, 1977), p. 190.

21. Possible instances of such a generalization can be found in Jean-Luc Marion's thought of givenness, where the "subject" is called the *interloqué* or *adonné*. See "L'interloqué," in *Who Comes after the Subject?* ed. Eduardo Cadava, Peter Connor, and Jean-Luc Nancy (New York: Routledge, 1991), and *Etant donné* (Paris: P.U.F., 1997). In a very different but surprisingly not so unlikely tone, Alphonso Lingis's attempt in *The Imperative* (Bloomington: Indiana University Press, 1998) to describe the various and multiple dimensions of existence (sensuous, ethical, technological, mechanical, artistic, etc.) in terms of a response to an imperative would also be such a generalization of Levinas's responsible self from the sphere of ethics to all spheres of subjective life. The reading of subjectivity in Levinas developed by Mark C. Taylor in *Altarity*, a reading which does indeed capture something essential in Levinas, seems already to have accepted the possibility of interpreting the subject in a nonethical context, though Taylor does not raise the question explicitly.

22. Jean-Luc Marion, in "The Saturated Phenomenon," *Philosophy Today* (spring 1996), proposes such a philosophy of religion. Marion claims that phenomenology is the form of philosophy best suited to thinking religious phenomena, on condition that phenomenology adopt a figure of subjectivity other than Husserlian consciousness. I am arguing that Levinas's responsible self provides such a subject.

1. Ethics as the End of Metaphysics

1. Robert Bernasconi has suggested that a reading of Levinas might develop an understanding of philosophy in terms of a "history of the face" that would parallel, but differ significantly from, Heidegger's history of Being. See "Levinas and Derrida: The Question of the Closure of Metaphysics," in *Face to Face with Levinas,* ed. Richard Cohen (Albany: State University of New York Press, 1986), pp. 193–98.

2. The text cited here is from "Is Ontology Fundamental?" which originally appeared in 1951 ("L'ontologie est-elle fondamentale?" *Revue de Métaphysique et de Morale* [January 1951]), ten years before *Totality and Infinity.* See also, on partial negation, *Totality and Infinity,* p. 198.

3. Alexandre Kojève, *Introduction to the Reading of Hegel* (Ithaca: Cornell University Press), p. 4.

4. See Hegel's *Phenomenology of Spirit* (Oxford: Oxford University Press, 1977), p. 102.

5. For a discussion of the possibility and consequences of distinguishing false from true otherness, see chapter 2, below.

6. Despite acknowledging that Franz Rosenzweig's *The Star of Redemption* (trans. William W. Hallo [Notre Dame: Notre Dame Press, 1971]) is "too often present in this book to be cited here" (TI, 28), Levinas seems on this point to set himself at a distance from Rosenzweig. Though Rosenzweig treats the breakup of the system from three different points of departure (God, man, and world), each of which resists the totality, he explicitly acknowledges that, of these, the human self is the privileged point of incision. Would the nature of Levinas's disagreement with Kierkegaard compel him to make similar claims against Rosenzweig?

7. This has been carefully noted by Jacques Derrida, who goes on to offer a

potential response by Kierkegaard: "Can one not wager that Kierkegaard would have been deaf to this distinction? And that he, in turn, would have protested against this conceptuality? It is as subjective existence, he would have remarked perhaps, that the other does not accept the system. The other is not myself—and who has ever maintained that it is?—but it is an Ego" (VM, 110).

8. In speaking of a transcendence without attributes, Levinas's thought resembles the Plotinian notion of the One. Elsewhere, Levinas will acknowledge explicitly the Plotinian thought of the One as a trace of the absolutely other (see DEHH, pp. 189, 201). In *Totality and Infinity,* Levinas does not speak of the beyond as the One, perhaps because he has collapsed unity and totality and so blinded himself to other resources contained in the word "one." In his later work, however, Levinas will devote much attention to the notions of singularity and uniqueness, discovering in them the possibility of resisting totalization (see chapter 5, below).

9. For Jean-Luc Marion, the thought of distance assumes a crucial role in passing beyond ontology. Hence, in his *L'idole et la distance* (Paris: Grasset, 1977), he considers the notion of distance as it appears in Levinas's work (p. 267). Though Marion acknowledges Levinas's naming of distance, he will subsequently distinguish his own theological approach to distance from the ethical approach of Levinas.

10. Here Levinas is profoundly influenced by Rosenzweig. For Rosenzweig, the breakup of the All maintained each of the elements—God, Man, and World—that had composed it but denied that one embraced or determined all the others. In themselves, each of the elements remains a totality; but this totality is not all-embracing. Each is an "excluding all" which is summoned to enter into a "constellation" with the excluded others. Levinas adopts a similar position when he speaks of a nonconjunctive "and" that joins, in distance, totality and infinity. For Levinas, as for Rosenzweig, the same, in the face of distance, can claim only a finite totality, a totality (if the word holds) that is not all-embracing.

11. Perhaps also to the degree that Heidegger has been misunderstood? See Derrida's "Violence and Metaphysics" (VM, 134–40) and chapter 2 below for some suggestions of how Levinas might have misrepresented Heidegger.

12. The importance of being-in-the-world and being-able-to question as fundamental determinations of *Dasein* is described by Jacques Derrida in *Of Spirit: Heidegger and the Question* (trans. Geoffrey Bennington and Rachel Bowlby [Chicago: University of Chicago Press], 1989).

13. In a certain sense, the phrase "Heideggerian ontology" is a misnomer, first because, as I have shown, *Being and Time* distinguishes its project, fundamental ontology, from ontology; and second because the later Heidegger will abandon even the term fundamental ontology. I still use it because Levinas does. It can be argued that Levinas's use of such a term reflects a profound, and profoundly productive, misreading of Heidegger's intentions. This misreading is exposed and called to account for itself by Jacques Derrida in "Violence and Metaphysics" (VM, 134–40). I will develop another reading of *Being and Time* in chapter 6, below.

14. "Letter on Humanism" in *Basic Writings,* ed. David Farrell Krell (New York: Harper and Row, 1977), p. 207.

15. The phrase "someone who is a being" [*quelqu'un qui est un étant*] merits further consideration. Can there be someone who is not a being? Certainly there can be a being that is not someone. But, is it violent to subordinate the relation to a being that is not someone, a stone for instance, to the relation to Being? And does

a being that is not someone present what is absolutely other than the same? Derrida asks this question in an interview ("Eating Well, or the Calculation of the Subject," in *Who Comes after the Subject?*) when he points out that within Levinas's thought a certain violence against beings is still permitted, namely the violent death of animal being which feeds or provides sacrifice for human-being. On Derrida's reading of Levinas, Levinas would have already accepted a determination of the other: it is this being and not that being. On this reading, what Levinas calls the absolute alterity of "someone who is a being" would be already relative to a prior difference among beings.

16. Martin Heidegger, *Basic Problems of Phenomenology* (Bloomington: Indiana University Press, 1982), p. 275.

17. Heidegger would respond that it is precisely *l'étant* in the context of the world or within the horizon of Being that is *l'étant* as such.

18. See the parallel passages in *Totality and Infinity*. For example, "an existent [*l'étant*] is comprehended in the measure that thought transcends it, measuring it against the horizon whereupon it is profiled. Since Husserl, the whole of phenomenology is the promotion of the idea of horizon, which for it plays a role equivalent to that of the concept in classical idealism; an existent [*l'étant*] arises upon a ground that extends beyond it, as an individual arises from the concept" (TI, 44; see also pp. 189–90).

19. Levinas frequently refers to the texts of the Phaedrus where Plato asserts the superiority of speech to writing; referring to Plato, he claims that speech better attends its own presentation. In "Violence and Metaphysics," Derrida notes this and adds a similar text of Nicholas of Cusa: "while the worker abandons his work, which then pursues its independent destiny, the verb of the professor is inseparable from the very person that proffers it" (see VM, 101). In the next chapter, I will treat more fully the significance of Derrida's attempt to position Levinas within the context of Neoplatonism and Christian theology.

20. It is characteristic of Levinas's thought that it continues to use "signify," "other," "metaphysics," etc., even after the meaning of these terms has been rent and broken from its traditional sense. One might well wonder if this compromises or qualifies the intended transcendence or movement beyond the totality comprehended by the tradition of metaphysics.

21. In naming "holiness," Levinas appeals to the sense of holy that is implied in the Hebrew word *kodesh*. The Hebrew word is formed from a root which means "separate" or "withdrawn." The biblical holy is that which is separated, just as, for Levinas, the absolutely other is met in separation and distance.

In Rosenzweig's *The Star of Redemption*, one finds a notion of holiness similar to that evoked by Levinas. In commenting on the notion of a "holy land," Rosenzweig weaves together the themes of desire, impossible possession, infinity and holiness in ways that one could show to be at work also in *Totality and Infinity*, especially in Levinas's critique of rootedness and the Site. Rosenzweig writes, "this people has a land of its own only in that it has a land it yearns for—a holy land. And so even when it has a home, this people is . . . only 'a stranger and a sojourner.' God tells it: 'The land is mine.' The holiness of the land removed it from the people's spontaneous reach while it could still reach out for it. This holiness increases the longing for what is lost, to infinity, and so the people can never be entirely at home in any other land" (p. 300). This passage can be compared with the following from *Totality and Infinity*: "The metaphysical desire does not long to return, for it is desire for a

NOTES TO PAGES 22–26

land not of our birth, for a land foreign to every nature, which has not been our fatherland and to which we shall never betake ourselves. The metaphysical desire does not rest upon any prior kinship" (TI, 34).

22. See Derrida's "Violence and Metaphysics" and my reading in chapter 2, below.

23. How does this notion of annihilation as resistance to totality compare to Bataille's anti-Hegelianism? At one point, Levinas claims that the other "sovereignly says no!" (TI, 199). What is the relation of this sovereignty to the sovereign in Bataille, a sovereign that is unquestionably a reading of the "master" in Hegel?

24. In reading "Violence and Metaphysics," I will have cause to ask if such an indifference in the approach of the face does not compromise the claim that the upsurge of language institutes peace with the other. If both murder and ethics leave the other uncomprehended, then by what authority does Levinas determine that the presentation of the absolutely other is purely ethical, purely nonviolent?

25. Earlier, I showed that the essence of language is the vocative; now, it appears the first words are in the imperative. There is thus in *Totality and Infinity* a double essence of language: when it is I who speak to the other, language is essentially vocative; when the other arises in the face, language is essentially imperative. The "double origin of language" is discussed by Bernasconi in "Levinas and Derrida." In addition to documenting this double origin or essence of language, Bernasconi notes further that each of the primordial languages arises as a response: the vocative arises in response to the appearance of the face, and the imperative arises in response to my interpellating the other. Since both beginnings are a response, the origin of language slips away.

26. See Hegel's *Phenomenology of Spirit,* chapter A1. Hegel refers to the "divine nature" of language on p. 66.

27. Edith Wyschogrod notes this "Hegelian conclusion" in her article "Emmanuel Levinas and the Problem of Religious Language," *Thomist* 36 (January 1972): 11.

28. When he says that "the *hic et nunc* itself issues from possession," Levinas refers to the subtitle of the chapter on sense-certainty, "The This and Meaning." In German, the word for "meaning" is homophonic with the word for "mine." Following Hegel, Levinas plays on this pun.

2. Theology and the Unthought Constitution of Ethical Metaphysics

1. Levinas's understanding of theology is presented without reference to historical figures. The author of *Totality and Infinity* seems to accept an understanding of theology that, upon historical examination, might be shown to apply only to certain figures of theological thought while others would escape it. I would suggest that within *Totality and Infinity*, the term "theology" functions by designating a form of intentionality or approach of the divine.

2. This passage is cited from a section of *Totality and Infinity* entitled "The Metaphysical and the Human." It is perhaps the strongest and most explicit treatment of theology in the work. It is also the section that is most inviting to those critics who seek to show "tribalism" or haughtiness and arrogance in Levinas's thought. In it, Levinas expresses scorn for "primitive" religions in which the I is "bewitched" by or immersed in mythic relations to God or the gods. I can see why some might see his attitude as hierarchical or Eurocentric, Judeocentric even, when they read such sentences as "there can be no 'knowledge' of God separated from the relationship with men. . . . Everything that cannot be reduced to an interhuman relation represents not the superior but the forever primitive form of religion" (TI, 78–79). A

passage like this debases certain forms of spirituality expressed even in Western religions. On this point, see David Tracy's remarks in *Ethics as First Philosophy*, ed. Peperzak, pp. 196–98.

3. Levinas's understanding of mysticism, like his understanding of theology, appears overly general and historically uninformed. His distaste for mysticism is similar to that of Rosenzweig, and it might be said, as one says of Rosenzweig, that it seems to deal more in types than in historical figures.

With regard to how *Totality and Infinity* understands both theology and mysticism, juxtaposition with historical scholarship or historically informed theological work might show that (1) certain forms of theology do not employ the concept and are not theoretical, and that (2) certain forms of mysticism do not privilege union or participation. This would certainly be the upshot of Jean-Luc Marion's work in theology and his reading of Dionysian mysticism. See in particular, *L'idole et la distance* and *God without Being*.

4. In ways that are neither entirely similar to nor dissimilar from those of Levinas, Marion, too, will attempt to describe the religiosity of the atheist. (In addition to *God without Being*, see "De la mort de la mort de Dieu," in *Laval théologique et philosophique* 41,1 [February 1985].) For Marion, however, the atheist is part of a religious process that is explicitly theological: atheism denies concepts of God and thus can be situated within the ascent to God found in the mystical theology of such figures as Pseudo-Dionysius. For Levinas, the atheist is not expressly identified with a negative moment in a movement to God.

5. On Marion tracing Descartes's naming of God to the theologian Lessius, see Jean-Luc Marion, *On Descartes' Metaphysical Prism*, trans. Jeffrey L. Kosky (Chicago: University of Chicago Press, 1999), pp. 208–10.

6. Whether or not every figure of theological thought is penetrated by ontology is, hence, precisely the question that must be asked if one wants to free theology from Levinas's positioning of it. In work subsequent to *Totality and Infinity*, theology is no longer an obstacle in the passage beyond ontology and totality but part of the goal, if not also an important vehicle—precisely because Levinas recognizes a nonontological element in it. In *Otherwise than Being, or, Beyond Essence*, it is a matter of hearing "a God not contaminated by Being" and hence of thinking a theology pure of ontology.

7. In his theological thought, Jean-Luc Marion is critical of subjecting the appearance of God to such an extended chain of conditions. In *God without Being*, he accuses Heidegger of idolatry for making the appearance of God depend on a set of conditions that are proper not to God but to Being. As evidence, he cites the passage from the "Letter on Humanism" in which Heidegger writes, "only from the truth of Being can the essence of the holy be thought. Only from the essence of the holy is the essence of divinity to be thought. Only in the light of the essence of divinity can it be thought or said what the word 'God' is to signify" (pp. 39–40). Parallels between this passage and the one I have cited from Levinas would form an indispensable starting point for a consideration of Marion's relation to Levinas on matters theological.

8. Jean-Luc Nancy, "Of Divine Places," in *The Inoperative Community* (Minneapolis: University of Minnesota Press, 1991), p. 113.

9. Ibid., p. 112.

10. Is it necessary for the words "God" or "theology" to appear in every discourse that is theological? Kevin Hart in *The Trespass of the Sign* argues that "we do not need God in a discourse for it to be theological in Derrida's sense" (p. 32). In the

first chapter, Hart offers an extensive discussion of what "theology" and "theological" mean in Derrida's thought. In subsequent chapters, he undertakes a rapprochement of Derrida's thought and certain forms of theology, arguing that, by deconstructing the metaphysical element of theology, Derrida leaves open the possibility of a theology free of metaphysics. On this reading, theology should welcome deconstruction as its liberator from onto-theology.

11. The integral connection of logocentrism and theology is considered throughout *Of Grammatology* (Baltimore: Johns Hopkins University Press, 1976) but is especially prevalent in part one, "Writing Before the Letter." For Derrida, "the sign and the divinity have the same place and time of birth. The age of the sign is essentially theological" (p. 14). This means that, in Derrida's thought, a charge of logocentrism includes a supposition of a theologically determined thought and vice versa. Thus, when Derrida discusses the debasement of writing in Levinas's thought, he also discusses a theological character of Levinas's thought. Again, readers should refer to the first chapter of Hart's *The Trespass of the Sign* for a more complete discussion of how logocentrism is essentially theological.

12. Though functionally similar, one difference that is perhaps not to be ignored is that for Derrida writing resists totalization and presence because signification is always lacking whereas for Levinas in the face signification exceeds the totality.

13. Though the author of *Totality and Infinity* explicitly rejects any suggestion of a theological determination of the face, more than twenty years after this work was published, Levinas seems to acknowledge that the face can be understood theologically. In the preface to the German edition of *Totality and Infinity,* Levinas writes of the face: "it also calls upon me from a strange authority—imperative, disarmed— the word of God and the verb in the human face. . . . The language of the inaudible, the language of the unheard-of, the language of the non-said. Scripture! . . . A commandment in the nakedness and poverty of the other, ordering responsibility for the other: beyond ontology. The Word of God. A theology which does not proceed from any speculation on worlds-behind-the-world, from any knowledge transcending knowledge. A phenomenology of the face: a necessary ascent to God" (EN, 198–99).

There is much to comment on in this passage, and many of the ideas introduced here will recur later (see parts 2 and 3 of this book, where I consider Levinas's later, more mature work). For now, I will remark only that in this critical reflection on *Totality and Infinity,* Levinas, like Derrida, acknowledges a theological significance of the face; but whether or not this theology is the same as that which Derrida describes must be decided later (see part 3, below).

14. Derrida cites this passage in "Violence and Metaphysics" (VM, 108) but does not give a page reference to *Totality and Infinity.* The passage is on p. 293. This is typical of how Derrida cites Levinas's work throughout the essay, and it is reminiscent of Levinas's own manner of referring to authors and ideas without citing references or naming names.

15. Despite the admonitions of Jean-Luc Marion, I retain the term "negative theology," marking it with "so-called" in order to register Marion's opposition to giving this thought a title that seems to dwell on only one part of the co-implicated process of positive, negative, and mystical theologies. I retain the phrase because it is used by Derrida in the essay under discussion here.

It is well known that in his later work Levinas frequently denies that his thought is a negative theology. What is less often remarked is that, at least once, when responding orally to questions posed of his essays, he claims, "I am treating emphasis as a method [*procédé*]. I think I have found there the *via eminentiae*" (GCM, 89). In thus characterizing his method as a retrieval of the *via eminentiae*, Levinas seems to admit a close relation between his thought and that of figures of so-called "negative theology," if we understand "negative theology" now *with* Marion's admonitions in mind—that is to say if we understand its mystical theology as (1) undoing the finality of the negative moment just as much as the negative moment undoes the finality of the affirmative, and (2) not reestablishing a hyperessential being beyond Being. For a discussion of the later Levinas's relation to mystical theology, see my "Contemporary Encounters with Apophatic Theology: The Case of Emmanuel Levinas," *Journal for Cultural and Religious Theory* 1.3 (August 2000) (www.jcrt.org).

16. Derrida cites the same passage from Eckhart in the essay on Pseudo-Dionysius that is part of his confrontation with the thought of Jean-Luc Marion. See "How to Avoid Speaking: Denials," in *Derrida and Negative Theology* (Albany: State University of New York Press, 1992), p. 78. Contrary to Derrida, Marion reads the hyperessential names as not referring to a being beyond beings or as supposing a more elevated Being but as beyond Being and beings entirely.

17. *Phenomenology of Spirit*, pp. 66, 60, 60.

18. Ibid., pp. 61, 63, 64.

19. Ibid., p. 66.

20. Cited in VM, p. 147. Though the reference to this specific passage is lacking, there are many passages in the section "Ethics and the Face" that could stand in for the passage Derrida cites: for instance, "The alterity that is expressed in the face provides the unique 'matter' possible for total negation"; "*Autrui* is the sole being I can wish to kill" (TI, 198).

21. In some of Derrida's more recent writings, he considers the ambiguous place of animal-being in the list of what can be killed. Animal-being, like the face, is, according to the evidence, a potential victim of murder; but, unlike the face, its murder would be legitimate, would be consecrated, or would even be the very act of consecration. See especially the interview "Eating Well, or the Calculation of the Subject," in *Who Comes after the Subject?* pp. 96–119.

22. In pointing out that the upsurge of language in the face is the condition also of violence, Derrida's remarks to Levinas closely parallel a comment that Gershom Scholem once made about Martin Buber's dialogical relation of I and Thou: "Buber could have pointed out—I often wonder why he never did—that the first dialogue among human beings mentioned in the Bible, the one between Cain and Abel, also leads to the first murder." See Gershom Scholem, *On Jews and Judaism in Crisis* (New York: Schocken Books, 1976), p. 159.

23. Here, Derrida seems closer to Rosenzweig than to Levinas, and closer to Rosenzweig than Levinas is to Rosenzweig. In *The Star of Redemption*, Rosenzweig separates the upsurge of language, Revelation, from messianic peace, Redemption. According to Rosenzweig, redemption, peace, is anticipated in the silent rite of liturgy and gesture practiced by the community, whereas revelation is lived in language and interpersonal dialogue. "The word unites, but those who are united fall silent" (p. 308). The word becomes silence when peace arrives. But can man, whose life is speaking, ever experience redemption, silence, outside of his anticipation of it? According to Rosenzweig, "it is God who experiences while man merely watches" (p. 394). The end, peace, would be inaccessible to man, who may only gaze on it or anticipate it in the silence of liturgy and rite.

24. At the end of the preface, the author of *Totality and Infinity* offers some re-

marks that could indicate the necessity of unsaying or undoing what is said of the infinite: "[the preface] belongs to the very essence of language, which consists in continually undoing its phrase by the foreword or the exegesis, in unsaying the said, in attempting to restate without ceremonies what has already been ill understood in the inevitable ceremonial in which the said delights" (TI, 30). However, I cannot see any explicit thematization or practice of these notions in the development of this book. I also note that this passage suggests unsaying to be necessary because of the inevitable misunderstandings that arise in communication, not because of the ethical essence of language or because of God.

25. In all fairness, "existent" is a perfectly fine translation of *étant*—if it is borne in mind that "existent" here has nothing to do with Heideggerian existence.

26. My reading of onto-theo-logy is based on Derrida's and not the original in Heidegger, not because I am ignorant of Heidegger's text or because I feel that Heidegger is more obscure than Derrida. I do so because the theses suggested by Derrida are not contested significantly among interpreters of Heidegger and because Derrida presents them in a fashion that is readily accessible to my discussion of Levinas.

27. This is why the only language that would avoid Being would be "a language of pure invocation, pure adoration, proffering only proper nouns in order to call to the other from afar" (VM, 147). It is either a cry or, perhaps, prayer, if prayer can be understood as nonpredicatory. For an attempt at this, see the reading of prayer developed by Jean-Luc Marion in *L'idole et la distance* in his discussion of Dionysius.

28. Derrida schematizes the difference between Heidegger and Levinas as follows: for Heidegger, "the first violence is this dissimulation. . . . Being is less the *primum cognitum*, as was said, than the *first dissimulated*. . . . For Levinas, on the contrary, Being (understood as concept) is the *first dissimulating*" (VM, 149).

3. Reduction to Responsibility

1. The following passages can also be cited: "essence properly so-called is the verb, the logos, that resounds in the prose of predicative propositions"; "in the verb of the apophansis, which is the verb properly so-called, the verb 'to be,' essence resounds and is heard" (OBBE, 41, 41).

2. It is not hard to see why these passages are important not only to Levinas's ethics but to Marion's theology as well. When Heidegger suggests that requesting (*euchē*) and prayer are not forms of apophantic logos, where something is pointed out, he opens the possibility that certain forms of theological address do not have an ontological significance. This seems to be precisely the insight that Marion puts to work in his interpretation of theological language in Pseudo-Dionysius as pointing beyond Being.

3. According to Levinas, this means that the Other appears to the subject only insofar as the subject has the capacity to receive him. The appearance of the Other would therefore not be absolute but conditioned by the capacity or preparedness of the ready subject. This marks one of the differences between *Otherwise than Being, or, Beyond Essence* and *Totality and Infinity*, where the revelation of the face is welcomed in the hospitality of the subject who receives it, warmly and with generosity. See below, chapter 5.

4. Preface to *Ideas: General Introduction to Pure Phenomenology*, trans. W. R. Boyce Gibson, 5th ed. (London: George Allen and Unwin, 1969), p. 23. This citation has been taken from the author's preface to the English edition, written in 1930, nearly

seventeen years after the original publication of *Ideas*. It is not reprinted in the more recent translation of Husserl's *Ideen* by F. Kersten.

5. I thus side with those who take Levinas to be a phenomenologist and against those who seek to emphasize his opposition to phenomenology. In an article discussing Levinas and Husserl, Stephan Strasser has argued that even though "the philosophy of Levinas differs essentially from all that has been up until the present conceived as phenomenology," nonetheless "it is a phenomenology, but a phenomenology of a new type. Perhaps, one should draw this conclusion more precisely as follows: *Levinas changed the phenomenological optics by adding to it a dimension of depth.*" See Stephan Strasser, "Antiphénoménologie et phénoménologie dans la philosophie d'Emmanuel Levinas," *Revue Philosophique de Louvain* 75 (February 1977): 124.

6. Adriaan Peperzak, "Dieu à travers l'être et le bien," in *Philosophie de la religion entre éthique et ontologie*, Biblioteca dell' "Archivio di Filosofia," CEDAM.

7. The term "supplement" and the phrase "originary supplement" are, of course, drawn from Jacques Derrida, especially *Of Grammatology* and *Speech and Phenomena and Other Essays on Husserl's Theory of Signs* (Evanston, Ill.: Northwestern University Press, 1973), where these categories are developed more extensively than anywhere else in his work.

4. Insight and Drift: Husserl

1. Jean-Luc Marion, *Reduction and Givenness* (Evanston, Ill.: Northwestern University Press, 1998), p. 1.

2. Cited by Jean-Luc Marion in "Le phénomène saturé," in *Phénoménologie et théologie*, ed. Jean François Courtine (Paris: Criterion, 1992), p. 81.

3. Cited ibid., p. 84.

4. Much will depend, of course, on how this appearing is interpreted. As Michel Henry has pointed out in "Quatre principes de la phénoménologie" (*Revue de métaphysique et de morale* [1991/91]), in the dictum "To the things themselves!" one can hear the urgency of a slogan or byword that would perhaps betray a certain uneasiness or ambiguity about the principle itself. Henry argues that as it has been historically interpreted in Husserlian phenomenology, this principle subordinates access to phenomena to the thing itself. That is, the principle establishes appearing on one side (the "To") and the things on the other ("the things themselves") such that phenomenological appearing is rendered second or a mere means of access to the priority of ontological investigation into the thing. This would contradict precisely Husserl's claim that "in the phenomenon . . . there is, in other words, no distinction between appearance and being" ("Philosophy as Rigorous Science," in *Phenomenology and the Crisis of Philosophy*, trans. Quentin Lauer [New York: Harper and Row, 1965], p. 106).

5. See *The Crisis of European Science and Transcendental Phenomenology*, trans. David Carr (Evanston, Ill.: Northwestern University Press, 1970), §48, p. 165.

6. Marion, *Reduction and Givenness*, p. 33.

7. "The Breakthrough and the Broadening" is a phrase coined by Jean-Luc Marion and used as a chapter title in his *Reduction and Givenness*.

8. Paul Ricoeur, *Husserl: An Analysis of His Phenomenology* (Evanston, Ill.: Northwestern University Press, 1967), p. 89.

9. For a penetrating reading of Descartes's "videre videor," see Michel Henry, *The Genealogy of Psychoanalysis* (Stanford: Stanford University Press, 1993), chapter 1.

10. Michel Henry, *Phénoménologie matérielle* (Paris: P.U.F., 1990), p. 66.

11. Ibid., p. 81.

12. Heidegger advanced the argument I am making when he too sought to explain why "in the basic task of determining its ownmost field, phenomenology is unphenomenological" (HCT, 128ff.). According to Heidegger, Husserl's fidelity to the traditional conception of philosophy as a science barred him from proceeding in a line of questioning that would have led phenomenology to the soil it sought: namely, the twofold question of the being of consciousness and the meaning of Being.

13. Henry, *Phénoménologie matérielle*, p. 77.

14. Robert Sokolowski, *The Formation of Husserl's Concept of Constitution* (The Hague: Martinus Nijhoff, 1964), chapter 4, section 3a–c.

15. Marion, *Reduction and Givenness*, p. 159.

16. Cubist painting, in its effort to see its subject from every perspective all at once, would be, as it were, the most Husserlian of all art forms. It paints not what is seen (when have you ever seen bathers on the beach looking like Picasso's bathers except in a Picasso?), but what is intended beyond each moment of appearing.

17. Henry, *Phénoménologie matérielle*, p. 71.

18. Ibid., p. 85.

19. Henry writes: "This disaggregation of the 'immanent' given of the reduction—the given which replaced the *cogitatio*—is acknowledged by Husserl as soon as, pushing his analysis further, he conceived the condition of the reduction and of reflection as retention" (ibid., p. 85).

20. "Signs and the Blink of an Eye" is the title of a chapter from Derrida's book on Husserl, *Speech and Phenomena*. For Derrida, the blink of the eye means that the moment [*Augenblick:* blink of an eye], the now or the present held under the gaze of the ego, is haunted by an absence. The phenomenological gaze, according to Derrida, cannot encompass a total presence, for the eye blinks.

21. Ricoeur, *Husserl: An Analysis of His Phenomenology*, p. 192. The suggestion that a radical otherness attaches to presence is interesting; for it suggests that the notion of presence becomes an ally of totality on condition that this presence be interpreted in terms of the present, the present which is found in me. I expect that much phenomenology will be written, and has been written, in an attempt to reconsider without abandoning the notion of presence.

22. The significance of this primal impression will be elaborated upon in Levinas's phenomenology. Whereas Husserl overlooks the passivity in which this impression is left in order to focus on the conscious work of generating a present from it, Levinas will isolate this passivity and seek to describe it without the terms suggested by a phenomenology of consciousness (see OBBE, pp. 31–34, where Levinas explicitly treats the ur-impression). Since the passivity of the primal impression precedes the activity of consciousness, it must be described by a phenomenology that does not take consciousness as its subject.

23. I should note, however, that while the passive genesis of temporal objects implies the activity of consciousness, the genesis of time itself may not.

24. In a characteristically close and careful reading, Derrida, in *Speech and Phenomena*, detects another movement of Husserl's argument, claiming that "the body of the description in *The Phenomenology of Internal Time-Consciousness* and elsewhere prohibits our speaking of a simple self-identity of the present." The duration of time, the stretch which is the present, is a compound of presence and nonpresence; "nonpresence and nonevidence are admitted into the *blink of the instant. . . .* This

alterity is in fact the condition for presence, presentation, and thus for *Vorstellung* in general" (p. 65). Derrida's claim is based on his demonstrating that the strict distinction between retention and recollection does not hold in Husserl's own text. According to Derrida, Husserl introduced this distinction in order to secure a more fundamental distinction between perception and nonperception—retention and recollection would differ in that the former *perceives* the past or nonpresent whereas the latter does not: "primary remembrance [retention] is perception. For only in [retention] do we see what is past" (PIT, §17). Thus, retention, as a perception of the *past,* makes the present by compounding presence with nonpresence. In other texts, Husserl disavows the claim that retention is a perception: "the antithesis of perception is primary remembrance and primary expectation (retention and protention) whereby perception and non-perception continually pass over into one another" (PIT, §16 [cited by Derrida, *Speech and Phenomena*, p. 65]). Seen in this way, the difference between retention and recollection is a difference in two modes of nonperception. Retention therefore admits nonpresence *and* nonperception into the present. The present endures only as a compound made of a perceived now and a nonperceived nonpresence. Though Derrida is able to develop this through a reading of Husserl's own text, such a reading is one which the dominant voice of *The Phenomenology of Internal Time-Consciousness* seeks to repress, put down, or silence.

25. Husserl's phenomenology thus is challenged by certain forms of psychoanalytic interpretation which seek to trace in the subject the effects of an unconscious so radical that it is not merely a pre-conscious or a not-yet-conscious but an unconscious that remains forever foreign to the conscious subject. This unconscious would obey laws wholly other than those which hold, as I am showing, in the domain of consciousness—the laws Freud laid out in his discussion of the dream work, for example—and would contain thoughts that no phenomenological interpretation of consciousness would ever be sufficient to recovering.

26. Henry, *Phénoménologie matérielle*, p. 8.

5. The De-posited Subject: Levinas

1. Derrida, *Of Grammatology*, p. 145.

2. I have modified the translation in order to make a distinction between the self (*le soi*) Levinas writes about here and the oneself (*le soi-même*) I was describing earlier. It is difficult to maintain this distinction with any consistency since Levinas himself seems sometimes to speak of *le soi* where we might expect *le soi-même*. For instance, given the distinction we here insist on, one might expect that the third section of the fourth chapter would be called *Le soi-même* (oneself), not *Le soi.*

3. This "inversion of intentionality" will prove central to Jean-Luc Marion's attempt to articulate a phenomenology of givenness, and especially the givenness of the subject as what Marion has called *interloqué* (see "L'Interloqué," in *Who Comes after the Subject?*) and now calls *adonné* (*Etant donné*). That Marion first developed such a notion through an interpretation of Levinas can be seen in the reading of Levinas that he develops in *Prolégomènes à la charité* (Paris: La Différence, 1986), pp. 89–121.

4. For Levinas's discussion of the relations between apodicticity and adequacy in Husserl and the changes that these relations undergo in the course of Husserl's work, see "From Consciousness to Wakefulness: Starting with Husserl," in *Of God Who Comes to Mind*. In brief, Levinas shows that in the *Ideas*, Husserl's discovery of

the apodicticity of internal intuition (reflection on consciousness) went hand-in-hand with the search for an evidence that dispelled uncertainty, ambiguity, and error. That is to say, the author of the *Ideas* sought apodicticity in an evidence whose intuition offered adequate fulfillment for the significative intention that sought it out. In short, apodicticity equaled adequacy of evidence. In *Cartesian Meditations,* however, Husserl suggests that apodicticity need not derive from adequacy of evidence; but Levinas notes, "the positive determination of apodicticity, which does not go 'together with adequation' is lacking in these perplexed pages in which, on various occasions, are acknowledged the difficulties attached to the notion apodicticity 'provisionally neglected' therein" (GCM, 22). According to Levinas, the lack of adequacy there where the apodicticity of the *cogito* is discovered can be seen in the infinite iteration whereby the ego reflects on its own reflection; as infinite, this iteration never reaches adequate evidence, though it remains in the sphere of the apodictic.

5. In emptying or renouncing itself, the responsible self is sacrificial. I will discuss the sacrifice of the self in chapter 8, where I show how the responsible self exhibits an unmistakably religious dimension.

6. Though Levinas intends these remarks as a criticism of Heidegger, they are founded on a debatable reading of *Being and Time.* As I will discuss in chapter 6 below, Levinas tends to minimize or alleviate the consequences that death, which utterly dispossesses me of my being, has on the meaning of my ownmost being. The ownmost being which Heidegger seeks from the opening section of *Being and Time* is found in death, a possibility of being to which I can never actually lay claim since when I do I am no longer. In seeming thus to discover my ownmost in the dispossession of my own, this reading of Heidegger would suggest a rapprochement with Levinas on the question of the authenticity, mineness, and uniqueness of the self.

7. This use of the term "recurrence" echoes its use in Nietzsche's doctrine of the eternal return, especially as that doctrine has been interpreted by Deleuze to mean the return of difference (what returns is not some identical thing; rather, return is the being of difference) and, similarly, by Klossowski to mean a return in which the coherence, established in a memory that represents, of my self with its self is undone. See Gilles Deleuze, *Nietzsche and Philosophy* (New York: Columbia University Press, 1983), and Pierre Klossowski, "Nietzsche's Experience of the Eternal Return," in *The New Nietzsche,* ed. David Allison (New York: Delta Books, 1977).

8. Exile would also be the meaning of *Dasein*'s thrownness. As Heidegger points out, thrownness issues in a not-at-home which is not reducible to the at-home. Thrown into its there, *Dasein* is not at home there where it finds itself. Its own there is thus irreducibly uncanny [*unheimlich*].

9. The notion of "exile" resonates with the history of the Jewish people. It is perhaps best read in contrast not with Husserl but with Hegel, for whom the phenomenology of spirit draws on either Christianity or Greece to uncover the image of its consummate adventure: in Christian terms, a fall or exile from paradise which is eventually overcome in a kingdom which is even greater than the Eden which we left; in Greek terms, an Odyssean journey home. For Levinas, on the other hand, the phenomenology of the subject draws its images from the Jewish tradition of an exile which is original and final, one whose end has not yet come but is always forever anticipated, like a utopia that has no place in the world. In chapter 8, I will have cause to discuss the place of religion and particularly the Jewish tradition in Levinas's thought.

10. It would be interesting to study further the ways in which Levinas articulates a negative theology that is deprived of the orientation which its reference to God offers. Such a study would want to explore the ways in which the reference to God is displaced (or replaced) by a reference to the responsible self; responsibility would be the image of God in man, which might be why Levinas calls it a "divine discomfort" (OBBE, 122).

11. Would the insanity defense acquit the guilty subject of his responsibility by rendering him unconscious of his deed or unable to intend it? Levinas seems to say, no, since I am responsible for what is done unconsciously and what I can never have meant to do. A world in which everyone feels guilty but no one is responsible for his guilt is one very much at odds with the sentiment of the subject in Levinas.

12. The English translation is flawed by a significant typographical error, which I have corrected here.

13. It is not hard to see here why responsibility might be a terror. Notions such as an accusation which strikes me in my innocence, a 'fault' for which I can never apologize, and the self as a hostage might lead one to read Levinas as describing not the responsibility of the self but the terror of the self; the other would not be "the widow, the orphan, and the poor" so much as a terrorist; or, "the widow, the orphan, and the poor" would be my jailers. Responsibility might also be a horror, and one should read Levinas as a master teller of ghost stories. Obsessed with absent others, heeding calls from time immemorial, haunted by the dead who still summon it, the responsible self is the protagonist of a horror tale straight from Poe or Lovecraft. As a horror story, responsibility would draw dangerously close to the "experience" that Levinas describes as the *il y a*. I will return to this at the end of this book.

14. See also OBBE, 121: "Phenomenology can follow out the reverting of thematization into anarchy in the description of the approach: ethical language succeeds in expressing the paradox in which phenomenology finds itself abruptly thrown."

15. See Taylor, *Altarity*, pp. 185–218.

6. The Affected Subject: Responsibility or *Dasein*?

1. Jean Greisch, *Ontologie et temporalité, esquisse d'une interprétation intégrale de Sein und Zeit* (Paris: Presses Universitaires de France, 1994), p. 60.

2. Jacques Taminiaux, *Heidegger and the Project of Fundamental Ontology* (Albany: State University of New York Press, 1991), p. 40.

3. As Jean-François Courtine writes in his *Heidegger et la phénoménologie* (Paris: Librairie Philosophique J. Vrin, 1990), "it is therefore on the basis of the Husserlian determination of phenomenology, but all the while realizing the fundamental omission from which it suffers by not elucidating any further 'the intentional comportment and all that implies,' that the question of Being is phenomenologically imposed as the question of the being of the intentional and the question of the meaning of Being in general" (p. 253).

4. As Jean Greisch notes, there is something of a circular or reciprocal foundation at work in the twofold way in which the question of Being is posed in *Being and Time:* the analytic of *Dasein* presupposes a fundamental ontology which has discovered the various senses of Being, while fundamental ontology presupposes an analytic of *Dasein* wherein the different senses of Being are understood (*Ontologie et temporalité*, pp. 87–88). This circle, or reciprocal foundation, would be explained, in part, by the way in which the central problem of *Being and Time* (the question of Being) arises out of an immanent critique of Husserl's phenomenology.

5. One might argue that *Dasein* gets its determination solely from the question of Being. *Dasein* is only what the question of Being requires. One can then imagine, with Levinas among others, that there is much more to man than what the question of Being might furnish him.

6. Courtine, *Heidegger et la phénoménologie*, p. 238.

7. Greisch, *Ontologie et temporalité*, p. 176. The reasons for my decision to translate *Befindlichkeit* as "affectedness" will become clearer as this chapter progresses.

8. Heidegger goes on to note that Aristotle investigates the affects in his *Rhetoric* and argues that such a location of the affects must be taken as "the first systematic hermeneutic of the everydayness of Being with one another." The work of Aristotle helps the orator to understand the moods which belong to the public in order that his speech might rouse them, create them, and guide them.

Heidegger also cites Augustine and Pascal as important investigators of the affects (BT, 178, H. 139, and BT, 492, n. 5). This citation suggests the possibility of a fruitful alliance among theological thinkers of a certain stripe and existential or ontological inquiry. On the one hand, it is fair to say that the existential analytic grows out of Heidegger's early attempts at a hermeneutic of primal or mystical Christianity; the existential analytic might never have disclosed the phenomena it does without the assistance of theology. On the other hand, the existential analytic makes possible a philosophical grounding of the intelligibility of the phenomena described in these theological texts; in and through the terms provided by the existential analytic, the phenomena of religious life become accessible to philosophical thought. In chapters 6 and 7, I suggest that a similar possibility is broached by Levinas's philosophy.

9. This is why it is so hard to answer when asked "how do you feel." Because an affect shows being as 'that-ness' and not as 'what-ness,' and since a word designates—'designates what-ness'—it is difficult to find a word for how one is doing as it is disclosed by the affect.

10. See Giorgio Agamben, "La passion de la facticité," in *Heidegger: Questions ouvertes* (Paris: Editions Osiris, 1988), pp. 66–67.

11. See also BT, 173, H. 134, where Heidegger first speaks of the Being disclosed in an affect as a burden that *Dasein* must bear: "It is in this [a mood which seems like a lack of mood] that *Dasein* becomes satiated [*überdrüssig:* bored or weary] with itself. Being has become manifest as a burden. Why that should be, one does not *know.* . . . A mood of elation can alleviate the manifest burden of Being; that such a mood is possible also discloses the burdensome character of *Dasein,* even while it alleviates the burden."

12. Greisch, *Ontologie et temporalité,* p. 235.

13. Jean-François Courtine, "Voice of Conscience and Call of Being," in *Who Comes after the Subject?* p. 81.

14. Here, it is not hard to see a prototype of Lacan's psychoanalytic reading of reflection as that reading has been expressed in his observations on the mirror stage. Also, for a fertile and insightful reading of the passage on which I am commenting, see Jacques Derrida, *Aporias* (Stanford: Stanford University Press, 1993), pp. 64–67.

15. Courtine, "Voice of Conscience and Call of Being," p. 86.

16. See his "A Note Concerning Ontological Indifference," in *Graduate Faculty Philosophy Journal* 20, 2–21, 1 (1998), p. 33.

17. Jean Greisch has suggested that Heidegger's *Dasein* analytic is not so closed to ethics as Levinas suggests: "Discovering itself exposed to the disquieting strange-

ness of Being, there is space for many more or less traumatizing experiences, among which the shock of the encounter with *autrui* would quite certainly occupy a central place" (*Ontologie et temporalité*, pp. 34–35). Affected passively and finding itself in the very instance where it loses itself, *Dasein* would be open to the trauma of responsibility; for this traumatic affection entails the positing of a de-posited subject such as *Dasein* is in its Being-towards-death. It would also be open to a great many other traumas.

18. The obvious objection arises that in dying for the other, am I not simply owning my death in another way? Isn't it still my death when I die even if I die for the Other?

19. It should be noted that only late in his career does Levinas come to accept the term "love" as a possible characteristic of responsibility.

7. The Death of God and Emergence of the Philosophy of Religion

1. Jean-Luc Marion, "Metaphysics and Phenomenology: A Relief for Theology," *Critical Inquiry* 20, 4 (summer 1994): 572.

2. Martin Heidegger, "The Ontotheological Constitution of Metaphysics," in *Identity and Difference* (New York: Harper and Row, 1969), pp. 59–60.

3. Marion, "Metaphysics and Phenomenology," p. 579. As evidence, Marion cites definitions of God from Aristotle, Aquinas, Descartes, and Leibniz.

4. Ibid., p. 577.

5. Friedrich Nietzsche, *The Will to Power* (New York: Vintage, 1968), p. 9.

6. Ibid., p. 16.

7. Ibid., p. 528.

8. *Thus Spoke Zarathustra*, in *The Portable Nietzsche* (New York: Penguin Books, 1982), p. 198.

9. Friedrich Nietzsche, *On the Genealogy of Morals*, trans. Walter Kaufmann (New York: Vintage Books, 1967), pp. 47–48.

10. *Thus Spoke Zarathustra*, p. 376.

11. If one doubts that the ugliest man is in fact also the Christian or the man of God, that the murderer of God is in fact the creator of God, one need only be reminded that Zarathustra encountered another ugly man—the ascetic: "one who was sublime I saw today, one who was solemn, an ascetic of spirit; oh how my soul laughed at his ugliness," and also that Nietzsche himself deplored "the consistency of Christianity in conceiving the good man as ugly" (*Thus Spoke Zarathustra*, p. 228; *The Will to Power*, p. 435).

12. Friedrich Nietzsche, *Beyond Good and Evil* (New York: Vintage Books, 1966), p. 67.

13. *The Genealogy of Morals*, p. 117.

14. See the opening pages of Derrida's *The Gift of Death* for an indication of how this connection is at play in the work of the Czech phenomenologist Jan Patočka.

15. Obviously, one need not take Levinas at his word when he claims that the responsible self does not discharge its will or have any intentionality. A suspicious approach might very well find a displaced expression of the will or of repressed anger/ressentiment. For some suggestions, see William J. Richardson, "The Irresponsible Subject," in *Ethics as First Philosophy*, ed. Peperzak.

16. Hegel, *Faith and Knowledge*, p. 190.

17. G. W. F. Hegel, *Lectures on the Philosophy of Religion* (Berkeley: University of California Press, 1988), p. 102.

18. *Faith and Knowledge,* p. 57.

19. While the "disenchantment" of the world was meant to protect divine tran-scendence, to protect against "reducing the sacred grove to mere timber," it had the opposite effect when the protected transcendence was simply forsaken and left to languish in its distance. As Hegel notes, "It is precisely through its flight from the finite and through its rigidity that subjectivity turns the beautiful into mere things—the grove into timber, the images into things that have eyes and do not see, ears and do not hear" (FK, 58). Hegel here would anticipate some of Max Weber's theses concerning unintended consequences in the life of ideas and the Protestant Reformers. See Max Weber, *The Protestant Ethic and the Spirit of Capitalism* (New York: Charles Scribner's Sons, 1958).

20. *Faith and Knowledge,* p. 59.

21. Ibid.

22. *Faith and Knowledge,* p. 65. This needs to be read in contrast with Hegel's determination of man as finite spirit, that is to say, as the manifestation of infinite spirit for itself. Man as finite spirit would be the self-othering of infinite spirit in and as the consciousness which knows it. Infinite spirit would thus return to itself in man's knowledge of God. See below for how this conception of finite and infinite spirit is related to the philosophy of religion.

23. Immanuel Kant, *Critique of Pure Reason* (New York: St. Martin's Press, 1965), p. 528.

24. *Critique of Pure Reason,* p. 29.

25. Walter Jaeschke, "Philosophical Theology and Philosophy of Religion," in *New Perspectives on Hegel's Philosophy of Religion,* ed. David Kolb (Albany: State University of New York Press, 1992), p. 110.

26. Walter Jaeschke, *Reason in Religion: The Foundations of Hegel's Philosophy of Religion* (Berkeley: University of California Press, 1990), p. 4.

27. Immanuel Kant, *Lectures on Philosophical Theology* (Ithaca, N.Y.: Cornell University Press, 1978), p. 42.

28. I should note that Hegel's interpretation of all this could not be put better than it is expressed in the following observation from Kant's own *Lectures on Philosophical Theology:* "We now have sufficient insight to tell that we will be satisfied from a practical standpoint, but from a speculative standpoint our reason will find little satisfaction" (p. 27)—and we are well aware of Hegel's attitude to dissatisfied reason.

29. *Critique of Practical Reason* (New York: MacMillan, 1956), p. 134.

30. *Lectures on the Philosophy of Religion,* p. 82.

31. *Faith and Knowledge,* p. 55.

32. Ibid., p. 56.

33. *Phenomenology of Spirit,* p. 355.

34. Martin J. De Nys, "Philosophical Thinking and the Claims of Religion," in *New Perspectives on Hegel's Philosophy of Religion,* p. 19. See also Jaeschke, "Philosophical Theology and Philosophy of Religion," pp. 1, 6 *et passim.*

35. Eberhard Jüngel, in *God as the Mystery of the World* (Grand Rapids, Mich.: Wm. B. Eerdmans, 1983), writes, "The first philosophical interpretations of talk of the death of God known to us neither deny nor forget the theological origin of this expression, but rather make it very plain. It was Georg Friedrich Wilhelm Hegel who introduced talk of the death of God into philosophy and in doing so was well aware that he was using a theological expression" (p. 63). See also Martin J.

De Nys in "Philosophical Thinking and the Claims of Religion": "Hegel overcomes the 'death of God' that Enlightenment philosophy brings about by philosophically appropriating and maintaining the insight into the death of God that belongs to the consummate religion," namely Christianity (p. 25).

36. *Faith and Knowledge*, p. 190.

37. *God as the Mystery of the World*, p. 74.

38. Ibid., p. 89.

39. Cited in Jaeschke, "Philosophical Theology and Philosophy of Religion," p. 8.

40. Ibid., p. 8.

41. *Lectures on the Philosophy of Religion*, p. 130.

42. Ibid., p. 129.

43. Ibid., p. 104.

44. *Thus Spoke Zarathustra*, p. 198.

8. Ethical Phenomenology and the Religiosity of the Subject

1. The notion of heresy is invoked by Derrida in *The Gift of Death* when he writes on the Christian logic deployed by the Czech phenomenologist Jan Patočka in one of the latter's *Essais hérétiques sur la philosophie de l'histoire* (see especially chapters 1 and 2). I will use the notion here and will return to it later in this chapter when discussing the role of Levinas's Judaism.

The notion of heterodoxy is employed by Cyril O'Regan in *The Heterodox Hegel* (Albany: State University of New York Press, 1994) to suggest the "systematic odd-ness of Hegel's renditions vis-à-vis the mainline theological and philosophical tra-ditions . . . ; it wishes to insist upon the sincerity of Hegel's Christian and Lutheran dispositions, while acknowledging divergence" (p. 25).

In my use of the terms, no reference to a hetero-praxis is being made. I refer to Levinas's thought as heretical or heterodox without making any claim as to wheth-er or not he practices orthodox or reform or any other form of Judaism. Whether or not he keeps Kosher, attends synagogue on Friday nights, etc., is not my concern.

With the terms heretic or heterodox, I mean to say that the religiosity uncov-ered by phenomenology is not based on any dogma or a dogmatic, rabbinically or theologically authorized, interpretation of religion; one need not subscribe to a faith or a creed, belong to a particular people, or respect the authority of a particu-lar body of texts and their interpretations to discover this religiosity. The usefulness of the term will be apparent, perhaps, when I contrast my reading with those who claim Levinas is a Jewish philosopher, for better or worse.

2. The translation of this text has been modified.

3. Levinas also refers to the "Scriptural reproach of Job" in NTR, 49. For some-thing of a theological criticism of Levinas's heterodox stance, see Jean-Louis Chré-tien's "La dette et l'élection," in *Emmanuel Levinas: Cahier de l'Herne* (Paris: Editions de l'Herne, livre de poche, 1991). Chrétien raises an objection to Levinas in the name of a more theological reading of Job's story: "When God reminds Job of his absolute transcendence and asks him 'Where were you when I created the world,' is it a matter of making him 'support the universe,' or on the contrary of manifest-ing to him what God alone does and can do, of saying what of the divine is incom-municable . . . ? Does He not evoke a meaning which does not enter the world through Job, but through Himself alone? . . . Does not God manifest that He alone supports the universe?" (p. 270). To Chrétien, Levinas's ethical reading of Job over-

looks or at least excessively narrows the difference between creature and creator when it makes man, in responsibility, the support of the universe. As an "ethical Atlas" (p. 268), the creature is too much like God. If the responsible self, the creature, were instead to admit or confess its own inadequacy, its inability to meet the infinite obligation assigned to it, the difference would be better instituted. According to Chrétien, then, humility is missing from the responsible self, and it is humility that acknowledges and admits man's difference from God.

4. "'That is my place in the sun.' That is how the usurpation of the whole world began" (Pascal) is an epigraph to *Otherwise than Being, or, Beyond Essence.*

5. The discussion of *me voici* is also taken up by Jean-Luc Marion in "L'interloqué."

6. This notion is obviously very fragile and susceptible of many responses. It seems difficult to maintain in the face of the Nazi persecution of the Jews, but such a difficulty is precisely what Levinas holds is constitutive of responsibility. On the other hand, one (a Nietzschean, for example) could see a certain grandiosity or revenge in the way that the sufferer becomes the salvation of mankind.

7. One wonders: Are all religious phenomena unconditional, absolute, and not given in plain evidence? Do all religious phenomena strike me by revealing themselves contrary to expectation and from, as it were, beyond the world? These are good questions, ones that the history of religions will surely be able to raise more fully through reference to non-Western, non-Abrahamic traditions. They suggest that Levinas's phenomenology of religion is a phenomenology of particular religions, thus that the pure possibility being probed might have been determined by the actual religions it is meant to have suspended.

8. Are other subjects ordered as the responsible self? Chapter 5 was meant to raise this question. There might be other notions of subjectivity, notions purged of the specifically ethical cast given by Levinas, in which phenomenology might find the possibility of religious phenomena. Such a subject is being sought by Marion under the name *interloqué* and *adonné.*

9. I have abused this passage slightly: where Levinas wrote *philosophie*, I have inserted "metaphysics or onto-theology." This insertion is perhaps overly interpretive, perhaps not. It has been made in order to make a clear distinction between Levinas's favorable use of the word "philosophy" and his less favorable use of the same word. When used with negative connotations, Levinas generally means metaphysics or onto-theology, including its consummation in Husserlian phenomenology of consciousness. When used with positive connotations, he means something like the phenomenology of ethics I have described in part 2.

10. Are these the only meanings of religion? Might there be religious phenomena that do not demand a phenomenology open to transcendence? For Hegel, the central message of religion was not transcendence but reconciliation or immanence —that is, incarnation and the cross, where God in heaven died in order to become a man, who then himself died in order that the spirit might enter the religious community here on earth. Nevertheless, it remains true that at least some religious phenomena—if not most in the tradition of Western religions—make a claim to transcendence, unconditionality, the absolute, etc.

11. Cohen, *Elevations,* p. 173.

12. Gibbs, *Correlations,* p. 4.

13. Ibid.

14. Ibid., p. 166.

15. Cohen, *Elevations,* p. 128.

16. Later in this chapter, I will suggest that these authors return in a new way. The research of Gibbs and Cohen might help point out the historical source of the notion of responsibility which phenomenology investigates. That is to say, if Levinas's phenomenological account of religiosity proceeds through a description of responsibility as such, the notion of responsibility might have been given by a historical tradition: namely Judaism. This is not to say that a commitment to Judaism guides Levinas's phenomenology or that Levinas intends to be a Jewish philosopher but that without the historical event of Judaism there would be no responsibility for phenomenology to articulate the subjectivity of the subject.

17. *Correlations*, p. 12; see also p. 17.

18. Janicaud, *Le tournant théologique*, p. 31. Janicaud treats mainly Levinas's *Totality and Infinity* and for that reason seems not to take into account many of the advances Levinas made in his practice of phenomenology.

19. Ibid., p. 16.

20. Ibid.

21. The distinction put forth by Derrida has also been adopted by Jean-Luc Marion who cites from the same texts as I have in his "Metaphysics and Phenomenology," pp. 589-91. Marion claims that the feared confusion between phenomenology and theology can be avoided if one makes a clear and rigorous distinction: "of itself, phenomenology can identify the saturated phenomenon of the being-given par excellence [the phenomenological name for God, according to Marion] only as a possibility—not only a possibility as opposed to actuality but above all a possibility of donation. . . . The intuitive realization of that being-given requires, more than phenomenological analysis, the real experience of its donation, which falls to revealed theology. Between phenomenology and theology, the border passes between revelation as possibility and revelation as historicity. There could be no danger of confusion between these domains" (p. 590). Marion thus follows Derrida's distinction, the distinction that I too have put to work, between revelation or religious phenomena considered phenomenologically as possible and considered theologically or experientially as actual or historical.

I should note, however, that Marion disagrees with Derrida's identification of the phenomenological doublet of religion as indifferently "philosophical, metaphysical." For Marion, and as I have suggested for Levinas, too, phenomenology opens a philosophical thought of religion which is not metaphysical. For a philosophy of religion, "phenomenology alone is suitable—and not at all metaphysics, which is thought of actuality par excellence" (p. 590).

22. Catherine Chalier, *L'utopie de l'humain* (Paris: Albin Michel, 1993), p. 96.

23. When Levinas claims, "The authentically human is the being-Jewish in all men" (ITN, 164), he seems to evidence such pride—unless one interprets this quote in the way I have been suggesting.

24. Rabbi Haim of Volozhin, *Nefesh haHayyim*, III, 10; cited in BTV, p. 157.

25. An interesting light could perhaps be shed on the inner life of the Neoplatonic and Christian mystics if one were to employ Levinas's phenomenology. Inversely, many interesting questions could be raised for Levinas by comparison with mystical thinkers. Most notably, comparison with the mystics might suggest that the subject described by Levinas in terms of responsibility might be quite similar to the subject described in terms of mystical theology. This would force one to ask (as I tried in the preceding chapter) about the necessity of an ethical cast to the very life of the subject and would lead to a more precise determination of the place where ethics enters phenomenology. For a first attempt, see Jeffrey L. Kosky, "Con-

NOTES TO PAGES 166–180

temporary Encounters with Apophatic Mysticism: The Case of Emmanuel Levinas,"
Journal for Cultural and Religious Theory 1, 3.

26. *Nefesh haHayyim*, I, 4; cited in BTV, p. 161.

27. Ibid., I, 3; cited in BTV, p. 160.

28. Ibid., I, 4; cited in BTV, p. 160. Again, I should add that the thaumaturgical impulse behind such texts is deeply rooted in Neoplatonic thought. What is unique here is the specifically ethical cast given it.

29. This divine discomfort again recalls Chrétien's theological criticism of Levinas. The divine discomfort of supporting the universe, the responsible self as an "ethical Atlas," makes man too divine; it elevates him too much, making his suffering a source of pride. Rather than confess his inability to meet an infinite responsibility, the responsible self insists that he alone is responsible for all and thus forgets the humility proper to man. Having seen how this notion of responsibility as a divine discomfort emerges first in Judaism, Chrétien's criticism now seems particularly Christian.

30. Buber is referred to in NTR, p. 42.

31. Tractate *Shabbat* 88a–b; cited in NTR, p. 45. The full text appears in NTR, pp. 30–31.

32. Ibid.; cited in NTR, p. 47.

33. "At This Very Moment in This Work Here I Am," in *Re-Reading Levinas*, ed. Robert Bernasconi and Simon Critchley (Bloomington: Indiana University Press, 1991), p. 18.

34. Hegel, *Lectures on the Philosophy of Religion*, pp. 129–30.

9. The Ethical Possibility of God

1. For more on the relation between Nietzsche and Husserl, see Jean-Luc Marion, *Réduction et donation*, pp. 30–33. See also Rudolf Boehm, "Deux points de vue: Husserl et Nietzsche," *Archivio di Filosofia*, 3rd ed. (1963).

2. Husserl's reduction of God seems all the more remarkable when one compares it to Descartes, Husserl's admitted model for philosophy. For Descartes, one who meditates in a Cartesian manner ought not to have suspended or reduced God, since Descartes himself in his own meditations relies on the irreducibility of God to explain the existence of the *cogito* and even the very possibility of his doubt.

3. See "On the Idea of the Infinite in Us," in *Entre Nous: Thinking of the Other* (New York: Columbia University Press, 1998), and "God and Philosophy," in *Of God Who Comes to Mind* (Stanford: Stanford University Press, 1998).

4. The first of these points is made in the Third Meditation itself. See *The Philosophical Writings of Descartes*, vol. 2, trans. John Cottingham, Robert Stoothof, and Dugald Murdoch (Cambridge: Cambridge University Press, 1984), p. 28; AT, 40 (henceforth, citations from Descartes will be taken from this translation and will include a reference to the page number in the edition of Adam and Tannery [AT]).

The second point is made in the fourth set of replies. Descartes claims, "We cannot develop this proof [the proof for the existence of God] with precision unless we grant our minds the freedom to inquire into the efficient cause of all things, even God himself. For what right do we have to make God an exception if we have not proved that he exists? In every case then we must ask whether a thing derives its existence from itself or from something else" (AT, 238).

5. This notion of desire appears close to that suggested by the mystical theologians. In particular, when Gregory of Nyssa describes *epektesis* as an unending move-

ment of the soul toward God, the impossibility of its ever having enough of God, he seems to foreshadow theological desire as described by Levinas. It is interesting here to compare Levinas's, and Gregory's, notion of desire (for the infinite) with that of Origen. For Origen, it was possible for the soul to be sated with God, precisely because infinity had been rejected as undivine. Because an infinite being could not be known, not even by itself, according to Origen, God cannot be said to be divine. In not recognizing the infinite as a name of God, Origen's theology included the possibility of the soul's desire being sated.

6. Robert Gibbs, "Jewish Dimensions of Radical Ethics," in *Ethics as First Philosophy,* ed. Peperzak, p. 18.

7. Ibid., pp. 22–23.

8. Hegel, *Phenomenology of Spirit,* p. 355.

9. It is characteristic of Levinas to ascribe two radically opposed meanings to a term. The term "atheism" is a good example. On the one hand, for Levinas "atheism" has the meaning that I am discussing here. On the other hand, he uses "atheism" to name a form of thought that is closed to transcendence; atheism is philosophy that reduces all affectedness by what transcends me to the immanence of consciousness—the atheism of Husserl's phenomenology as discussed above.

10. See also OBBE, 121: "The trace is significant for behavior, and one would be wrong to forget its anarchic insinuation by confusing it with an indication or a monstration of the signified in the signifier. For that is the itinerary by which theological and edifying thought too quickly deduces the truths of faith."

11. In "L'obsession de l'autre," *Cahiers de l'Herne* (Paris: Editions de l'Herne, 1991), Michel Haar has suggested that the violence and trauma suffered by the responsible self is at least equal to that which is suffered by obedience to the anonymous. Also, Jean-Louis Chrétien, in "La dette et l'élection," *Cahiers de l'Herne* (Paris: Editions de l'Herne, 1991), suspects such a confusion of the *il y a* and the beyond Being when he asks, "is it the *il y a* which is chaos or the hither side of Being and nothingness?" (p. 273).

12. In this way, the responsible self resembles Abraham as the father of faith has been described in Kierkegaard's *Fear and Trembling*—with this exception: for Kierkegaard, the ethical is the realm of the universal, and the singularity of the self is found in the religious. For Levinas, on the other hand, the ethical is not the universal but is already the birth of the singular self. For a remarkable reading of Kierkegaard's story of Abraham, and also some suggestion of a possible comparison with Levinas, see Derrida, *The Gift of Death,* especially chapters 3 and 4.

13. "Obligation happens," "there is obligation," "*es gibt/il y a* obligation"—these phrases are repeated throughout John Caputo's remarkable and provocative work, *Against Ethics.* Caputo uses them to suggest that one does not know the origin of one's obligation, which nonetheless happens, and that any attempt to designate the origin of this obligation is an attempt by ethics or morality to secure the force, legitimacy, or righteousness of a responsibility which is wholly ungrounded. Caputo suspects such attempts of possessing a certainty or knowledge of good and evil which makes responsibility too easy, too comfortable, and too self-congratulatory; in these attempts, responsibility is the mere application of a technique and so does not call for any real response.

14. While I agree with much of what John Caputo argues in *Against Ethics* (namely the introduction of an element of undecidability and the possibility that there is obligation without uttering the name of God), I disagree to some extent

with his reading of Levinas, especially when he claims that for Levinas God sends the Other to me, that in some way God orders me to be responsible and thereby designates the origin of responsibility. The preceding discussion in this chapter intends to show that God is not indispensable from responsibility as its source or origin but that responsibility is the subject for whom the meaning of God takes on significance. Here in the conclusion, much of what Caputo argues for through reference to Derrida and Kierkegaard is argued for solely by a reading of Levinas, a reading of Levinas against himself, as it were.

15. "Save the Name [*Sauf le nom*]" is the French title of a work by Derrida that first appeared in English with the title "Post-Scriptum." I am referring obliquely to a passage that is presented in several voices. It runs as follows:

> — . . . . Certainly, the "unknowable God" ("*Der unerkandte GOtt*[*sic*]," 4:21), the ignored or unrecognized God that we spoke about says nothing; of him there is nothing said that might hold . . . [ellipses in original]

> —Save his name . . . [ellipsis in original]

> —that names nothing that might hold, not even a divinity [*Gottheit*], nothing whose withdrawal [*dérobement*] does not carry away every phrase that tries to measure itself against him. "God" "is" the name of this bottomless collapse, of this endless desertification of language. ("Post-Scriptum" in *Derrida and Negative Theology*, p. 300)

WORKS CITED

Agamben, Giorgio. "La passion de la facticité." In *Heidegger: Questions ouvertes*. Paris: Editions Osiris, 1988.

Autrement que savoir, Emmanuel Levinas. Paris: Editions Osiris, 1988.

Berger, Gaston. *The Cogito in Husserl's Phenomenology*, trans. Kathleen McLaughlin. Evanston, Ill.: Northwestern University Press, 1972.

Bernasconi, Robert. "Fundamental Ontology, Metotology, and the Ethic of Ethics." *Irish Philosophical Journal* 4 (1987): 76–93.

———. "Levinas and Derrida: The Question of the Closure of Metaphysics." In *Face-to-Face with Levinas*, ed. Richard Cohen. Albany: State University of New York Press, 1986.

———. "The Trace of Levinas in Derrida." In *Derrida and Difference*. Evanston, Ill.: Northwestern University Press, 1988.

Bernet, Rudolph. "Phenomenological Reduction and the Double Life of the Subject." In *Reading Heidegger from the Start*, ed. Theodore Kisiel and John van Buren. Albany: State University of New York Press, 1994.

Biemel, Walter. "L'idée de la phénoménologie chez Husserl." In *Phénoménologie et métaphysique*, ed. Jean-Luc Marion and Guy Planty-Bonjour. Paris: P.U.F., 1984.

Buber, Martin. *I and Thou*, trans. Walter Kaufmann. New York: Charles Scribner's Sons, 1970.

Cadava, Eduardo, Peter Connor, and Jean-Luc Nancy, eds. *Who Comes after the Subject?* New York: Routledge, 1991.

Cahiers de la nuit surveillée, no. 3: Emmanuel Levinas. Lagrasse: Verdier, 1984.

Caputo, John. *Against Ethics: Contribution to a Poetics of Obligation with Constant Reference to Deconstruction*. Bloomington: Indiana University Press, 1993.

———. *The Prayers and Tears of Jacques Derrida: Religion without Religion*. Bloomington: Indiana University Press, 1997.

Chalier, Catherine. *Levinas: L'utopie de l'humain*. Paris: Albin Michel, 1993.

———. "The Philosophy of Emmanuel Levinas and the Hebraic Tradition." In *Ethics as First Philosophy*, ed. Adriaan T. Peperzak. New York: Routledge, 1995.

Chrétien, Jean-Louis. "La dette et l'élection." In *Cahier de l'Herne: Emmanuel Levinas*, ed. Catherine Chalier and Miguel Abensour. Paris: Editions de l'Herne, 1991.

Ciaramelli, Fabio. "Le rôle du judaïsme dans l'œuvre d'Emmanuel Levinas." *Revue Philosophique de Louvain* 81 (1983): 580–99.

Cohen, Richard. *Elevations: The Height of the Good in Rosenzweig and Levinas*. Chicago: University of Chicago Press, 1994.

Collins, James. *The Emergence of the Philosophy of Religion*. New Haven: Yale University Press, 1967.

Courtine, Jean-François. *Heidegger et la phénoménologie*. Paris: Librairie Philosophique J. Vrin, 1990.

———. "L'idée de la phénoménologie et la problématique de la réduction." In *Phénoménologie et métaphysique*, ed. Jean-Luc Marion and Guy Planty-Bonjour. Paris: P.U.F., 1984.

————. "Voice of Conscience and Call of Being." In *Who Comes after the Subject?* ed. Eduardo Cadava, Peter Connor, and Jean-Luc Nancy. New York: Routledge, 1991.

Critchley, Simon. *The Ethics of Deconstruction: Derrida and Levinas.* Cambridge, Mass.: Basil Blackwell, 1992.

Davies, Paul. "On Resorting to Ethical Language." In *Ethics as First Philosophy,* ed. Adriaan T. Peperzak. New York: Routledge, 1995.

de Boer, Theo. "Theology and the Philosophy of Religion according to Levinas." In *Ethics as First Philosophy,* ed. Adriaan T. Peperzak. New York: Routledge, 1995.

de Nys, Martin J. "Philosophical Thinking and the Claims of Religion." In *New Perspectives on Hegel's Philosophy of Religion,* ed. David Kolb. Albany: State University of New York Press, 1992.

de Vries, Hent. "Adieu, à dieu, a-Dieu." In *Ethics as First Philosophy,* ed. Adriaan T. Peperzak. New York: Routledge, 1995.

Derrida, Jacques. *Aporias,* trans. Thomas Dutoit. Stanford: Stanford University Press, 1993.

————. "At This Very Moment in This Work Here I Am." In *Re-Reading Levinas,* ed. Robert Bernasconi and Simon Critchley. Bloomington: Indiana University Press, 1991.

————. "Eating Well." In *Who Comes after the Subject?* ed. Eduardo Cadava, Peter Connor, and Jean-Luc Nancy. New York: Routledge, 1991.

————. *The Gift of Death,* trans. David Wills. Chicago: University of Chicago Press, 1995.

————. *Of Grammatology,* trans. Gayatri Chakravorty Spivak. Baltimore: Johns Hopkins University Press, 1976.

————. "How to Avoid Speaking: Denials." In *Derrida and Negative Theology,* ed. Harold Coward and Toby Foshay. Albany: State University of New York Press, 1992.

————. "Post-Scriptum." In *Derrida and Negative Theology,* ed. Harold Coward and Toby Foshay. Albany: State University of New York Press, 1992.

————. *Speech and Phenomena, and Other Essays on Husserl's Theory of Signs.* Evanston, Ill.: Northwestern University Press, 1973.

————. "Violence and Metaphysics." In *Writing and Difference,* trans. Alan Bass. Chicago: University of Chicago Press, 1978.

Descartes, René. *Meditations on First Philosophy with Objections and Replies,* trans. John Cottingham. In *The Philosophical Writings of Descartes,* vol. 2. Cambridge: Cambridge University Press, 1984.

Fackenheim, Emil. *The Religious Dimension in Hegel's Thought.* Bloomington: Indiana University Press, 1967.

Gibbs, Robert. *Correlations in Rosenzweig and Levinas.* Princeton: Princeton University Press, 1992.

————. "Jewish Dimensions of Radical Ethics." In *Ethics as First Philosophy,* ed. Adriaan T. Peperzak. New York: Routledge, 1995.

Greenberg, Clement. *The Collected Essays and Criticism,* vol. 3. Ed. John O'Brian. Chicago: University of Chicago Press, 1986.

Greisch, Jean. Ethique et ontologie: Quelques considérations 'hypocritiques.'" In *Emmanuel Levinas: L'éthique comme philosophie première,* ed. Jean Greisch and Jacques Rolland. Paris: Editions du Cerf, 1993.

————. *Ontologie et temporalité.* Paris: P.U.F., 1994."

Haar, Michel. "L'obsession de l'autre." In *Cahier de l'Herne: Emmanuel Levinas,* ed. Catherine Chalier and Miguel Abensour. Paris: Editions de l'Herne, 1991.

Hart, Kevin. "Jacques Derrida: The God Effect." In *Post-Secular Philosophy,* ed. Philip Blond. London: Routledge, 1998.

———. *The Trespass of the Sign: Deconstruction, Theology, and Philosophy.* Cambridge: Cambridge University Press, 1989.

Hegel, G. W. F. *Faith and Knowledge,* trans. Walter Cerf and H. S. Harris. Albany: State University of New York Press, 1977.

———. *Lectures on the Philosophy of Religion,* trans. R. F. Brown, P. C. Hodgson, and J. M. Stewart. Berkeley: University of California Press, 1988.

———. *The Phenomenology of Spirit,* trans. A. V. Miller. Oxford: Oxford University Press, 1977.

Heidegger, Martin. *Basic Problems in Phenomenology,* trans. Albert Hofstadter. Bloomington: Indiana University Press, 1982.

———. *Basic Writings,* trans. David Farrell Krell. New York: Harper and Row, 1977.

———. *Being and Time,* trans. John Macquarrie and Edward Robinson. New York: Harper and Row, 1962.

———. *History of the Concept of Time: Prolegomena,* trans. Theodore Kisiel. Bloomington: Indiana University Press, 1992.

———. *Identity and Difference,* trans. Joan Stambaugh. New York: Harper and Row, 1969.

Henry, Michel. *Genealogy of Psychoanalysis,* trans. Douglas Brick. Stanford: Stanford University Press, 1993.

———. *Phénoménologie matérielle.* Paris: P.U.F., 1990.

———. "Quatres principes de la phénoménologie." *Revue de Métaphysique et de Morale* 1 (1991): 3–26.

Husserl, Edmund. *Cartesian Meditations: An Introduction to Phenomenology,* trans. Dorion Cairns. The Hague: Martinus Nijhoff, 1960.

———. *The Crisis of European Science and Transcendental Phenomenology,* trans. David Carr. Evanston, Ill.: Northwestern University Press, 1970.

———. *The Idea of Phenomenology,* trans. William P. Alston and George Nakhnikian. Dordrecht: Kluwer Academic Publishers, 1990.

———. *Ideas Pertaining to a Pure Phenomenology and to a Phenomenological Philosophy, First Book, General Introduction to a Pure Phenomenology.* The Hague: Martinus Nijhoff, 1982.

———. *The Phenomenology of Internal Time Consciousness,* trans. James S. Churchill. Bloomington: Indiana University Press, 1964.

Jaeschke, Walter. "Philosophical Theology and the Philosophy of Religion." In *New Perspectives on Hegel's Philosophy of Religion,* ed. David Kolb. Albany: State University of New York Press, 1992.

———. *Reason in Religion: The Foundations of Hegel's Philosophy of Religion,* trans. J. Michel Stewart and Peter C. Hodgson. Berkeley: University of California Press, 1990.

Janicaud, Dominique. *Le tournant théologique de la phénoménologie française.* Paris: Editions de l'Eclat, 1991.

Jüngel, Eberhard. *God as the Mystery of the World,* trans. Darrell L. Guder. Grand Rapids, Mich.: Eerdmans, 1983.

Kant, Immanuel. *Critique of Practical Reason,* trans. Lewis White Beck. New York: St. Martin's Press, 1965.

————. *Critique of Pure Reason,* trans. Norman Kemp Smith. New York: St. Martin's Press, 1965.

————. *Lectures on Philosophical Theology,* trans. Allen W. Wood and Gertrude M. Clark. Ithaca, N.Y.: Cornell University Press, 1978.

————. *Religion within the Limits of Reason Alone,* trans. Theodore M. Green and Hoyt H. Hudson. New York: Harper Torchbooks, 1960.

Kierkegaard, Søren. *Fear and Trembling,* trans. Howard V. Hong and Edna H. Hong. Princeton: Princeton University Press, 1983.

Kojève, Alexandre. *Introduction to the Reading of Hegel,* trans. James H. Nichols Jr. Ithaca, N.Y.: Cornell University Press, 1969.

Kosky, Jeffrey L. "After the Death of God: Emmanuel Levinas and the Ethical Possibility of God." *Journal of Religious Ethics* 24, 2 (fall 1996).

————. "Contemporary Encounters with Apophatic Theology: The Case of Emmanuel Levinas." *Journal of Cultural and Religious Theory* 3 (fall 2000).

————. "The Disqualification of Intentionality: The Gift in Derrida, Levinas and Michel Henry." *Philosophy Today* (1997, supplement).

————. "The Phenomenology of Religion: New Possibilities for Philosophy and for Religion." In *Phenomenology and the Theological Turn.* The Bronx: Fordham University Press, 2000.

Landgrebe, Ludwig. *The Phenomenology of Edmund Husserl,* ed. Donn Welton. Ithaca, N.Y.: Cornell University Press, 1981.

Levinas, Emmanuel. *Autrement que savoir, Emmanuel Levinas.* Paris: Editions Osiris, 1988.

————. *Beyond the Verse: Talmudic Readings and Lectures,* trans. Gary D. Mole. Bloomington: Indiana University Press, 1994.

————. *En découvrant l'existence avec Husserl et Heidegger.* Paris: Librairie Philosophique J. Vrin, 1967.

————. *Dieu, la mort, et le temps.* Paris: Grasset, 1993.

————. *Difficult Freedom: Essays on Judaism,* trans. Sean Hand. Baltimore: Johns Hopkins University Press, 1990.

————. *Entre Nous: Thinking of the Other,* trans. Michael B. Smith and Barbara Harshav. New York: Columbia University Press, 1998.

————. *Ethics and Infinity,* trans. Richard A. Cohen. Pittsburgh: Duquesne University Press, 1985.

————. *De l'existence à l'existant,* 3rd ed. Paris: Librairie Philosophique J. Vrin, 1990.

————. *Of God Who Comes to Mind,* trans. Bettina Bergo. Stanford: Stanford University Press, 1998.

————. *In the Time of the Nations,* trans. Michael B. Smith. Bloomington: Indiana University Press, 1994.

————. *Nine Talmudic Readings,* trans. Annette Aronowicz. Bloomington: Indiana University Press, 1990.

————. *Otherwise than Being, or, Beyond Essence,* trans. Alphonso Lingis. Dordrecht: Kluwer Academic Publishers, 1991.

————. *Totality and Infinity,* trans. Alphonso Lingis. Pittsburgh: Duquesne University Press, 1969.

Lingis, Alphonso. *The Imperative.* Bloomington: Indiana University Press, 1998.

Marion, Jean-Luc. "De la mort de Dieu aux noms divins: L'itinéraire théologique de la métaphysique." *Laval Théologique et Philosophique* 41, 1 (February 1985).

———. *Etant donné*. Paris: P.U.F., 1997.

———. *God without Being*, trans. Thomas A. Carlson. Chicago: University of Chicago Press, 1991.

———. *L'idole et la distance*. Paris: Grasset, 1977.

———. "L'interloqué." In *Who Comes after the Subject?* ed. Eduardo Cadava, Peter Connor, and Jean-Luc Nancy. New York: Routledge, 1991.

———. "Metaphysics and Phenomenology: A Relief for Theology." *Critical Inquiry* 20, 4 (summer 1994): 572–91.

———. "A Note Concerning Ontological Indifference." *Graduate Faculty Philosophy Journal* 20, 2–21 (1998): 1.

———. *On Descartes' Metaphysical Prism*, trans. Jeffrey L. Kosky. Chicago: University of Chicago Press, 1999.

———. *Reduction and Givenness*, trans. Thomas A. Carlson. Evanston, Ill.: Northwestern University Press, 1998.

———. "The Saturated Phenomenon." *Philosophy Today* (spring 1996).

Marx, Karl. *Selected Writings*, ed. David McLellan. Oxford: Oxford University Press, 1988.

Nancy, Jean-Luc. "Of Divine Places." In *The Inoperative Community*, trans. Peter Connor et al. Minneapolis: University of Minnesota Press, 1991.

Nefesh haHayyim by the Rabbi Hayyim Volozhin, trans. Benjamin Gross as *L'âme de la vie*. Lagrasse: Verdier, 1986.

Nietzsche, Friedrich. *Beyond Good and Evil*, trans. Walter Kaufmann. New York: Vintage Books, 1966.

———. *Gay Science*, trans. Walter Kaufmann. New York: Vintage Books, 1974.

———. *On the Genealogy of Morals*, trans. Walter Kaufmann. New York: Vintage Books, 1967.

———. *Thus Spoke Zarathustra*, trans. Walter Kaufmann. In *The Portable Nietzsche*. New York: Penguin Books, 1982.

———. *The Will to Power*, trans. Walter Kaufmann and R. J. Hollingdale. New York: Vintage Books, 1968.

O'Regan, Cyril. *The Heterodox Hegel*. Albany: State University of New York Press, 1994.

Peperzak, Adriaan T. "Dieu à travers le bien et l'être." In *Philosophie de la religion entre éthique et ontologie*. Biblioteca dell'Archivio di Filosofia, CEDAM.

———. *To the Other*. West Lafayette, Ind.: Purdue University Press, 1993.

Richardson, William J. "The Irresponsible Subject." In *Ethics as First Philosophy*, ed. Adriaan T. Peperzak. New York: Routledge, 1995.

Ricoeur, Paul. *Husserl: An Analysis of His Phenomenology*. Evanston, Ill.: Northwestern University Press, 1967.

———. *Oneself as Another*. Chicago: University of Chicago Press, 1994.

Rosenzweig, Franz. *The Star of Redemption*. Notre Dame: University of Notre Dame Press, 1985.

Sokolowski, Robert. *The Formation of Husserl's Concept of Constitution*. The Hague: Martinus Nijhoff, 1964.

Strasser, Stephan. "Antiphénoménologie et phénoménologie dans la philosophie d'Emmanuel Levinas." *Revue Philosophique de Louvain* 75 (February 1977): 101–25.

———. "Le concept du phénomène chez Levinas et son importance pour la philosophie religieuse." *Revue Philosophique de Louvain* 76 (August 1978): 328–42.

———. "The Unique Individual and His Other." In *Analecta Husserliana* 6. Dordrecht: D. Reidel, 1983.

Taminiaux, Jacques. *Heidegger and the Project of Fundamental Ontology.* Albany: State University of New York Press, 1991.

Taylor, Mark C. "Infinity, Emmanuel Levinas." In *Altarity.* Chicago: University of Chicago Press, 1987.

Tracy, David. "Mystics, Prophets, Rhetorics: Religion and Psychoanalysis." In *The Trials of Psychoanalysis,* ed. Françoise Meltzer. Chicago: University of Chicago Press, 1988.

———. "Response to Adriaan Peperzak on Transcendence." In *Ethics as First Philosophy,* ed. Adriaan T. Peperzak. New York: Routledge, 1995.

Wyschogrod, Edith. *Emmanuel Levinas: The Problem of Ethical Metaphysics.* The Hague: Martinus Nijhoff, 1974.

———. "Emmanuel Levinas and the Problem of Religious Language." *Thomist* 36 (January 1972): 1–38.

———. "How to Say 'No' in French: Derrida and Negation in Recent French Philosophy." In *Negation and Theology,* ed. Robert Scharlemann. Charlottesville: University Press of Virginia, 1992.

———. *Saints and Postmodernism.* Chicago: University of Chicago Press, 1990.

INDEX

Accusation, 98–101

Accusative, 86

Adequation: intuition and intention, 65, 90, 177, 209n4; intuition of death, 121–122

À-dieu, 187–188, 191, 195

Affectedness: of Dasein and fear for the other, 126–127; and disclosure, 112–116; as ground, 88; passivity of responsibility, 93–94, 96; phenomenological function in *Being and Time*, 112, 116; of subject, 87; translates *Befindlichkeit*, 112

Affectivity: Dasein's fundamental, 118; and double intentionality, 115–116; theological, 212n8

Agamben, Giorgio, 114

Anonymity, xxiii, 192, 193, 194, 195

Anxiety, 116–119

Apodicticity, 209n4; of responsibility, 89–90. *See also* Certainty

Apology, 100

Apophansis, 50–52, 54, 55

Appearing: of appearance, 62–64; confined, 65; of the I, *see* Summons; in Levinas, 84; made by the I, 67–70; and phenomenology, 56–57; and reduction, 55, 65; unconditional, 66, 100–101. *See also* Phenomenality; Phenomenon

Asceticism, 95, 135. *See also* Dispossession; Renunciation

Assignation. *See* Summons

Asymmetry, 30

Atheism, 26–27, 143, 186–187, 188, 203n4, 219n9

Augustine, Saint, 112, 114, 212n8

Authenticity, 91–92, 127–128

Autrui, 4, 17–21, 33–42, 43, 181. *See also* Being(s); Other; Otherness

Bataille, Georges, 202n23

Being: amphibology with beings, 49–52; of animals, 200n15, 205n21; beyond, 34–35; comprehension of, 4, 10–11, 15–16, 17; of Dasein, 109–110; in Heidegger, 45; in *Totality and Infinity*,

44–45. *See also* Beings(s); Existential analytic; Ontology, fundamental; Question of Being

Being(s) [*l'étant*]: as *Autrui*, 32–33, 43, 200n15; in existence, 13–14; and expression, 19, 22; neutralized, 4, 15–16; otherness of, 6, 15–16; par excellence, 132–133; in question of being, 12–13; in question Who?, 18–19. *See also* Being; Existential analytic; Ontology, fundamental; Question of Being

Being and Time: as phenomenological, 104, 107, 211n4. *See also* Existential analytic; Ontology, fundamental

Belatedness: of Dasein, 115; of responsible self, 97–98, 186

Bernasconi, Robert, 199n1, 202n25

Bible, 36, 126, 169–170

Bloom, Harold, xv

Bonaventure, Saint, 27

Buber, Martin, 53–54, 168, 169, 205n22

Call, 150, 153

Caputo, John D., xvi, xviii, 195, 219n13, 219n14

Cause, 132–133, 176, 190

Certainty: of death, 121–122. *See also* Apodicticity

Chalier, Catherine, 164

Chrétien, Jean-Louis, 215n3, 218n29, 219n11

Christianity, 142, 143, 144, 164, 171, 210n9, 212n8

Citation, 167–168

Cogitatio: as appearing, 66–70

Cogito: as appearing, 68, 69; breakup of, 176, 179; insufficiency of, 175, 177–178, 179; priority of, 73. *See also* Consciousness; Ego; Gaze; I

Cohen, Richard, 157–158, 159, 164, 198n16

Conditions for the possibility: of appearance, 56, 70; of experience, 62–63, 100–101. *See also* Unconditionality

Consciousness: as a priori, 72–73; more than, 83–84; stage of appearing, 69,

232

JEFFREY L. KOSKY has published articles in religious studies and philosophy. He is the translator of Jean-Luc Marion's *On Descartes' Metaphysical Prism: The Constitution and the Limits of Onto-theo-logy in Cartesian Thought*. He has taught at Williams College.